www.wadsworth.com

wadsworth.com is the World Wide Web site for Wadsworth and is your direct source to dozens of online resources.

At *wadsworth.com* you can find out about supplements, demonstration software, and student resources. You can also send email to many of our authors and preview new publications and exciting new technologies.

wadsworth.com
Changing the way the world learns®

Political Thought

A GUIDE TO THE CLASSICS

LAURIE M. BAGBY
Kansas State University

WADSWORTH

THOMSON LEARNING

Australia • Canada • Mexico • Singapore • Spain • United Kingdom • United States

WADSWORTH

THOMSON LEARNING ™

Political Science Publisher: Clark G. Baxter
Development Editor: Julie Iannacchino
Editorial Assistant: Jonathan Katz
Marketing Manager: Diane McOscar
Marketing Assistant: Kasia Zagorski
Signing Representative: Shelley Murphy
Print/Media Buyer: Christopher Burnham
Permissions Editor: Joohee Lee
Production Service: Peggy Francomb,
         Shepherd, Inc.
Text Designer: Adriane Bosworth

Copy Editor: Carey Lange
Cover Designer: Bill Stanton
Cover Image: © Bettman/CORBIS:
The cover images are:
Aristole in the background,
top left—Jean Jacques Rousseau
top right—John Stuart Mill
bottom left—John Locke
bottom right—Immanuel Kant
Compositor: Shepherd, Inc.
Printer: Webcom Limited

Printed in Canada
1 2 3 4 5 6 7 05 04 03 02 01

For permission to use material from this text, contact us by
Web: http://www.thomsonrights.com
Fax: 1-800-730-2215
Phone: 1-800-730-2214

ISBN 0-534-55877-1

Wadsworth/Thomson Learning
10 Davis Drive
Belmont, CA 94002-3098
USA

For more information about our products, contact us:
Thomson Learning Academic Resource Center
1-800-423-0563
http://www.wadsworth.com

International Headquarters
Thomson Learning
International Division
290 Harbor Drive, 2nd Floor
Stamford, CT 06902-7477
USA

UK/Europe/Middle East/South Africa
Thomson Learning
Berkshire House
168-173 High Holborn
London WC1V 7AA
United Kingdom

Asia
Thomson Learning
60 Albert Street, #15-01
Albert Complex
Singapore 189969

Canada
Nelson Thomson Learning
1120 Birchmount Road
Toronto, Ontario M1K 5G4
Canada

To Hunter.
May his character be formed to love what is true,
even if all around him seem indifferent.
Or, to put it another way, may he always be happy.

Contents

Part Two

REALISM   47

Chapter 3

Machiavelli (1469–1527)   48

Chapter 4

Hobbes (1588–1679)   66

Part Three

LIBERALISM   85

Chapter 5

Locke (1632–1704)   86

Chapter 6

Rousseau (1712–1778)   112

Chapter 7

John Stuart Mill (1806–1873)   148

Part Four

HISTORY AS PROGRESS   169

Chapter 8

Kant (1724–1804)   170

Chapter 9

Marx (1818–1883) and Engels (1820–1895)   188

Appendix   215

The Discipline of Political Thought: A Brief Introduction   215

Bibliography   220

Preface

A NOTE TO PROFESSORS

Professors who teach political thought have a particularly difficult time finding textbooks to suit their needs. Typically, they want to use original works in their classes and they approach these texts idiosyncratically. They do not want to be boxed into the generic approach of many introductory textbooks. Often, such professors either do not use a textbook or, when they do, supplement it with materials that reflect their own approach that goes beyond the textbook. If they do without a textbook entirely, they face yet another, growing, problem. Students are often discouraged when they try to read the classics of political thought because their education has focused on the present. Understandably, they have difficulty approaching classic works replete with unfamiliar words, styles, and historical references. Sometimes students simply give up or refuse to read the assignments and rely on their professors' lectures to help them understand the material.

For students analyzing the classics of political thought, a textbook that gives them historical context is useful but does not raise their understanding to a level at which they can truly appreciate what they are reading. They need to learn the idiosyncracies of particular philosophers and how to read carefully authors whose writings are often multifaceted. They need to learn how to interpolate, to ask questions of the author while reading, and to look for answers. This book is intended for those professors who want to give their students this extra help—not a way out of reading the great works of political thought, but a way to access them.

The introduction that follows outlines the features of this book. My purpose is to provide a vehicle that can be used in different ways and in different situations for classes large and small. This book can serve as an introductory textbook or a resource for upper-level courses in political thought and philosophy. The *Guide* feature is particularly flexible. A professor can give a writing assignment based on a guide to one of the classics (particularly valuable if the class is small and/or at the upper level), or can simply recommend that the students use the guides to prepare for their exams (especially useful in larger and introductory courses). A professor can also use the guides to generate questions and discussion. He or she can emphasize historical context by focusing on the *background* feature, or stress hermeneutics through the *careful reading* feature.

A NOTE TO STUDENTS

This book is written with today's student in mind, someone who is bright and, in some ways, better educated than ever but less familiar with the classics of literature and philosophy than their college-educated parents. On first encountering a classic, today's student tends to seek out an expert, either a textbook or a professor whose lectures, they hope, will provide all the necessary information. You will discover, however, as you use this book, that there is no substitute, no matter how expert, for thoughtful and individual reading of the text. When you read these books with a sense of curiosity, and humility, you will find yourself asking questions for which you have no immediate answers. At first this experience is rather uncomfortable. You may be used to having most of the answers. But the classics that you are about to encounter are so rich, so powerful, that scholars who have devoted their entire lives to studying them continue to achieve fresh insights and discover new interpretations. The first thing to remember is that if you feel like you do not understand everything you read, or if you have more questions when you finish than when you began a reading, you are in excellent company. These books are considered classics because of this very quality. Reading them is more like being on an exciting journey than reaching any definite destination. Of course, your ultimate destination is better knowledge about such fundamental concepts as justice, government, and human nature. But reading these books will teach you to understand, as Socrates did, that you ultimately do not *know*.

This book's purpose is to teach you how to read better and understand more thoroughly. It will raise questions for you to explore with your professor and fellow students and give you some of the tools you need to achieve greater understanding. But it will not tell you what opinions to form. Because learning is easiest when curiosity is genuinely aroused, I hope that this book can help you discover that curiosity.

A NOTE OF ACKNOWLEDGMENT

Many people helped me during this project. Marsha Frey, professor of history at Kansas State University, extensively reviewed the draft and suggested historical references; professor of classics, Haydn Ausland of the University of Montana, provided criticisms of the sections on Plato and Aristotle; Mark F. Griffith, professor of political science at the University of West Alabama, Livingston, wrote a useful review, as did Kenneth B. Peter, San Jose State University, and Paul Thomas, University of California, Berkeley. Any errors that remain are solely my own.

A special thanks must go to my undergraduate student assistant, Mellissa Rundus, who helped with the research. Her insights and suggestions on what would prove interesting to students were invaluable. Her work was funded during the summer of 1999 by a McNair scholarship for which we are both grateful. That scholarship led to the coauthored appendix to this book on research in the academic discipline of political thought. Laine Rundus, my graduate teaching assistant in the fall of 1999 and spring of 2000, provided essential library assistance. He also read the draft manuscript and made useful suggestions for improving readability.

A special word of thanks must go to Ann Hill and my parents, Ken and Nina Johnson, who often took care of our son, Hunter. Their excellent care assured me that Hunter was having fun and learning new things. Nina also read a draft of the manuscript and provided a useful perspective on how to communicate its ideas effectively.

I also want to thank my husband, Tim, for his love and support. He has extensive training in political thought and made suggestions at crucial stages in the production of this book. I am grateful to Jim Franke and Dale Herspring, whose support and friendship was important during a very difficult and challenging year.

Thanks also to Hunter, who is the source of my commitment to the enterprise of learning.

Introduction

ORGANIZATION

This book is divided into four major parts, each dealing with a particular category of political thought: *idealism, realism, liberalism,* and *historical progress.* These categories are not exclusive nor are they necessary to understanding the featured authors, but they do provide an initial means of thinking about the authors in comparative terms. At the beginning of each section I will offer a more thorough explanation of these terms, but I will briefly define them here.

Idealism   In political thought, an idealist is a philosopher who sees his job as discovering true standards of thought and behavior, standards that can provide the philosopher with a way of thinking about and improving the political condition. In other words, although idealists know that people often act badly, especially in politics, they nonetheless think that people can improve. Strangely enough, although idealists acknowledge that people can never be perfect, they still believe in the moral imperative to fight for more justice to the political arena. Consequently, idealists often strongly criticize the existing order.

Realism   Realists disagree profoundly with idealists. They do not see themselves as standard-bearers attempting to make politics morally better. If we go the way of the idealists, say realists, we are apt not only to fail, but to be destroyed by all those around us who are not so scrupulous. Only if we accept human nature as it is—selfish, passionate, power-hungry—can we find a political formula for change that will actually work. Realists, acknowledging that human nature is flawed, want to channel its destructive energies by building laws and institutions that constructively use self-interest.

Liberalism   In contemporary American politics, to be a liberal is to acquire a partisan label. But in political thought, the term *liberal* means to liberate human beings so that they can become the best that they can be. Liberals see their task as not simply controlling human nature through channeling self-interest, but as constructing social contracts that draw on the human capability to reason effectively. These schemes, most often based on self-interest, assume that people enter freely into an agreement to form a government to protect their rights and freedoms. Liberals believe that, given the proper laws, people can use these rights and freedoms constructively.

Historical Progress   There are political theorists who focus on history and who see that history as having a definite end or final state. A prime example is the Christian belief in the apocalypse, but secular thinkers, as well, prophecy an end. These philosophers see patterns of conflict and progress in human history and argue that humanity is inevitably evolving socially, politically, and economically toward a state of peace and prosperity around the globe. This way of thinking differs from the other three schools of thought most notably in its rejection of the claim that political change happens because individuals make choices. Rather, change results from forces of nature outside of our individual or even collective control.

Admittedly, all of these categories are artificial. Hobbes, for example, spans realism and liberalism. Nevertheless, most political ideas from ancient times to the present can be better understood, at least initially, in terms of these categories that provide reference points upon which we can build.

You will notice that the categories chosen for this book have an historical sequence. Even though we can find most of these categories of political thought during all historical periods (for example, we can find many realists in the birthplace of idealism, ancient Greece), the strongest and most formative examples of each type of thought can be found during a particular historical time. Idealism was most profoundly articulated in ancient Greece, realism most strongly and fully worked out in Renaissance Europe and beyond, liberalism most complete with the flowering of the Enlightenment thought, and the perspective on history as progress in the aftermath of Enlightenment liberalism.

CHAPTER ORGANIZATION

Each part divides into chapters devoted to a given philosopher and each chapter breaks down into the following components.

Background

In this section I provide the historical context for each philosopher. To fully understand an individual's ideas it is helpful to understand their social, political, and economic context. However, understanding political thought requires more than knowing the history surrounding it. In our own times, elements of all four types of thought abound and compete for our attention and allegiance. Because these philosophies have lasting meaning, we will spend more time analyzing their reasonableness. We will ask what they have to say to us today.

Understanding

Following the historical background, students will find a brief section on understanding the particular author. Each philosopher has idiosyncrasies in writing style and references that can mystify a first-time reader. How does Machiavelli use historical examples? Why does Locke quote the Bible so much? If a philosopher was threatened with persecution for making his ideas public, this fear may have affected the way he wrote. Sometimes, cultural beliefs and practices unfamiliar to us today must be explained in order for certain passages to make sense.

Careful Reading

Most of our authors do not always write in a completely straightforward way. They use terms figuratively, not literally. They rely on allusions, symbols, and metaphors. They engage in irony and sarcasm. Students who have not had much exposure to classics of literature and thought may not know exactly how to understand these forms of writing, and often make the mistake of taking them too literally. In this section I will alert students to the particular literary tendencies of the author and analyze two or three extracts as examples of these literary devices.

Careful reading means reading with full concentration and thinking about what you read. This may seem obvious—how could we not think while we read? However, if you observe yourself while reading you will notice that sometimes your brain goes on autopilot. We all do this. Occasionally, we do not have the foggiest idea what we have just read. Even when we are aware of every word we are reading, our thinking powers are only half engaged. We are trying to absorb and retain the information, but we are not asking questions. We have not noticed that two pages back, the author seemed to say the opposite of what he is saying on this page. So, actually, to read carefully with full concentration requires a lot of effort.

Please note that in this section and in the section below, I may be using a particular translation or edition of a work and you may be using another. This might mean that I will refer to specific words that you cannot find in your text. Even in works originally written in English, an edition will treat punctuation and spelling differently. My use of brief selections and quotations from the texts is meant to *guide you back to your own book.* Also, my interpretations of selected passages are meant only to illustrate for you how to carefully decipher a work. They are not meant to be the final word on what a particular passage means.

Guide to. . .

At the end of each chapter are guides to the important texts by each author. In the section on Plato, for example, there are guides to the *Apology, Crito, Republic,* and *Gorgias.* These guides include brief commentary on difficult passages. Each one is a little different, designed with the idiosyncracies of the particular text in mind, so briefly familiarize yourself with the plan of the guide (how it is arranged, how it refers to the text) before beginning. It is essential when reading works of such depth to get a clear understanding at each step before moving on. If you use the guides as you read, you will more thoroughly grasp (and I hope more thoroughly enjoy) the material. Read a section of the philosopher's text, then refer to the guide and answer the questions about that section. If you record your answers to each question you will compile a useful set of notes that you can use as a resource for asking questions and participating meaningfully in class discussion. Remember that when you run into an unfamiliar word, a few seconds spent with a dictionary can clear up hours of confusion.

USING THE WORLD WIDE WEB

Materials that may be useful in your research into political thought will appear on the website for this book at *www.wadsworth.politicalscience.com*—especially materials that relate each thinker to current issues. There are hundreds of classic electronic texts in political thought that you can read or download, such as Plato's *Apology.* Because of *Project Gutenberg* and other internet projects, readers have unparalleled access to the greatest works of thought and philosophy. Many universities have created websites that offer historical and biographical material about particular philosophers or philosophies, and these websites are accessible. In addition, some sites carry scholarly commentary, articles previously published on pertinent topics, sections from books, and book reviews. Because of the transitory nature of web materials, some web pages may cease to exist—be removed from the site and new ones added.

IDEALISM

An idealist in political thought is not someone who expects human goodness at every turn. Indeed, an idealist can be fairly worldly, even pessimistic. The ancient Greek philosopher Socrates and his pupil, Plato, often expressed disappointment with humanity. Socrates seemed to love people and yet in his dialogues with them was all too aware of their flaws. When individuals criticize others, it is because they hold certain standards against which others fall short. For Socrates, the entire visible world failed to measure up to his ideals.

Idealists perceive certain standards of what is good and right and then apply those standards to the world around them. Because the world often disappoints, idealists see their job as raising others to those higher standards through logical persuasion. Notice that idealists believe in an external, absolute Truth and an individual's ability to use reason to approach that Truth. This claim that Truth is out there, that indeed there is one true definition of the Good Life, one true notion of Justice, is controversial and rejected today as arrogant and even dangerous. There are many definitions of right and wrong, the critics argue. Today, ancient idealists would have to look to conservative intellectuals or perhaps religious thinkers to find anyone who fervently holds this idea of objective truth. Unlike religious thinkers, however, the ancient philosophers believed that Truth could be approached through reason without revelation.

PLATO (C. 427–347 B.C.)

BACKGROUND

To understand Plato, one must understand his teacher Socrates—the personality that towers in so many of Plato's dialogues. Socrates' influence on Plato was so extensive that scholars still dispute which ideas in the dialogues, if any, came from Plato and which came from Socrates. Indeed, we know Socrates primarily through Plato's dialogues.[1] From these and a few other sources we get a fairly good idea of Socrates' origins and character.

Born in 470 B.C., Socrates was the son of a stonemason. At one time his father may have been wealthy, but by the end of his life he was rather poor. We know little else of Socrates' youth because he never wrote anything down (at least nothing that has survived). We do know that he served as a *hoplite* (a foot soldier) during the Peloponnesian War, a great war between his city of Athens and the city of Sparta. This war left an indelible impression on Socrates; he was critical of the Athenians imperialism and their ambition for more power, land, and wealth. It is said that though he fought well in the war, Socrates was a philosopher even then. He would stop in mid-march to think, and catch up with his fellow soldiers hours later.

Socrates married a woman named Xanthippe, who bore him several children and had the reputation of being a shrew. She complained that he talked too much and made too little money.

Athenian politics during Socrates' and Plato's lifetimes were interesting but often treacherous. Athens was a direct democracy in which each citizen of

---

[1] All quotations from Platonic dialogues in this chapter are from *The Collected Dialogues of Plato,* edited by Edith Hamilton and Huntington Cairns, Bollingen Series LXXI, Princeton: Princeton University Press, 1961. Selections from *The Republic* are translated by Paul Shorey, and selections from *Gorgias* are translated by W. D. Woodhead. Quotations in the study guides for the *Apology* and *Crito* are translated by Hugh Tredennick. The numbers and letters that appear after these quoted portions of text appear on the margins of many classic works of philosophy as the standard method of citation.

Athens could come to the Assembly and vote directly on the issues of the day. Only adult males who had citizen mothers could participate, but it was in some ways more democratic, although less equal, than our own system.

The Athenian system produced political problems that were sometimes frightening, sometimes ludicrous. During the Peloponnesian War, for example, the Athenian Assembly voted to put all adult male Mytilenaeans to death and sell the women and children into slavery because Mytilene had revolted against Athens. The next day, another speaker came before the Assembly, won the debate because of his superior speaking skills, and convinced the Athenians to send another ship with orders to overtake the first ship and stop the executions. Fortunately, it succeeded.

Suffice it to say that the Athenian Assembly often changed its policies because of the eloquence of the speaker before it. Socrates truly deplored the ability of rhetoricians to sway the Assembly. In fact, much of Plato's dialogues addressed opposition to one aspect or another of *sophism*, the philosophy embraced by the power-elite of Athens. In this philosophy (as you will hear from Thrasymachus in *The Republic*), right and wrong are determined solely by who is in power. For those who accepted this premise, selfishly relying on emotional or deceptive rhetoric to sway the democracy was perfectly natural, and even admirable. Plato apparently thought that such an attitude in leadership would lead to the downfall of civilization.

Another unfortunate aspect of pure democracy, at least for Socrates, was the absence of individual protections, what we would term a bill of rights. In a pure democracy, whatever the majority said prevailed, even if it meant fining, exiling, or even executing an innocent man. Socrates' constant questioning and criticism of democracy angered many, in particular some Athenian leaders such as Meletus, who swore out an indictment against him. He accused Socrates of failing to recognize the gods of the city and of introducing new gods. He also accused Socrates of corrupting the young men of the city, with whom he frequently held philosophic discussions. Meletus was not entirely wrong on either count. Although Socrates paid homage to the local gods, many of his well-known discussions called into question the traditional Greek pantheon (as you will see in Plato's *Republic*). Socrates also tried to persuade the promising young men of Athens not to follow the path of their elders who used democracy for their own gain. To that extent, he was corrupting their minds against the system as it then operated.

When it came time for his trial, Socrates was true to what he had taught his entire life. He did not rely on eloquence to convince the jury they should have mercy on him. Rather, he proclaimed his innocence and told them that, in fact, he had been doing the Athenians a favor by alerting them to their flaws. He suggested that the appropriate punishment for this crime was to be feasted for life at public expense. This suggestion had the effect one might imagine. He was executed in 399 B.C. by ingestation of hemlock. Socrates' fate underscores the frequent unpopularity of intellectuals who have innovative ideas even within the most democratic of regimes.

Obviously, Socrates would be the kind of teacher who would influence his students, as he certainly influenced Plato (427–347 B.C.). Most of Plato's dialogues feature Socrates, and of those that do not, some feature a stranger who is similar to Socrates in many ways. Most scholars point out that Plato's most characteristic philosophy appears in *The Republic*. How much of Socrates' influence is in this dialogue is unknowable. Certainly Socrates' spirit is still evident in the quest for the definition of justice in the soul and in the city, as well as in many of his arguments about why injustice does not pay. It is not really necessary to separate the ideas of Socrates from those of Plato when reading *The Republic* or other dialogues—it is more necessary to *learn* from this spectacular display of artistry and reason.

Plato came from an aristocratic family, some of whose members held office in Athens. Plato, however, was not involved in the government. There is some evidence in letters attributed to Plato that he once tried to fulfill his dream of influencing political leaders by becoming a tutor to the son of the tyrant of Syracuse, thus indirectly advising the tyrant. If the letter is to be believed, this experiment ended when Plato was no longer needed for tutoring and left the city. Later, Plato founded a school known as the Academy (c. 387 B.C.) to continue and further the philosophic work begun by Socrates. This school branched out beyond political philosophy to incorporate the sciences, mathematics, and other useful studies, and it became an important model for universities. Plato's Academy operated until A.D. 529, when Roman Emperor Justinian closed the pagan schools of philosophy. The head of the school at that time, Damascius, was a teacher of Neoplatonism. He took many of the books from the Academy's libraries and fled to the ruler of Persia for protection. If you visit Greece today, you can still see ruins in or near the place where Plato taught his students.

Plato's philosophy inspired early Roman Catholic Fathers of the Church such as St. Augustine. Plato's thought—some belief in and arguments for the existence of an afterlife and eternal standards of Justice and the Good—spoke to Christian ideals. Although Platonic philosophy was largely unknown to the people during the medieval period, when the vast majority was illiterate and poor, it was preserved by the Church (which sometimes saw its role as protecting the people from dangerous philosophy while at the same time preserving that philosophy). Platonic and Aristotelian philosophy was also preserved and fostered in the Islamic world.

UNDERSTANDING PLATO

To communicate his philosophy, Plato wrote dialogues. Initially, you can think of a dialogue as a kind of play. A dialogue reads like a recording of the give-

and-take among people who are holding a conversation—engaging in argument. Imagine the characters, where they are sitting, what they look like. There are clues in the dialogues about the ages of the participants, which helps our imagination flesh them out. Occasionally, Plato will manage to throw in a little background about where the participants are speaking or how they are behaving; but much of the time there is nothing but conversation. You can tell a lot about the character of the actors by what they say: Some are angry, some uninterested, some drip sarcasm. Indeed, one of the best things about reading a Platonic dialogue is the humor that lies beneath the surface. It may take awhile to catch all of it, but it is well worth the effort.

The dialogues are unusually rich. Unlike treatises, which fully develop only one side of an argument, dialogues anticipate and include counterarguments, thus making the central argument stronger. An argument is always stronger if it has stood the test of questioning and counterarguments, which is what Plato is hoping to show. The challenge for a new reader of Plato is to sort out the arguments. Because Plato is arguing through Socrates, try to concentrate first on what Socrates says, especially in those places where he summarizes his argument for those with whom he is conversing (his interlocutors). As you get comfortable with Socrates, search to understand the challenges to his point of view. You may sometimes get bogged down in the long strings of questions and answers. It is not as important to remember every fragment of the argument as it is to understand generally the interlocutors' reasons for their thinking. In other words, to read a dialogue you need to relax—even scholars who have devoted their entire careers to Plato argue with each other about what this or that passage is really about.

Another way to discover Plato's point of view is to watch the reactions of the interlocutors to each other. Because Plato and his teacher most admired logical discussion, and believed that emotions often blinded people to the truth, it is safe to say that a display of emotion in one of the participants is meant to show the irrationality of his position. If Socrates says something that another interlocutor cannot dispute, that person is likely to get angry and even call Socrates names. In the dialogue *Gorgias,* for instance, a man named Callicles calls Socrates childish and insinuates that he is not a real man. He says that Socrates can be easily "struck hard," or taken advantage of in a legal dispute. He advises him to become a real man by leaving philosophy for a career in business! Remember that when people start shouting, calling names or mocking others in a debate, it is usually because they have run out of arguments and thus make this their last defense. So these outbursts are not just humorous but meant by Plato to teach us a lesson about the character of those who are sophists or hold other wrong-headed views.

Plato has another advantage in using a dialogue rather than a treatise. Unlike the treatise, the dialogue shows that it is very difficult to be *absolutely* certain about one's conclusions. There is always a challenge, often a tough one, and there may be some truth within that challenge to be acknowledged by a rational person, no matter how strongly he believes in his side. This attitude toward certainty has become known as Socratic humility. It should not be confused, however, with the view that all arguments are equally valid. For Socrates, and Plato, all arguments certainly were not equally valid. Arguments that stood the test of logic were to be provisionally accepted as true; arguments that were exposed through questioning as illogical were to be rejected. In this way alone could philosophers come closer to the truth, but they must always be ready to back away from their conclusions if someone else could show them to be illogical. This humility bears some resemblance to the much later idea held by liberal political thinkers—the free marketplace of ideas, in which the public is trusted to distinguish better arguments from worse arguments without being protected from wrong ideas by censorship.

CAREFUL READING

Plato is famous—some say infamous—for his use of metaphorical references. If students have read little of this type of literature, they may be thrown by Plato's seemingly picturesque way of putting things. However frustrating this may be at first, the fact that Plato is a subtle and even artful writer is one reason why his works are so intriguing. Learning to enjoy this type of writing is like learning to enjoy fine wine—and the journey is just as enjoyable.

Indeed this last sentence is an example of metaphorical writing, which is simply to compare something with something else. Usually people use metaphors when they find it hard to put into words directly what they are trying to communicate. The bigger and more complex the ideas we attempt to relate, the more we tend to use metaphors. Religious texts are full of metaphors because they are about the biggest and most unfathomable of concepts—God. So it should come as no surprise that a philosopher like Plato, who is concerned with the Good Life, Truth, and Justice, might occasionally resort to a metaphor.

Often, Plato actually warns us that a metaphor is coming, or is already underway. Near the beginning of *The Republic*, for instance, Socrates says that in order to define what justice is in the individual soul, it might help to define what justice is in a much larger body, a city. Much of the rest of the dialogue concerns the construction of that city. In a way, then, the entire *Republic* is a metaphor. We have to keep in mind as we read Socrates' recommendations for the ideal city that he is also commenting somehow on justice in the soul. The accompanying guide to *The Republic* will remind you of this metaphor. Following are two examples of other, smaller metaphors that appear in *The Republic,* along with analysis of a myth that appears in the *Gorgias.*

The Allegory of the Cave

This metaphor appears at the beginning of Book VII. (Each of the ten parts of *The Republic* is generally referred to as a book.) Socrates is talking:

> Next, said I, compare our nature in respect of education and its lack to such an experience as this. Picture men dwelling in a sort of subterranean cavern with a long entrance open to the light on its entire width. Conceive them as having their legs and necks fettered from childhood, so that they remain in the same spot, able to look forward only, and prevented by the fetters from turning their heads. Picture further the light from a fire burning higher up and at a distance behind them, and between the fire and the prisoners and above them a road along which a low wall has been built, as the exhibitors of puppet shows have partitions before the men themselves, above which they show the puppets. (7.514–514b)

Socrates then describes the experience of one man freed from his fetters. He would find the light painful, and at first be unable to see. After awhile, however, he would begin to see the world as it really was. Socrates describes the reaction of such an enlightened man to the petty games and contests of those who are still in the cave. He expresses the opinion that such a man is likely to consider personal honors and awards meaningless.

This metaphor is probably the most famous in Plato's *Republic*. What are we to make of it? It will help to read the six books that come before this scene. You will find that Socrates highly values the life of philosophy and that he sees his role as an educator, attempting to draw his interlocutors toward the Truth. You will also find that he considers this task difficult; even the smartest humans are often difficult to persuade. From reading his background you know that Socrates was disliked by many of the elite in Athens, who viewed him as a troublemaker and an agitator against rule by the people. So the first thing to keep in mind when interpreting any metaphorical passage is the context you have learned thus far.

Next remember the clues that are laid there for you, some of which are fairly obvious. The first sentence in Book VII reads, "Next, said I, compare our nature in respect of education and its lack to such an experience as this." Here, Socrates has given you a large clue about his intent in this metaphor.

Remember to read the entire metaphor for its application to the issue of the philosopher's task of educating people, especially Socrates' own role. The men dwelling in the cave are perhaps common people. But do they also include the smarter ones to whom Socrates is talking? He later talks about the liberated prisoner returning to the cave to persuade others to make the ascent. He predicts that such a man will at first be unable to see in the darkness and thus appear ridiculous to those who have never left. He states that he will seem silly if he has to testify in the cave about the "shadows of justice" with those who have never themselves seen it. (7.517d–e) Socrates is obviously referring here, through Plato, to his later demise at the hands of the Athenian elites; however, he could also be talking about his interlocutors who wind up ridiculing him instead of continuing a civil conversation, or more generally, to all those he fails to persuade.

Think about the content of this metaphor. Why are the prisoners fettered so they can see nothing but shadows? Why are they in the dark, seeing things they think are real, but are not real? Our expression "in the dark" is apt here—these prisoners represent people who are in the dark intellectually. Their concerns are not real, yet they truly believe they are real. Next, think about how this statement might be applied today. Some people have called television "the cave." People watch its flickering images, entertained for hours by sit-coms and dramas, while important world events pass them by. They take as truth the political opinions they hear on the nightly news, without investigating further. Could our entire popular culture be the cave, dominating much of our waking hours with its TV shows, music, fashions, trends? Inasmuch as we are in touch with that culture, do we lack reflection of what is more important, including our own family relationships? Is consumerism the cave, leading us to desire the latest product with false promises of improving our lives? Plato would probably answer yes to all of these questions.

Think of what Socrates is saying about himself. He is telling his interlocutors that he considers himself to be in the cave when talking to them. He is trying to draw them up out of their own ignorance, and risking their ridicule to do so. They might take this self-identification as an insult, but they do not. Socrates may see himself as a lonely man, talking to people out of a sense of duty, when he could be enjoying himself more in divine contemplations. He understands why he is misunderstood—he is talking about things that others have never experienced and that threaten their chosen way of life—and yet he continues to want to talk to them.

What is the light? The ultimate Truth, no doubt. But since we can only see it fully when we are dragged up out of the cave by a philosopher, we must be content now with what Socrates calls the "likenesses and reflections" of the light as he describes them through metaphor. Could it be that those interlocutors who can follow his argument are out of the cave, but still squinting and groping in the blinding light?

Luckily for us, Plato often gives us an interpretation of his own to accompany the metaphor, and he does here as well. He does not, however, explain each nuance but leaves all of them to his readers to ponder on their own. Socrates tells Glaucon that the cave image he has constructed must be applied to Glaucon's world. The world we can see is like the cave, and our sun is like the fire in the cave. The ascent of the prisoner is like "the soul's ascension to the intelligible region . . ." He tells Glaucon that "in the region of the known" (the intelligible region), "the last thing to be seen and hardly seen is the idea of the good . . ." which would correspond to the sun outside the cave. The idea of the Good, he says, is "the source of truth and reason." (7.517b–d)

This passage tells us that Plato thinks what we see around us, illuminated by the sun, is not as real as that which is visible only with our mind—the intelligible region. What is something we can see only with our mind? Geometry is an entire field built upon ideas that only appear in their perfection in our mind. No circle exists on earth that corresponds to the perfect circle as defined by geometry. No matter how precise our instruments for drawing the circle—even if they are computerized—it will always have minute flaws. So Socrates is not saying that everything around us is not real, because we can after all see and touch it. Rather, he is saying that those things intelligible to the mind only are *more* real in the sense that they are perfect and do not change. It is easy enough to see how this might be the case in geometry, but Plato thought this insight applied to all kinds of ideas. The idea of the Good is pure, and can only be approximated by humans who try to be good and build sound political institutions.

You can see why the Church was later attracted to Plato's thought. He mentions God once in this passage, as well as an "author of light." It is never clear what kind of God Plato is writing about, but we at least can say that this God appears to be the author of both the light and the idea of the Good. The idea of the Good makes everything else in the world comprehensible to the philosopher. It is the true standard by which he can see the world as it truly is. Socrates argues that a leader can only be a good one if he has some knowledge of this eternal, unchanging idea of what is good. What a bold political statement for any philosopher to make! Because most leaders in Athens and elsewhere were not philosophers, nor did they usually listen to philosophers, there were probably no leaders in Athens or elsewhere that Socrates would call good.

The Ship of State

The city that Socrates constructs has three classes: the workers, the soldiers, and the philosopher-rulers. Justice in the city is defined as each class doing its own job well, and not interfering in the work of others. In Book V, Socrates discusses the special role of the guardian and the ruling classes in three shocking suggestions. The first suggestion is women should be allowed into the military and ruling classes. The second is all relationships within those classes should be communal—marriages should happen at the command of the state and should not be permanent, and children should be raised not by their parents but communally. Children who are born defective should be "exposed" or left to die. Some of these suggestions, when you read them, ought to cause dismay. They could be taken metaphorically, as the guide to *The Republic* will indicate, but they nevertheless also should be pondered as actual political proposals. The third suggestion and perhaps the most sweeping is philosophers should be the rulers. Indeed, he says that unless philosophers are rulers, none of the rest of his proposals will be realized (5.473d–e).

Plato presents the third suggestion in such a way that it raises strong doubts about the plan's feasibility. Unless philosophers become kings or actual kings become philosophers, he says, his plans cannot be fulfilled. Book VI of *The Republic* finishes the argument by showing just how difficult it is to become a true philosopher—few are actually born and bred to be true "suitors of philosophy." It is also unlikely that a true philosopher, once found, would ever want to rule. Philosophers, suggests Socrates, are far more interested in pure contemplation than in taking on the responsibility of ruling. A far more difficult obstacle in the way of philosopher-kings also is discussed in Book VI. Socrates uses the image of the ship of state to get the point across.

> Picture a shipmaster in height and strength surpassing all others on the ship, but who is slightly deaf and of similarly impaired vision, and whose knowledge of navigation is on a par with his sight and hearing. Conceive the sailors to be wrangling with one another for control of the helm, each claiming that it is his right to steer though he has never learned the art and cannot point out his teacher or any time when he studied it. And what is more, they affirm that it cannot be taught at all, but they are ready to make mincemeat of anyone who says that it can be taught, and meanwhile they are always clustered about the shipmaster importuning him and sticking at nothing to induce him to turn over the helm to them. And sometimes, if they fail and others get his ear, they put the others to death or cast them out from the ship, and then, after binding and stupefying the worthy shipmaster with mandragora or intoxication or otherwise, they take command of the ship, consume its stores and, drinking and feasting, make such a voyage of it as is to be expected from such, and as if that were not enough, they praise and celebrate as a navigator, a pilot, a master of shipcraft, the man who is most cunning to rule, while the man who lacks this craft they censure as useless. They have no suspicion that the true pilot must give his attention to the time of the year, the seasons, the sky, the winds, the stars, and all that pertains to his art if he is to be a true ruler of a ship, and that he does not believe that there is any art or science of seizing the helm with or without the consent of others, or any possibility of mastering this alleged art and the practice of it at the same time with the science of navigation. With such goings on aboard ship do you not think that the real pilot would in very deed be called a stargazer, an idle babbler, a useless fellow, by the sailors in ships managed after this fashion? (6.488b–489a)

We already know that in Socrates' view, most of the politicians of Athens were mere rhetoricians or demagogues who used their eloquence and force of personality to sway the voters to support plans that would make them more powerful and wealthy. Socrates knew that most, if not all, actual governments were based on "force or fraud," to borrow a phrase from another philosopher, Machiavelli. We also know that, ideally, Socrates thought philosophers make the best rulers. His image of the ship of state illustrates graphically the impossibility of philosopher-kingship. We in a democracy may not like to contemplate this argument because it can easily be seen as a critique of our own situation.

Notice that the original shipmaster mentioned here cannot be the philosopher because he is described as slightly deaf and somewhat blind, with navigation skills to match. Yet this shipmaster is not depicted as a demagogue, but rather a ruler with good intentions. He is easily removed from power by the sailors, who are willing to be forceful and ruthless. Somehow the sailors manage to convince him to turn over the helm to them. How could this happen, unless the shipmaster or ruler did not have the knowledge, foresight, or backbone to understand the serious threat to his power (and the safety of his ship) posed by the sailors? This is the image of a well-meaning but imprudent people, who do not suspect that their leaders will abuse their power and try to take more.

The sailors who take over the ship are the rhetoricians. As soon as they have control, they misuse it to indulge their desires—for pleasure, wealth, and of course more power. What does this say about why most democratic leaders strive to achieve power? Most say they are interested in the people's welfare, but when they obtain power, Socrates sees them using it only for their own selfish interests. Is this unattractive image not confirmed in our modern politics every time we find corruption?

Notice that in the corrupt democracy Socrates depicts, the sailors praise the man who is the most cunning, the man who has the skills to seize the most power from others. But, says Socrates, these are not the same skills that are actually needed to be a ship's pilot, or a good ruler. A real pilot studies everything related to navigation, just as a good ruler would constantly study everything related to leadership. Socrates says that the art of seizing power is completely different from the true art of ruling, and in fact points out the difficulty of finding a leader skilled in both seizing power and in ruling well. Socrates is probably suggesting that seizing power by force and fraud is incompatible with true leadership. Leadership, then, is not a technical skill but depends on the quality of the mind and moral character of the leader.

Finally, Socrates tells us how real philosophers (those who could serve the common good) are badly treated by those who pretend to be capable leaders. Not surprisingly, this was exactly the way Socrates himself was treated by the leaders of Athenian democracy. Such a philosopher (the true pilot) would be treated like someone who knew nothing about politics—"a stargazer, an idle babbler, a useless fellow . . ." In the dialogue *Gorgias*, when Socrates' chief opponent Callicles calls Socrates childish or unmanly for pursuing philosophy instead of business or the worldly life of rough and tumble politics, Socrates concludes that those most qualified to rule are considered least qualified by those around them, those who have a more sophisticated view of what leadership entails. Unfortunately, as Socrates knew, power trumps wisdom. There is no way for a philosopher to rule if the people and their leaders do not want it.

Before you dismiss this as an old-fashioned indictment of democratic politics by an elitist philosopher, consider the roles played by polling and by focus groups in our own democracy. Politicians routinely use polls, focus groups, and other mechanisms for measuring public opinion, not so much as a means of finding out the people's will, but of skillfully shaping or pacifying that will by using the right words, phrases, and appeals in their speeches. People's reactions to various words and phrases are used to shape the rhetoric of our leaders. Consider the typical rhetoric offered the public in ten-second campaign sound bites created by public relations teams to fit into the nightly news broadcasts. Consider also the often lamented reality that a politician who lacks charisma (or one who is physically unattractive) cannot be elected to national office in the age of televised campaigns. Or consider that politicians who are seeking national office often think they must take money from just about any source, legal and illegal, thereby potentially obligating themselves to particular organizations and interests. Democracy may still be the best system among many bad ones (a reality that even Plato recognized), but it has its flaws.

The Myth in Gorgias

In the *Gorgias,* a dialogue on the value of political rhetoric as it was typically practiced in Athens, Socrates has just concluded a rather nasty, but also humorous exchange with his chief rival Callicles. Callicles has become non-communicative because of his disgust with Socrates' stubborn advocacy of selfless leadership. In the face of Callicles' snide and brief responses, Socrates tells the men assembled a concluding myth to make his point about good leadership in one more way.

Socrates says that when the god Zeus first ruled, mortals were in charge of judging other mortals on the day of their death. The god Pluto told Zeus that the judges were making bad decisions and the wrong people were going to the Isles of the Blessed and Tartarus (Hell).

> Then Zeus said, "Well, I will put a stop to that. Cases are judged badly now," said he, "because those who are tried come to judgment with their clothes on, for they are still alive when judged. And therefore many," said he, "who possessed evil souls are invested with fine bodies and lineage and wealth, and when the trial takes place, many witnesses come forward to testify that they have lived righteous lives. So the judges are dazzled by these, and at the same time they are clothed themselves when they give the sentence, their eyes, their ears, and their whole bodies acting as a screen before their souls. They have all these hindrances before them, both their own clothing and that of those on trial. First of all then," said he, "men must be stopped from foreknowing their deaths, for now they have knowledge beforehand. Prometheus has already been told to stop this foreknowledge. Next they must be stripped naked of all these things before the trial, for they must be judged after death. And the judge must be naked too and dead, scanning with his soul itself the souls of all immediately after death, deprived of all his kinsmen and with all that fine attire of his left on earth, that his verdict may be just." (523–524)

Socrates goes on to say he believes that the souls of human beings are now seen by the gods as they truly are. So a king's soul may be seen by the gods in its true condition, which may be scarred, crooked, and unjust. According to Socrates, there are three types of people—those whose souls are curable with punishment prescribed by the gods, those whose souls are incurable, and those whose souls are pure or unscarred. The curable souls will spend a time in punishment and then be admitted to the Isles of the Blessed. The ancient Church saw this image as an example of a pagan philosopher who already knew about purgatory. The incurable souls spend eternity in Tartarus. These are souls who apparently cannot turn away from their evil convictions. Socrates says "it is among the most powerful that you find the superlatively wicked" most likely to go to Tartarus and stay there. (525e) Most people in power prove to be evil, he says, because the temptations of power are too great for them; but sometimes the god sees a soul "that has lived in piety and truth." Philosophers are especially likely to appear this way to the god because they have minded their own business instead of "playing the busybody." Such a soul will go straight to the Isles of the Blessed. (526c)

This myth is not the only one Plato ever included in a dialogue. *The Republic* includes a different myth about the afterlife. Given that several of the dialogues have different myths, it is difficult to believe that Socrates thought this particular myth was fact in the absolute sense, despite what he says. After reading *Gorgias*, you may wonder why Socrates needed to add this myth at all, particularly as he had already made several strong arguments for just leadership without any reference to the gods or the afterlife. There are several ways of explaining its presence, however. The important thing to remember is that it is quite all right, and even necessary, to speculate about the purpose of this and other nonliteral parts of Platonic dialogues.

It could very well be that Plato thinks this myth is true in its essentials. Indeed there is quite a bit of evidence that Plato did believe in eternal life; he certainly believed in a realm of higher reality that encompassed eternal ideas. Perhaps he thought it was quite reasonable to believe the human soul was eternal, because men could obtain knowledge of eternal ideas through philosophy. Perhaps he also thought it was reasonable to believe in a god or gods because it is hard otherwise for even a philosopher to explain the existence of everything we experience. It would then be reasonable to think that the god or gods meted out eternal justice. Another way of viewing this myth, not incompatible with the first way, is to see it as a bit of Socratic rhetoric. Earlier in the dialogue, Socrates says that a "true orator" or a good rhetorician would be a "moral artist," one who uses rhetoric to shape people's souls for the better and to lead them toward Justice. Socrates may think that such a myth is an example of the good form of rhetoric, especially for those who cannot follow all the intricacies of philosophical debates. Others may see this myth as a rather convenient form of self-justification. Whatever its purpose, predictably, the myth has no effect on Callicles.

Let us look at some of the details. Originally, judgment took place on earth, but Zeus found this system flawed because appearances were getting in the way of seeing people's souls as they really were. Accordingly, Zeus instituted a new system in which souls were judged after death, when completely "naked." The real importance of this idea, of course, is all earthly things that Callicles admires—power, wealth, appearances—do not matter in the final judgment. Real Justice, according to Socrates, is blind to these things that do unfortunately matter in this lifetime. Think for a moment about the advantages a person has in this lifetime by being born into a wealthy or politically powerful family, or sometimes simply by being born beautiful. We are attracted to people who appear successful and are beautiful. Although Socrates does not say that it is impossible for such people to be just, he does claim that it is difficult because (as we have already seen in *The Republic*) they are so tempted. In any case, he here denies any positive relationship between these earthly marks of success and real success, that of achieving Justice in the human soul.

Indeed, the person most apt to be scorned by society as useless—the philosopher—is most likely to go straight to the Isles of the Blessed. Notice he says that such a person has "not played the busybody in his life." Now if we were to take this statement too literally, we would have to accuse Socrates of hypocrisy because he certainly criticized throughout his life Athenian politics and leaders. But why would Plato want to make his teacher look like a hypocrite? Read carefully. Not playing the busybody to Socrates means only to mind your own business well. Socrates' business is being a philosopher, and being a critic of the political system is part of being a philosopher; but Socrates has never actually tried to become involved in politics. He has been advocating that those who do actually participate in politics be just. In his view, then, he has been minding his business and doing justice his entire life. Indeed, earlier, he tells Callicles that he has been engaged appropriately in the political art (as opposed to Athenian politics) all along.

> I think that I am one of very few Athenians, not to say the only one, engaged in the true political art, and that of the men of today I alone practice statesmanship. Since therefore when I speak on any occasion it is not with a view to winning favor, but I aim at what is best, not what is most pleasant, and since I am unwilling to engage in those 'dainty devices' that you recommend, I shall have nothing to say for myself when in court. (521d–e)

The "dainty devices" refer to deceptive rhetoric, and "when in court" is a foreshadowing of the fact that Socrates did not try to escape punishment when he was convicted by using any of these devices.

GUIDE TO *APOLOGY*

The *Apology* is Plato's account of the trial and sentencing of Socrates. It raises some major questions about the meaning of life and the uncertainty of death, and less metaphysical issues such as the relationship of the political philosopher to the state.

The Charges (17a–20a)

1. Who has brought the charges against Socrates?
2. What are the charges that the jury must consider?
3. Who are his real accusers? Socrates claims that his real accusers are not the men who have brought the specific charges he must address at his trial.

Defense against Socrates' Real Accusers (20a–24b)   Socrates begins this part of his speech by claiming he is not an expert in the same sense as the sophists, who charge for lessons in subjects such as rhetoric and law. He tries to explain why he has a reputation for being a kind of sophist when he is not.

1. Socrates says he has gotten a bad reputation because he has a "kind of wisdom." What is this wisdom?
2. Recount Socrates' tale of how he got his mission from the god or oracle at Delphi.
3. After hearing the god's opinion, what did Socrates think was his religious duty?
4. Do you believe Socrates is entirely sincere in his account of the god's pronouncement and his reaction to it?

Defense against Meletus' Charges (24b–28)

1. How does Socrates answer the charge that he has corrupted the youth? (24b–26b)
2. Meletus also charged Socrates with not believing in the gods. How does Socrates prove that he does believe in the gods? (26c–28)

Socrates' Integrity (28–30b)   Here Socrates defends not only his integrity but also the value of integrity per se. Throughout this dialogue and in *Crito,* it is evident that it was very important for Socrates to never contradict his principles in either speech or action.

1. Socrates asks his accusers "if you think that a man who is worth anything ought to spend his time weighing up the prospects of life and death." Explain why Socrates thinks he should disregard the danger of execution when living his life and in defending himself in court.
2. Do you think Socrates is wise to disregard the possibility that he may die if he does not please the court?

Socrates' Warning (30b–33)

1. In what sense does Socrates think he is a gift of God? What service has he provided the city of Athens by philosophizing there?
2. Socrates claims that he has always had within him a divine voice which sometimes stops him from saying or doing something, but never urges him to do anything. Why does he think the voice has usually stopped him from participating directly in the political life?

3. What minor political offices has Socrates held, and what did he do to offend his colleagues? What is his point in recounting these episodes?

Socrates' Bold Proposal (36–38c)   The jury has decided that Socrates is guilty. Now he must argue with them about why he should not receive the death penalty for his crimes, but Socrates maintains his integrity and refuses to plead for leniency as expected.

1. How does Socrates characterize the vote of the jury? Why does it surprise him?
2. What does Socrates think he deserves for his "crimes"? What do you think of his proposal?
3. Why does Socrates eventually propose a fine?

Socrates' Response to the Death Sentence (38c–42)

1. Who does Socrates consider to be the true loser as a result of what he considers an unjust sentence?
2. Why is it better to escape doing wrong than to escape death?
3. What does Socrates predict will happen soon after his death?
4. What does Socrates have to say to those who voted for him? In particular, why does he consider death a blessing?

GUIDE TO *CRITO*

Socrates' friend and student, Crito, has come to his prison cell to convince him to escape. Socrates has been imprisoned for approximately a month and is waiting for a ship, which has been sent upon a sacred voyage, to return home (no executions could take place until its return). The ship is now nearing Athens. It is evident that Socrates' friends had the willingness and means to help him leave Athens. This dialogue provides Crito, and the rest of us, Socrates' explanation for why he will not disobey the sentence he himself considers wrong.

Greetings (43–44b)

1. Why does Crito not wake up Socrates? Why would Socrates have preferred to be awakened?
2. What bad news does Crito bring?
3. What dream has Socrates had, and what does it mean to him?

Crito's Plea (44b–46b)

1. Why does Crito think others will think ill of him if he does not succeed in helping Socrates to escape? What is Socrates' response to this concern?

2. What is Socrates' response to Crito's claim that he must pay attention to what ordinary people think and do?

3. What arguments does Crito use to try to shame Socrates into leaving?

Dialogue with Crito (46b–50)

1. What principle is Socrates trying to establish by talking to Crito about the value of expert advice?

2. What is that "part of us" that is "mutilated by wrong actions and benefited by right ones"? (47e–48) Why is life not worth living when this part is ruined?

3. Why would it be wrong for Socrates (and even harmful to him) to disobey the sentence of the jury?

Dialogue with the Laws (50–)

1. Why do you think Socrates personifies the laws so that he is in effect having a conversation with them?

2. For the sake of argument, Socrates supposes that he tells the laws that he intends to "destroy" them by disobeying them. In what sense would he be destroying the laws by escaping justice?

3. What reasons do the laws give for why Socrates should stay and take his punishment? Which if any of these reasons do you find convincing?

4. Do you agree with the laws that a person owes the state obedience to its laws, even the unjust ones, because that person has benefitted from years of protection and the privileges of a citizen?

5. Do you think that Socrates agrees with everything the laws say, or do you suppose that Socrates may be in only partial agreement (since he has in the past—as recounted in the *Apology*—disobeyed direct orders from the government because he did not think they were just)?

GUIDE TO *THE REPUBLIC*

As you know by now, Plato's *Republic* is not always a book to be taken literally. It is full of analogies, metaphors, and figurative turns of phrase. Indeed, it is possible to argue that the entire book, including all of the proposals for the city in speech, is a metaphor to describe Justice in the individual soul. As you read the book, then, keep in mind that Socrates is trying to find out what this Justice is. On top of that goal, Socrates is trying to make some points about political power and types of government that may not be obvious. Remember, do not read the book simply to answer the following questions, but concentrate on these questions as you move through the text to help you eventually obtain the bigger picture.

Book I

1. How does the question of justice arise? What are the answers given to the question by Cephalus, Polemarchus, and Thracymachus?
2. How does Socrates respond to each of these answers? (It is worthwhile to recount his response to each specific answer instead of summarizing.)

Book II

1. Why do Glaucon and Adimantus get into the discussion? What do they say about Justice?
2. After Glaucon's and Adimantus' arguments, Socrates shifts the conversation to the question of the just city, as opposed to the just individual. Why does Socrates do this?
3. Describe the first city Socrates develops. Why does Socrates' friend call it a city fit for pigs and thus unsatisfactory? Why does Socrates nonetheless say that it may be the most just city?
4. When Socrates begins to discuss the more luxurious city, he says that it will need to have a military. Why does the luxurious city need a special class of soldiers?
5. What qualities does Socrates say the soldiers (or guardians) should possess to set them apart from the rest of the city?

Book III

1. What is the goal of the guardians' education?
2. Describe the "myth of metals." In this passage we have the first clear glimpse of the metaphor between the just soul and the just city. What parts of the individual soul do you think these metal-classes represent?
3. How do you think this three-class system would work in an actual city?

Book IV

1. Why does Adimantus object to the arrangements in the just city that Socrates is building?
2. How are the four virtues (Justice, Wisdom, Courage, Temperance or Moderation) distributed among the people in the just city?
3. How do these virtues correspond to the three classes in the city and the three parts of the soul?

Book V   Book V is central, both in place and importance. In it we find the "three waves," or three shocking proposals, that would seem to make the city more of a fantasy than an actual proposal. In Plato's time, for instance, women were expected to remain hidden from the view of other men, to stay at home, and to attend only to household needs. Here in the first shocking wave, however, Socrates calls for female soldiers. In the second wave, Socrates proposes a sort of communism which includes the elimination of the family—guardian marriages will take place at the rulers' command, and the guardians' children will be raised collectively, not by their parents. Finally, Socrates argues that philosophers should rule over the city, a proposal he thinks is the most incredible of all.

1. Why do Socrates' friends think women are unfit to be soldiers? What arguments does Socrates use to contradict this belief?
2. The guardians or soldiers are that class out of which the rulers will emerge. To that end, and to keep the soldiers' stock strong, Socrates recommends strange marriage, mating, and child-rearing practices. How do you think these ideas would work in practice?
3. Keeping in mind that the rulers represent reason in the individual soul, and that these marriage, mating, and child-rearing proposals would apply particularly to them, what do you suppose might be the metaphorical meaning of these proposals for reason or philosophy? (Here and elsewhere Plato uses images of procreation, birth, and abortion to discuss the process of "conceiving" ideas, evaluating, and keeping/rejecting them.)
4. Look up the word *eugenics* if you are unfamiliar with it. Socrates recommends a form of eugenics when he says that unsuitable children of the guardians should be exposed or left to die. The ancient Greeks often practiced infanticide: When an unwanted child came along, it was left up to the gods to decide the child's fate. Keeping in mind the ongoing metaphor about the soul, and that Plato sometimes uses images of exposure or abortion to discuss the rejection of ill-formed ideas, what metaphorical point might Socrates be making with this proposal?
5. What are obstacles to the kingship of philosophers discussed in Book V?
6. If it is almost impossible, as Socrates says, to imagine philosophers consenting to kingship and having the people accept them (and hence the ideal city is almost impossible), then what *political* points do you think he is making in Book V?

Book VI

1. What is the difference between true and false philosophers? In what way are philosophers useless?
2. How does the analogy of the sun and the Good help to clarify your understanding of Socrates' argument?
3. How do you think the idea of the Good relates to Justice?

Book VII The cave parable, as discussed in this chapter, is another key to understanding Socrates' purpose in this dialogue. It tells us what Socrates thought his own position was in relation to most of the people around him, including the other interlocutors in this dialogue.

1. What is the situation of the men in the cave? What do they *think* is their situation?
2. Why is it so hard for one of these men to be drawn up to the light? What does the light represent?
3. Why is it so hard to get the man who knows what the real world is like to come back into the cave?
4. How do the men still chained in the cave greet their freed partner upon his return? Why?
5. What do you think Socrates is saying about his own situation and role with this parable? Why do you think Socrates continues to draw others into the light?

Book VIII

1. What are the four kinds of corrupt constitutions? How do the types of constitutions correspond to the types of human beings?
2. What is the historical sequence of constitutions? Do they get better or worse over time?
3. Does Socrates consider democracy the best form of government? Why or why not?

Book IX

1. What is tyranny? How can Socrates argue that the tyrant is really unhappy, even if he is unaware of the fact?
2. What is Socrates trying to depict with his analogy of the many-headed monster?

Book X

1. What are Socrates' arguments against poetry? What is his purpose?
2. Is philosophy an alternative to poetry? Explain.
3. Why do you think Socrates discusses an afterlife at the end of the dialogue? Is this discussion essential to Socrates' arguments on justice?

GUIDE TO GORGIAS

The *Gorgias* is a dialogue about political rhetoric (political speech making). There was certainly plenty of speech making in ancient Athens. Men who excelled at making speeches were able to persuade the Athenian Assembly to vote their way. Eloquent lawyers won cases. If anything, the ability to use words well has only become more important in today's democracies. In U.S.

politics, one awkward gaffe can earn a politician everlasting shame and one catchy phrase can ring in the ears of the voters for an entire campaign. Is this talent for public speaking, almost made into a science by politicians in our information age, really serving the public? Or, is rhetoric mostly used to obscure issues and sway audiences with emotive rather than factual appeals? These are questions Socrates was already asking.

Socrates argues that most political rhetoric is deceptive and harmful to the public, because it serves the selfish interests of the power brokers. What may surprise you is that Socrates also argues that such rhetoric is harmful to the politicians as well, that it leads them astray and makes them unhappy. Gorgias is a successful teacher of rhetoric. In Socrates' and Plato's day, teachers of rhetoric promised to make young men into successful lawyers and politicians. In a way, Socrates is arguing that he is teaching something far more useful than what Gorgias is teaching.

Introductory Section (447–449)   This section runs from the beginning of the dialogue to where Socrates starts asking Gorgias, "What is rhetoric?" It involves Socrates and two interlocutors. Chaerephon is an admirer of Socrates who wants to hear him defend the teaching of philosophy against the teaching of rhetoric. Polus is an admirer of Gorgias and wants to defend the practice of rhetoric.

1. What does Gorgias do for a living?
2. What does Socrates want to know from Gorgias?
3. How does Socrates react to the idea of Gorgias' giving a demonstration of his speaking abilities?
4. Why does Polus think that he is good enough to answer Chaerephon's questions?

Dialogue with Gorgias (448–461)   Here Gorgias enters the fray and is fairly generous (though not at first straightforward) with his answers. Ask yourself why Socrates persists in not being satisfied with Gorgias' answers.

1. What kind of answers does Gorgias initially give to the question, "What is rhetoric?"
2. Gorgias finally offers Socrates a decent definition (persuasion in the law courts and assembly). Look this definition over carefully. Why does Socrates continue with his questions?
3. Explain the distinction Socrates makes between knowledge and belief. What type of communication produces knowledge and what kind produces mere beliefs, according to Socrates?
4. Why does Gorgias claim that rhetoric is the most powerful of arts, even though the rhetorician is not an expert in any area but speaks on every topic?
5. Why does Gorgias think that the teacher of rhetoric should not be blamed if his students use rhetoric to promote an unjust cause?

6. Socrates seems to think that the teaching of rhetoric is not morally neutral, as Gorgias would claim, but that the teachers transmit certain undesirable values to their students. Gorgias had previously told Socrates that the skillful rhetorician can speak on any topic, and persuade the vast majority to believe anything the rhetorician desired. He has also admitted that the rhetorician needs no knowledge of the topic about which he is speaking, in part because he is speaking to audiences who are even more ignorant of the topic than he. If Gorgias advertises his classes to students with this description of rhetoric, can he really be teaching a morally neutral skill, as he claims?

7. Near the end of his exchange with Gorgias, Socrates suggests that much of what rhetoricians talk about are matters concerning what is right and wrong, just or unjust. (Should we raise taxes to build a stronger military? Should we make war?) Do you believe it is realistic to want politicians to know what is right or just before they start making recommendations to the public?

Polus (461–481)   Soon, Polus interrupts and tries to give Gorgias a rest from his efforts (though he had earlier boasted that Gorgias could speak about anything without any preparation, and had offered Gorgias' services without asking him first). Polus decides to go on the offensive and question Socrates.

1. Why is Polus apparently so angry at Socrates?
2. Why does Socrates deny that rhetoric is a true art?
3. Why does Socrates call rhetoric a form of flattery and compare it with cooking or putting on makeup?
4. Why does Polus admire rhetoricians so much?
5. Read Polus' story about King Archelaus and then read Socrates' reaction to Polus' story. Why does Polus think that a man like Archelaus is happy? Why do you think Socrates says such a man is likely to be very unhappy?
6. Socrates soon persuades Polus to agree with the idea that doing wrong is ugly or unattractive and that doing justice is beautiful. He then defines *ugly* and *beautiful* in ways that do not advance Polus' argument. What is the overall point Socrates is trying to make by persuading Polus to agree with these definitions?
7. Polus has agreed to all of Socrates' points, so how can he reject Socrates' conclusions at the end of it all?

Callicles (481–523)   Callicles is the toughest opponent of Socrates in this dialogue. When he enters into the argument, he scoffs at Gorgias and Polus for caving into the "conventional" (merely man-made) morality that Socrates is advocating, and for being ashamed to say what they really think. Callicles has a complete theory of morality and politics, unlike Polus and Gorgias. It is important that you understand the view that all morality is man-made—a creation of whoever is in power. This theory is still held by many people today.

1. What sense do you get about Callicles' opinion of human nature from his opening comments?
2. What does Callicles mean when he says that Socrates has been advocating values or ideas that are merely "conventional" or man-made?
3. How does Callicles explain why conventional morality and democratic ideas are so strongly advocated?
4. What opinion does Callicles have of Socrates? What advice does he give Socrates?
5. Who does Callicles think should rule, and why? How would Athenian rhetoricians fit into his vision?
6. Socrates points out that in Athenian democracy the people are stronger because of their numbers and that, according to Callicles' own argument, they therefore deserve to rule. Socrates uses what is known as a rhetorical argument, that is, one designed to show the flaws in Callicles' reasoning more than to reflect Socrates' own views. It is highly unlikely that Socrates would actually agree that the people should rule because of their strength of numbers. How does Callicles revise his definition of who should rule, after he is challenged by Socrates?
7. Socrates and Callicles get into an argument about what is the best way to live one's life. Socrates says the best way is to live a temperate or moderate life. For Callicles, the best way is to indulge your desires. Explain each man's argument.
8. Socrates tries to point out to Callicles that his idea of pursuing pleasure endlessly might actually end up hurting him. How does Socrates try to get this point across to Callicles?
9. Socrates argues that rhetoricians have to spend most of their time trying to figure out how to please their audience. They are really not pleasing themselves, but have become slaves to the crowd. If this is the case, why do you think that so many politicians continue to think that they are happy and in control of the people instead of the other way around?
10. Why does Socrates bring up past Athenian leaders and ask Callicles if he knows any who advised the people to do what was right and best for them?
11. It would certainly seem as though Socrates has no use for rhetoric, but then he finally mentions the possibility of a speaker who uses rhetoric to promote the Good. Why would a good leader need to use rhetoric? What goals would he try to reach for the people? Do you think Socrates is talking about himself here? Is he also talking about possible political leaders? (Remember, he is trying to persuade others here—such as Polus or Chaerephon—who might be politically powerful in the future.)

12. Why does Callicles become so angry toward the end of his dialogue with Socrates?

13. Socrates summarizes his position after Callicles' angry outburst. Use this summary to add to your own understanding of Socrates' position. Why does Socrates maintain that a person is more likely to feel free and happy if he or she lives a just life?

14. How does Socrates depict previous, supposedly great, leaders of Athens? What type of leadership would he prefer for Athens? How does he view his own role in Athenian politics?

Myth (523–end)   In this section you will find an unusual addition to Socrates' other arguments. Socrates thinks that it is important to tell his listeners a story about justice in the afterlife. This story is just one facet of a multifaceted argument. Given that, it is important to try to understand its purpose and why Plato felt it should be included.

1. In what manner were people originally judged and how did Zeus change that system?

2. How does the new system of judgment affect people who have power, wealth, health, and so on?

3. Who is more likely to go to the place of punishment (Tartarus) and stay there forever? Who is most likely to go to the Blessed Isles? Why?

4. In your estimation, does this myth strengthen or weaken Socrates' overall argument? Why does he include it here?

BIBLIOGRAPHY

Julia Annas, *An Introduction to Plato's Republic,* New York: Oxford University Press, 1981.

Ernest Barker, *The Political Thought of Plato and Aristotle,* New York: Russell & Russell, 1959.

Thomas C. Brickhouse and Nicholas D. Smith, *Plato's Socrates,* New York: Oxford University Press, 1994.

John Burnett, *Early Greek Philosophy,* London: A & C Black, 1952.

George Klosko, *The Development of Plato's Theory,* New York: Methuen, 1986.

C.D.C. Reeve, *Philosopher-kings: The Argument of Plato's Republic,* Princeton: Princeton University Press, 1988.

Gregory Vlastos, *Socrates, Ironist and Moral Philosopher,* Cornell University Press, 1991.

ARISTOTLE (C. 384–323 B.C.)

BACKGROUND

Aristotle's influence on Western culture and especially the development of classical republicanism is immense because his philosophy, more than any other, was welcomed by the Roman Catholic Church. The Church found his teachings largely compatible with its theology because of the analysis of St. Thomas Aquinas, a thirteenth-century scholastic. Imagine this one person, Aristotle, having a formative impact on the politics of an entire civilization.

Aristotle was born in 384 B.C. in Stagira in northern Greece. Unlike Socrates' family, Aristotle's was fairly noteworthy. His parents were wealthy and influential. His father was the physician of King Amyntas III of Macedonia. Because of his father's occupation, Aristotle, for better or worse, always had a connection to royalty. When his father died, young Aristotle became the ward of his guardian, Proxenus, who decided that the young man would go to Athens to complete his formal education. Once in Athens, Aristotle chose Plato's school, the Academy. Going to school in ancient Athens was somewhat like going to college today. Aristotle paid tuition. He listened to lectures. He was required to write and speak about what he was learning. As time went on, he was even asked to do some teaching of his own, particularly on the subject of rhetoric. Unlike our modern colleges, however, the school granted no degrees and Aristotle had more control over what classes he would take. For twenty years, Aristotle stayed at the Academy, listening to lectures and doing research in areas such as the natural sciences, mathematics, rhetoric, and of course, philosophy.

Aristotle became Plato's best student, constantly listening to the great philosopher and eventually learning enough to diverge from and go beyond Plato's teachings. When Plato died in 347 B.C., Aristotle would have been the most natural choice to replace his old teacher as head of the Academy, except that, by then, there was enough of a difference between what Plato thought and what Aristotle held that other philosophers at the Academy objected. Instead, Plato's nephew Speusippus became head of the Academy. Aristotle then went out on his own. First, he stayed for three years at the court of his friend Hermeas, king of Atarneus and Assos, where he met and married the king's niece, Pythias. When Hermeas's lands were conquered by the Persians, Aristotle left for Mytilene. There he received an invitation from Philip of Macedonia to become the tutor of his son, Alexander, later known as Alexander the Great. Aristotle happily accepted Philip's invitation and spent the next five years, until Alexander turned eighteen, instructing the young man and conducting his own research and writing with the king's ample support.

When Philip died and Alexander assumed the throne of Macedonia, Alexander considered his formal schooling at an end. He began his remarkable career as world conqueror, but not without paying Aristotle special homage for his service by rebuilding Aristotle's hometown of Stagira where he lived for a time. By 335 B.C., however, Aristotle was back in Athens, preparing to start his own school in an area of town called the Lyceum. The school Aristotle founded came to be known as the Peripatetic School because of its members' tendency to teach their classes while walking around. The teacher would lead, and the students would walk alongside and behind, probably according to their rank and accomplishments. Students would listen, ask questions, and occasionally add their own opinions. Aristotle's school resembled the modern college or university even more than Plato's. Lecturers tended to be permanent residents, always actively engaged in research and teaching. There was a library and other support for both activities.

At some point, Aristotle's first wife died and he married a woman named Herpyllis. Their son Nichomachus edited the work now known as the *Nichomachean Ethics* after his father's death. With the exception of the *Politics,* the *Nichomachean Ethics* tells us the most about Aristotle's political teaching. His comfortable and honored life was about to take a dramatic change for the worse when his old student, Alexander, died in 323 B.C. Alexander's Macedonia had dominated Greece, but now that he was gone, the Greeks felt freer to rebel openly against Macedonia's control. Because of his long association with Macedonian royalty, Aristotle now not only felt unwelcome in Athens but also threatened by a fabricated charge of impiety. Vowing not to let Athens sin against philosophy twice by killing another philosopher, Aristotle fled to Chalcis in Euboea where he lived on his deceased mother's estate. Within a year of his arrival in Chalcis, however, Aristotle died of an undefined stomach illness. Such was the humble end of a man whose work was to have so much influence on future thought.

A few words must be said about Aristotle's times. Aristotle believed he was living through the decline of Athens, a state that once dominated Greece. While politically dominated by Macedonia, Athens was still a democracy; but for Aristotle, that democracy was becoming more and more corrupt, its citizens lacking an understanding of good citizenship. Class conflict, always an important element in Greek politics, became more pronounced as imperialism and commercialism challenged the old aristocracy which had lost the traditional base of power. Although the common man gained more political influence, he did not proportionately gain more political wisdom. The popular philosophies of the day valued the accumulation of wealth and the pursuit of pleasure rather than duty to the city as a whole or to fellow citizens. Certainly the value of the intellectual or contemplative life was evermore downplayed in favor of the life of action and acquisition.

Aristotle nostalgically idealized the fifth century, a time in which he thought Athenians, though democratic, were less corrupted by excessive wealth and more influenced by love of the city. But Athens was never the city Plato or Aristotle would have wanted, and both philosophers criticized it. By Aristotle's time, however, Athenian decline was more apparent. The *Politics* is, among other things, a call for a return to older notions of virtue and citizenship. In this way Aristotle shares with many commentators today the conviction that true citizenship has fallen into decline, and that the reinvigoration of democratic institutions is only possible through the inculcation of citizen virtue.

Aristotle's written work was supposedly kept by his student and the second head of the Lyceum after Aristotle left, Theophrastus. When Theophrastus died, one of his students received his library, and when that student died, his family hid the books in a vault to protect them from theft. Apparently forgotten, they stayed in the vault until they were discovered, somewhat damaged, circa 100 B.C. by a man named Apellicon, who brought them back to Athens. When Emperor Sulla conquered Athens in 86 B.C., the Romans took them back to Rome as part of the spoils. There, scholars discovered how deep and wide ranging these works of philosophy were. Copies of these books were then made more accessible to scholars. Unfortunately, not all of Aristotle's works survived. Given their route to Rome, it truly is a wonder that so much remained.

UNDERSTANDING ARISTOTLE

Aristotle's lost works include dialogues of the type written by Plato and meant for a more general audience, and collections of information for further analysis. We have what scholars call Aristotle's "systematic treatises." Other ancient scholars praised Aristotle's beautiful prose, but this is probably on the basis of the dialogues. The treatises that we have, including Aristotle's most famous political work, the *Politics*, often seem plain and even clumsy and disjointed.

In the case of the *Politics* and several other works, a very good case has been made that Aristotle did not craft a planned book with a beginning, middle, and end. Instead, the *Politics* probably constitutes a collection of notes from which Aristotle gave lectures during his headship of the Lyceum. These notes center around the theme of politics and may have been put together by Aristotle, but more likely were collected by a student.

Lectures do not read like a book. Usually, with even the most talented lecturer, there are no smooth transitions from the lecture of one day to the lecture of another day. Certain digressions that would not usually be permitted in a consciously constructed work are perfectly suitable for lectures. The reader then should expect to find changes in tone, emphasis, reasoning, and even opinion within the *Politics*, especially since these lectures may have been given over a period of several years. Thus we may not be able to subject the *Politics* to the same level of critical scrutiny as works that were intended as one coherent argument. Changes may not indicate a flaw in Aristotle's logic if his arguments used in class changed over the course of time.

The *Politics* is considered a mature work of Aristotle, because it was written in the latter part of his life and thus possibly less influenced by Plato. As with so many other philosophers, Aristotle addresses the ideas of his great teacher, the man who set him on the path toward his own philosophy. A reader can tell much about what Aristotle thinks by paying close attention to which ideas of Plato Aristotle accepts and which ones he rejects. For instance, in the *Politics*, Aristotle discusses communism among the guardian class in Plato's *Republic* and concludes that such a system is practically impossible. In explaining his rejection of this communistic ideal he reveals his ideas about human nature, justice, and the role of government. In another instance, Aristotle agrees with Plato that the state must shape the young, formative years of an individual in order to produce a virtuous citizen. Aristotle also emphasizes habituation or actually practicing virtuous deeds rather than the purely intellectual route Plato advocates of knowing virtue and thus acting virtuously. Aristotle's self-conscious comparisons with his mentor reveal a great deal about his views.

Aristotle's understanding of politics, as his understanding of plants and animals, was teleological. In Greek, *telos* means "end" or "final state," and *logos* means "reasoning" or "thinking." Teleological thinking thus scrutinizes and evaluates something according to its natural ends. For example, when we see an acorn, we think of an oak tree. The acorn is not evaluated for its own sake but for what we know it can become given the right conditions. Teleological thinking is an integral part of the pro-life position in today's abortion controversies. The pro-life advocate sees the potential of a fully developed person in the fertilized egg or zygote and can thus claim that abortion even at this very early stage is the unjust killing of a human being. Applying the teleological mode of thinking to biological matters is fairly straightforward, but applying it to politics is more difficult and controversial.

To apply teleology to politics, one would first have to claim that political associations are natural to human beings. One would then have to know the final end or most perfect state of political order. Claiming to know what is the best human political order is always going to be controversial. What is best or natural is simply not as clear for human associations as it is for the animal kingdom. The ant must help build an anthill and a bee belongs in a hive, but because human beings have reason and are not driven by instinct but have free will, there are many different claims about the best political order. Some claim that all such orders are artificial and that humanity would be better off without any political order. Aristotle therefore gives himself a very difficult assignment. Pay close attention when he discusses what is natural for human beings, especially when he compares human beings with other animals. Aristotle understands what makes human beings different from animals driven by instinct, but he still maintains that teleological thinking can be applied to human beings.

Many have criticized Aristotle for his seemingly blatant sexism and advocacy of slavery. (Aristotle's views do not seem as open to women's equality as Plato's. We have seen, however, that Plato's views are not as open as they seem, and we will see that Aristotle's views are not as closed as they first appear.) Part of the reason for the difference in tone between Plato and Aristotle on the issue of women is a difference in their way of thinking. When Plato was formulating his ideals, practical considerations carried little weight. Plato knew what the world as we know it was like, but he thought that the philosopher should set aside that world when formulating absolute standards of justice, for instance. However, Aristotle did not think that the philosopher could or should remove himself from the world as we know it. Aristotle was much more likely to start with observations of actual human behavior and then logically deduce standards of virtue and justice. This approach has its strengths and weaknesses.

Aristotle observed that the women in his world were less accomplished in most areas and less courageous than men, that they attended to domestic tasks, and that they were more nurturing. He did not see these traits as possibly the result of faulty or unjust socialization. Within this seemingly universal female behavior, Aristotle discerned the essence of female nature, her *telos;* thus, the virtue of a woman was different from that of a man and had to be treated separately. Despite his tendency to mistake common practice for what was natural, Aristotle tried to deal with these issues objectively. He retains Plato's view that all subjects must be treated objectively, that it is not good enough to simply receive and transmit existing folklore and prejudices, and that society should not be ordered on the basis of tradition but on what makes sense in the light of reason. This view of society is essential in the development of later thought, which challenged in a more radical way the inequality between the sexes, classes, and races that many saw as eternal and natural.

CAREFUL READING

As with many other works, parts of Aristotle's *Politics*[1] will leave one impression if skimmed and another impression if carefully read and pondered.

Aristotle on Women

Aristotle's views on the role of women in the family and society often make modern readers uncomfortable. His views on women as well as slaves were no doubt influenced by the unequal relationships he saw around him. Nonetheless, in both cases Aristotle manages to depart from a superficial assessment of the subject matter based solely on the practices of his day. Aristotle does not equate women's intelligence with that of either slaves or children, but exactly what he thinks of women's intelligence and virtue is a matter of much speculation.

Aristotle tells us that the husband's rule over the wife is constitutional, while his rule over his children is royal. He claims a general rule that the male is naturally "fitter for command," although there may be some exceptions to this rule. He seems to imply that women are in some sense the equals of their husbands (such that they cannot be ruled over like a king rules over his subjects), but that they are not equal enough to share in his rule. Nevertheless, the husband's rule remains constitutional. (1259b1–15) This may mean that, unlike children, wives must give consent before they can be ruled. Luckily, Aristotle continues along these lines, giving us a better chance of grasping what he thinks of the relationship between husbands and wives.

> But the kind of rule differs—the freeman rules over the slave after another manner from that in which the male rules over the female, or the man over the child; although the parts of the soul are present in all of them, they are present in different degrees. For the slave has no deliberative faculty at all; the woman has, but it is without authority, and the child has, but it is immature. So it must necessarily be supposed to be with the excellences of character also; all should partake of them, but only in such manner and degree as is required by each for the fulfilment of his function. Hence the ruler ought to have excellence of character in perfection, for his function, taken absolutely, demands a master artificer, and reason is such an artificer; the subjects, on the other hand, require only that measure of excellence which is property to each of them. Clearly, then, excellence of character belongs to all of them; but the temperance of a man and of a woman, or the courage and justice of a man and of a woman, are not, as Socrates maintained, the same; the courage of a man is shown in commanding, of a woman in obeying . . . All classes must be deemed to have their special attributes; as the poet says of women,

---

[1] Here and elsewhere the author will be using the Everson translation, Aristotle, *The Politics*, edited by Stephen Everson, Cambridge: Cambridge University Press, 1989. Reprinted by permission of Princeton University Press.

"Silence is a woman's glory, but this is not equally the glory of man."
(1260a10–30)

First, notice that Aristotle distinguishes the rule of a husband over a wife from that of a father over his children. Both wife and children are free (not slaves), but the father's rule over his children is royal, which implies no consent on their part is necessary for him to make decisions regarding their welfare. The husband's rule over his wife is constitutional, which we will find here and elsewhere means that it involves at the very least consent and may involve ruling and being ruled in turn. Aristotle elsewhere advocates exactly this form of government as preferable to all others under most circumstances. In so saying, Aristotle departs from the view that wives are to be treated as slaves (and given Aristotle's reasoning on slavery, this means that he does not think women are like natural slaves, with no ability to reason). He also disagrees with the idea that a woman's reason is as immature as that of a child; however, the question of why women must be in a subordinate position remains.

Aristotle does say that there are "exceptions to the order of nature." Some women truly are fit to lead instead of being led. In most cases, however, the man is "by nature fitter for command, just as the elder . . . is superior to the younger and more immature." Perhaps female reason is immature, just not as immature as that of a child. Aristotle brings in again the analogy of husband-rule to the constitutional state. In such a state, citizens rule and are ruled by turns, and the natures of the citizens are considered equal. However, when one citizen rules, the others accord him a certain respect because of his role, such as our president or senator. Aristotle brings up the image of Amasis and his foot-pan in this context. In this story, King Amasis's subjects treated him disrespectfully because they knew he was not born of royal blood. He made a god for them to worship, and only later told them the god was fashioned from a foot-bath. This story brings home the point that it is not a person's origins that should earn his respect, but the individual's performance. In other words, respect should be truly earned. Aristotle says that the relationship of male and female is always this kind of relationship.

Aristotle goes on to explain the difference between men and women and why men are usually more suited to rule in marriage and elsewhere. Dealing with the souls of men, women, children, and slaves, Aristotle says that the (natural) slave has no ability to reason. The woman has the ability to reason, "but it is without authority." The child has reason, too, but "it is immature." Here, Aristotle does not refer to women's reason as immature, only without authority. What does this notoriously ambiguous phrase mean? Man, "the ruler," must have virtue in its perfection; that is, he must have excellent reason to be the "master artificer." An artificer is one who creates things, which involves thinking, deciding, planning. So the male usually must be a superior decision maker and planner, according to Aristotle.

Aristotle then separates out men, women, and children by saying that although they have the same type of souls, and they have virtue, but their virtue is shaped by their role. Remember Aristotle's teleological view that all are to be measured by the role or function they ultimately fill. A woman's virtue of courage, for example, is shown through her presumably natural function of obeying. A man's courage is shown through his function of commanding. Aristotle concludes this selection with a not-so-appealing statement that "silence is a woman's glory," but not a man's.

Aristotle never satisfactorily explains what he means by women have reason, but no authority. Some have said that Aristotle, looking around him, saw that women simply did not take the lead in households and concluded that leadership was not in their nature. He certainly would have seen the men around him as much bolder. Aristotle may have mistaken a cultural phenomenon for something natural. Some take seriously Aristotle's argument that women by nature are generally not leaders and either attempt to prove or disprove his conclusions. Others maintain that Aristotle is making a genuine distinction between the general quality of women's reason as opposed to men's. This conclusion would seem to be bolstered by his depiction of women's reason as immature, though not as immature as children's. In our day some have attempted to support or disprove this position using empirical research.

If seen through the eyes of Aristotle's contemporaries, his thoughts are different, even path breaking. In his ensuing discussion on the relationship of the family to the state, he underscores the importance of educating women because their excellences "must make a difference: for . . . half the free persons in a state are women." Aristotle follows his teacher Plato in concluding that women's roles as citizens must be taken seriously, and that women must be educated because they are an important part of what makes the city virtuous.

The Active versus the Contemplative Life

At a certain point in Book VII of the *Politics,* Aristotle asks which is best, the active or contemplative life. What he means by active and contemplative might seem obvious at first—the political versus the philosophical life. However, Aristotle is more ambiguous than Plato, not only making his preference clear but also in defining these terms.

> Now it is evident that that form of government is best in which every man, whoever he is, can act best and live happily. But even those who agree in thinking that the life of excellence is the most desirable raise a question, whether the life of business and politics is or is not more desirable than one which is wholly independent of external goods, I mean than a contemplative life, which by some is maintained to be the only one worthy of a philosopher. For these two lives—the life of the philosopher and the life of the statesman—appear to have been preferred by those who have been most keen in the pursuit of excellence, both in our

own and in other ages. Which is the better is a question of no small amount; for the wise man, like the wise state, will necessarily regulate his life according to the best end . . . (1324a25–1324a35)

But perhaps someone, accepting these premises, may still maintain that supreme power is the best of all things, because the possessors of it are able to perform the greatest number of noble actions . . .

If we are right in our view, and happiness is assumed to be acting well, the active life will be the best, both for every city collectively, and for individuals. Not that a life of action must necessarily have relation to others, as some persons think, nor are those ideas only to be regarded as practical which are pursued for the sake of practical results, but much more the thoughts and contemplations which are independent and complete in themselves; since acting well, and therefore a certain kind of action, is an end, and even in the case of external actions the directing mind is most truly said to act. (1325a35–1325b30)

Aristotle combines the topic of the best life with the topic of the best form of government. This may seem strange to us, because we often thoroughly separate our private pursuit of happiness from the government and its role. For Aristotle, however, the two were very much related: Good people made a good government, but also a good government could shape better people. He starts off by affirming that the best government is one in which every citizen can "act best and live happily." What does Aristotle mean by "act best"? Certainly it does not mean doing whatever the individual thinks is best.

Aristotle starts out, as he often does, with other people's opinions. The active life for most people means the life of business and politics. The contemplative life is thought to be a life wholly independent of external goods. This is probably also a fairly good description of Plato's view, but the phrase "wholly independent" should give the reader pause. Certainly Plato thought that the contemplative life was the only one worthy of a philosopher, but the distinction between philosopher and statesman is not as clear as it seems at first. In Plato's *Gorgias,* the truest statesman was the moral artist, probably the philosopher, whether or not he was actually in a position to rule.

Aristotle goes on to say that there are those who think despotic or tyrannical rule is the greatest injustice, yet to rule over men constitutionally is a "great impediment to a man's individual well-being." This is probably a direct reference to Plato's teaching in *The Republic* and other dialogues that tyranny is the worst form of government, whereas the ideal rule of philosophers might make the best government (if people would accept it). This position would be a great burden to the philosophers, though, who would rather not depart from their philosophical speculations to perform the task of ruling. Thus, the Republic was a state in which the best life (unbounded contemplation) was incompatible with the best form of government (philosopher-rule).

Aristotle juxtaposes this stance with another: The best life is active or political and all excellences and virtues can be practiced by all citizens. This view downplays the value of the purely contemplative life. Yet a third view is that tyranny leads to happiness. The happiness Aristotle is referring to here is the happiness of one individual, the tyrant, who enjoys having "despotic power over [his] neighbors." In such a state, the laws do not promote the virtue of citizens but serve to maintain the tyrant's power and happiness.

Aristotle gives us a fourth view: Absolute power can lead to happiness because those with it can perform the most noble actions. This view seems similar to the view of Cephalus in the beginning of *The Republic:* A rich man can more easily be just because he has enough money to pay his debts, honor the gods, and be generous. Aristotle thinks this view is ludicrous and says that if this is so, then no one should have any regard for anyone else who gets in the way of noble actions. A robber could live the best life if he did noble actions with his stolen loot (such would be the situation of Robin Hood). For a ruler's actions to be honorable, Aristotle says, he must be as superior to other men as men are to women or fathers are to children. That cannot happen if the means the ruler uses to get his power and money are not noble. Aristotle states his view of what is just—a person should receive obedience from others only if he truly deserves it. To deserve obedience, a person must be excellent or virtuous and also have the "capacity for action . . ." Here Aristotle closes the gap between the contemplative and the active life. Apparently, in his view, it is possible to have both in one person.

Aristotle continues to build on this impression. Happiness, he says, is "acting well," and so the active life is best for the city and for individuals; but the active life does not, surprisingly, have to be the life of business or politics after all. Indeed, Aristotle seems to turn common notions of these two lifestyles around by saying that the active life can be a life that pursues contemplation for its own sake. He seems to deny the original opinion that a contemplative life is or can be cut off from all action. Thinking is action, and external actions are good because of the thinking that precedes them. Hence, the philosophical life is a kind of active life, not the opposite of active life. Aristotle's life involved that philosophy. He was first and foremost a philosopher, but he was also a teacher who had an impact on other people's actions. He was a tutor to a future world leader; certainly that position gave him practical influence.

The greatest, most excellent action of all for Aristotle seems to be the action of the mind in contemplation. Aristotle simply does not accept the distinction between active and contemplative life. He compares the contemplative life to a city that has cut itself off from relations with other states. Such a state can still be active because different parts of the state (the intellectuals, the businessmen, the politicians, the women, and so on) have relationships with each other just as the parts (that is, different aspects of the soul) can act upon each other. Later, Aristotle compares the contemplative life with that of the gods. They have no "external actions over and above their own energies." If the gods are the source of all things, then in a sense nothing they can do in the world is outside of themselves or external to them. Yet, reasons Aristotle, we would not want to say the gods are not perfect simply because they do not lead lives of typical worldly action.

For Aristotle, the same life is best for individuals, states, and all of humankind. Obviously Aristotle thinks that the best life for individuals is one of contemplation, with or without practical action. Similarly, we know that the best government is that in which those who deserve to rule do so because of their virtue. It would seem that the best state must be ruled by wisdom, but Aristotle does not adopt Plato's view that philosophers should rule, and in a communistic setting. Perhaps in Aristotle's best regime, the wise would not resent taking part in ruling, seeing no major clash between thinking and acting.

GUIDE TO *POLITICS*

You will find Aristotle's political philosophy in the *Politics* more practical than Plato's. Pay particular attention to the fact that he is also more of an economic thinker.[2]

Book I

Section 1

1. What is the aim of the state or political community?
2. What is Aristotle's method and purpose?

Section 2

1. What are the first two human relationships?
2. How does Aristotle describe the proper relationship between men and women?
3. Describe the development of society from family to the state.
4. Why is man the most political animal?
5. How does Aristotle prove that the state is natural and actually in some way prior to the individual and family?
6. How is man both the best and worst of animals?

Section 3

1. What are the three relationships in the family that Aristotle considers?
2. What popular opinions about slavery does Aristotle recount?

---

[2] The translation from which we took our selections in the Careful Reading section of this chapter use the term *excellence*, but others use the term *virtue* or in some cases *goodness*. In the guide to *Politics*, the author typically uses the term *virtue*, but be aware that your translation may use *excellence*, *goodness*, or other terms.

Section 4

1. Why is the art of acquiring property so important for the household?
2. What type of instrument is a slave, and what kind of property is he?

Section 5

1. Describe in general Aristotle's hierarchical view of the world in its various aspects.
2. Describe the "natural slave."

Section 6

1. What is conventional, as opposed to natural, slavery? Why is conventional slavery wrong?
2. What is the proper relationship between master and slave?

Section 7

1. How does Aristotle distinguish constitutional rule from monarchy?
2. How does Aristotle describe the science or knowledge the master must have?

Section 8

1. Why does Aristotle say that acquiring property is natural to man?
2. For what purpose do plants and animals ultimately exist? For what purpose do you suppose he will say man exists?

Section 9

1. Define the natural art of acquiring wealth. Define the unnatural art of acquiring wealth.
2. What kind of person is Aristotle criticizing in his discussion of unnatural wealth?

Section 10

1. Toward the end of this section, Aristotle condemns usury or money-lending. Why?

Section 11

1. What does Aristotle mean by the practical side of acquiring wealth, as opposed to the theoretical side of acquiring wealth?
2. Do you have any sense as to whether Aristotle approves or disapproves of the business tactics of Thales the Milesian (monopoly)?

Section 12

1. What is the difference between the rule of a father and the rule of a husband?
2. How does Aristotle describe constitutional rule?

Section 13

1. Every person has some virtue, according to Aristotle. How does virtue manifest itself in each case?
2. How does Aristotle link the virtue of the citizens with the virtue of the state?

Book II

Section 1

1. What is Aristotle's purpose in this book and what methods will he use?
2. What is the first question Aristotle is going to answer?

Section 2

1. What is Aristotle's chief criticism of Plato's *Republic?*
2. What kind of government must there be if the citizens are naturally equal? What kind of government is better?

Section 3

What are Aristotle's chief complaints about Plato's proposal in *The Republic* that the guardians have in common (1) possessions and (2) children?

Section 4

1. Why would assaults and murders increase if we followed Plato's wish and did not know who were our own children?
2. What does Aristotle say about homosexual love, which he thinks Plato endorses?

Section 5

1. What kind of arguments does Aristotle use against common property?
2. In what sense should property be held in common? What is the relationship between private property and generosity or benevolence?
3. Why does Aristotle show respect for what people have done for ages (custom)?

Section 6

1. What do you consider Aristotle's top three complaints against Plato's book, *The Laws?*
2. If you have read *The Republic* or *The Laws,* how do you now assess Aristotle's interpretation of either or both of these works?

Section 7   In the third paragraph of this section, Aristotle begins his critique of Phaleas's ideas on the equalization of property. Aristotle critiques Phaleas's ideas in order to advance his own ideas.

1. What are the three desires that can cause crime, according to Aristotle? What are the three cures?
2. What other criticisms does Aristotle level at Phaleas's ideas?

Section 8

1. What are the chief features of Hippodamus's model of government? Why does Aristotle reject them?
2. Aristotle takes an opportunity to discuss the role of change in government, particularly in changing laws to fit changing circumstances. Sum up his philosophy on changes in laws.

Section 9   We can find out what Aristotle thinks should be done by examining his critique of the Spartans. The Spartan constitution had many defects.

Provide Aristotle's critique of the following:
—Spartan women
—laws on property
—the Ephors
—the Council of Elders
—the kings
—the common means

Section 10

1. How do the Cretans better manage their common meals? What do you suppose is the social benefit of common meals?
2. What problems does Aristotle see with the Cretan Cosmi?

Section 11

In the context of criticizing the Carthaginian government, Aristotle takes the opportunity to discuss aristocracy. What is aristocracy, and how does it differ from oligarchy? What are the advantages of aristocracy?

Section 12

Aristotle finally speaks of the Athenian government, and then only in the first half of this section. What reform does Aristotle think Solon enacted? How and why was this reform perverted as time went by?

Book III

Section 1

1. What is Aristotle's best definition of a citizen?
2. What is Aristotle's definition of a state?

Section 2

Compare the common definition of citizenship with Aristotle's definition of a citizen.

Section 3

What makes a state a state?

Section 4

1. Why does Aristotle make a distinction between the virtue of a good citizen and a good man?
2. Why, even in the good state, are the virtues of the good man and good citizen not the same (with some exceptions)?

Section 5

1. Should mechanics/laborers, who have no leisure, be citizens?
2. Aristotle mentions mothers/women as citizens, yet this inclusion does not correspond to his definition of citizen in the first section of this book. Why do you think he fails to explain this discrepancy?
3. In the last paragraph, Aristotle explains when the good man and the good citizen are the same. What are those situations?

Section 6

1. What is Aristotle's definition of a constitution?
2. Explain Aristotle's statement that man is a political animal.
3. Aristotle distinguishes between true forms of government and defective forms. What is the difference?

Section 7

Provide definitions of the three true forms of government and the three defective forms.

Section 8

The real difference between democracy and oligarchy is not numbers, according to Aristotle. What is the real difference?

Section 9

1. Explain Aristotle's statement that the purpose of the state is to ensure the good life for its citizens.
2. Aristotle answers the question of who should have more influence in any good state. Who should, and why?

Section 10

What objections does Aristotle raise to each claim for power?

Section 11

1. What are the arguments for and against the rule of the many?
2. In the final paragraph, what does Aristotle say about the source of just and unjust laws?

Section 12

For Aristotle, what type of inequality is important when assigning leadership positions to those in the state?

Section 13

Under what circumstances is ostracism reasonable, and how can it be misused?

Section 14

Define the five forms of kingship.

Section 15

1. Aristotle takes the opportunity to compare kingship with rule by the many. Which does he seem to prefer? Why?
2. How do governments usually deteriorate from kingship to democracy?

Section 16

Which do you think Aristotle prefers—the rule of one man or the rule of law? Why? When is the rule of law inadequate?

Section 17

1. What type of people are suited for kingship, aristocracy, and constitutional government, respectively?
2. How likely is real kingship in the real world?

Section 18

Note that Aristotle concludes that the virtue of the good man is the same as the virtue of the citizen in the perfect state. If the perfect state is so unlikely, why does Aristotle mention its qualities?

Book IV   Aristotle will discuss the development of the perfect state. Keep in mind he is quite realistic about the chances of the perfect state coming into existence.

Section 1

What is the purpose of political science? (Does Aristotle's definition differ at all from what Plato's might have been?)

Sections 2–3

1. What is the perfect state?
2. What is the most tolerable of the three defective states? Why?

Section 4

Why must a democracy be ruled by laws to be good and what happens when it is not?

Section 5

What type of oligarchy is like a tyranny? Why?

Section 6

In both democracies and oligarchies, under what circumstances do the citizens set up laws to govern themselves?

Section 7

What makes a regime aristocratic?

Section 8

In general, what is a polity? What distinguishes an aristocracy from a polity?

Section 9

Discuss two different ways in which democracy and oligarchy can be combined in a state to form a polity.

Section 10

How does Aristotle define the third and most common form of tyranny?

Sections 11–12

1. Why is the middle class most able to follow rational principle?
2. What are the political benefits of a city having a large middle class?

Section 13

How do governments that include the people actually deceive the people? What would need to be done to involve the people?

Section 14

1. In general, how does the deliberative function operate in a democracy and in an oligarchy?
2. Which branch of the U.S. government has the deliberative function?

Section 15

1. Which branch of the U.S. government would correspond to Aristotle's magistrates?
2. Why is a magistracy that controls women generally impracticable?

Section 16

In effect, we select jury members by lot in the United States. What are the advantages and disadvantages of this system?

Book V

Sections 1–2

1. What types of problems stir up revolutions?
2. Why does Aristotle call a democracy with a large middle class the safest of the imperfect forms of government?

Sections 3–4

1. What do you think of Aristotle's inclusion of feelings such as insolence, fear, and contempt in his causes of revolution?
2. What does Aristotle mean that revolutions are either done by force or by fraud (deception)?

Section 5

Aristotle deals with demagogues in a democracy. What is a demagogue and what motivates him to stir up revolution?

Section 6

In general, why do oligarchies have revolutions? How can a (peaceful) revolution happen by accident?

Section 7

Why is equality on the basis of merit the only stable principle of government?

Section 8

1. Aristotle advises rulers who want stable government to invent emergencies and dangers to keep on full alert. Do you think this is a useful and justifiable policy?
2. In order to increase stability, how does Aristotle advocate that the rich should treat the poor?

Section 9

What advice would Aristotle give to U.S. voters today about how to select a president and how to view their democracy?

Sections 10–11

1. Given everything he says here about monarchies and tyrannies, how would Aristotle advise a king to maintain his power?

2. Aristotle gives the tyrant advice about how to maintain his power, including deceiving people. Why does Aristotle do this when he clearly disapproves of tyranny?

Section 12

What criticisms does Aristotle level at Socrates' approach to change and revolution in government?

Book VI

Sections 1–2

1. What is the chief aim of democracy? What is the democratic definition of justice?
2. Based on what he has said elsewhere, do you think Aristotle approves of majority rule and the democratic principle that everyone should live as they please?

Section 3

Aristotle discusses oligarchical and democratic views of justice. How do we come closer to true justice, according to Aristotle?

Section 4

1. Why do agricultural people make the best candidates for democracy?
2. At a certain point it becomes clear that Aristotle's best democracy is actually a polity. How does he mix the democratic elements with oligarchical/aristocratic elements?

Section 5

Aristotle recommends considerable redistribution of property to make the poor in a democracy rise into the middle class. What is your opinion of this advice?

Section 6

What type of oligarchy is the most long-lasting? Why?

Section 7

What is the relationship between the type of military and the type of government?

Section 8

1. What offices that Aristotle discusses are familiar to us today in city, state, or federal government? Are any not familiar?
2. Are you surprised that the various functions of government in Aristotle's time were very similar to those now?

Book VII

Section 1

Aristotle makes a comparison, as did Plato, between the individual and the city. What makes individuals happiest, according to Aristotle, and how does this observation relate to his teaching on the best city?

Section 2

1. Aristotle asks the question whether a state should foster more the contemplative (thinking) life or the life of business and politics. Does he answer this question here?
2. Why is it irrational to tyrannize over others? Does Aristotle's answer give us any further insight into the value of the contemplative life?

Section 3

Do Aristotle's comments on the thinking life as active life help to clarify further what type of activity the state should value and foster?

Sections 4–5

Why does Aristotle counsel against too large a state?

Section 6

Why does Aristotle favor a city having access to the sea? How should it control the harmful effects of this access?

Section 7

Why does Aristotle think the Greeks are best suited for good government?

Section 8

Here Aristotle lists the functions of a self-sufficient state. Do you think the list is complete? Is there any part not necessary?

Section 9

Why does Aristotle exclude farmers, artisans, and laborers from citizenship?

Section 10

Does Aristotle's treatment of farmers as slaves further clarify his view of slavery as discussed in Book I?

Sections 11–12

From reading the requirements Aristotle lays down in these two sections for a good city, can you tell what his aims are for the city?

Section 13

Aristotle concludes that a happy city is one made up of happy individuals. What makes people happy and how do they maintain happiness?

Section 14

Aristotle claims that what makes individuals truly happy is honor. Does this section shed any light on how the state can encourage its citizens to lead an honorable life?

Section 15

Should education in early life be mainly based on reason or on habit (habituation)?

Section 16   Note: Exposure is the abandoning of newly born infants to the natural elements—infanticide.

Discuss a few of the laws the legislator should make regarding marriage and children. What kind of community would endorse this much regulation of private life, as opposed to the type our society has?

Section 17

Do you think Aristotle's advice about the early treatment and education of children, especially keeping them from vulgar language and entertainment, is generally sound even today?

Book VIII

Section 1

What is Aristotle's reason for preferring public education?

Section 2

In general, what type of learning should a free man avoid? Why?

Sections 3–4

1. How much importance does Aristotle assign to the enjoyment of leisure? What should we do with our leisure?
2. How much physical education should be given to boys? What can happen with excessive training?
3. Why do you think Aristotle specifies boys when giving his advice here, but does not explicitly exclude girls?

Sections 5–7

1. What is the connection Aristotle sees between music and morals?
2. Would Aristotle agree with critics of some rock and rap music who say it damages the character of the young? Why or why not?

BIBLIOGRAPHY

D.J. Allan, *The Philosophy of Aristotle,* London: Oxford University Press, 1970.

Abraham Edel, *Aristotle and His Philosophy,* Chapel Hill, NC, University of North Carolina Press, 1982.

Werner W. Jaeger, *Aristotle: Fundamentals of the History of his Development,* London: Oxford University Press, 1962.

Curtis N. Johnson, *Aristotle's Theory of the State,* New York: St. Martin's Press, 1990.

Donald Kagan, *The Great Dialogue: A History of Greek Political Thought from Homer to Polybius,* Westport, Conn.: Greenwood Press, 1986.

Carnes Lord, *Education and Culture in the Political Thought of Aristotle,* Cornell University Press, 1982.

REALISM

Realism is perhaps best understood in contrast with idealism. Realists reject the methods and goals of idealists. Knowing that idealists avoid believing that everyone is good, realists understand that the idealist philosopher considers it his duty to try to change people for the better, precisely because they are not good. Realists criticize idealists for that exact goal—trying to change people.

Realists tend to think that you cannot fundamentally change most people, at least not in their hearts. Realists believe that people's behavior can be changed—a task that is both achievable and important to them. After all, if only a few saints can really change their hearts and become truly good, what about the rest of humanity? Political change, if it is to be solid and permanent, must take into account the nature of the vast majority. If leaders and their people are given unreachable goals of goodness and justice, and if some of them actually try to reach these lofty goals, they will fail. They will fail either because their hearts are not up to the task of transformation or because the world is filled with people who will take full advantage of their moral principles. Thus, realists consider it irresponsible to offer idealistic advice that could get people hurt.

The realist is actually more optimistic than the idealist about the possibility of achieving lasting and positive political and social change. Different realists see different aspects of human nature as determining—self-interest, power, greed, and so on—but they all believe that if we accept human nature as it is, we can devise political institutions that channel and use that human nature to positive results. The realist wants to use the so-called bad parts of human nature to channel destructive energies through laws and institutions that will constructively use self-interest.

Machiavelli (1469–1527)

Background

Niccolò Machiavelli (1469–1527) wrote *The Prince* and *The Discourses* in the early part of the sixteenth century, during the Italian Renaissance. The term *renaissance* literally means "rebirth," and the men of the Renaissance saw their times as the rebirth of the ancient world. They derided the Middle Ages as a time of darkness and superstition. The Renaissance was certainly a time in which ideas and ideals were reborn. During the Renaissance, the works of ancient philosophers such as Plato and Aristotle, and the Roman philosopher Cicero, were rediscovered by scholars outside the Church. The ancient admiration for things human in art, music, poetry, and literature was revived in society generally.

If you go to a museum with adequate medieval and Renaissance art collections, you will see the difference in attitudes immediately. Medieval art is usually not very realistic, but symbolic; it concentrates on presenting certain religious themes clearly. The Madonna and Child are frequent subjects of medieval art, for instance, and in many works, the baby Jesus is depicted as more of a little adult teaching people on the lap of his mother. Renaissance art also frequently depicts biblical figures, but they are depicted with more realism and greater attention to physical beauty. Renaissance art also includes many more themes, including ancient pagan ones such as depictions of gods and mythical heroes and secular images of people and things. In other words, the Renaissance was a time during which people, especially artists and intellectuals, turned their attention from a wholehearted focus on Christian themes to a celebration of things human and natural, deploying greater realism and more attention to beauty for its own sake.

However, Renaissance man could not totally escape his medieval past. For Machiavelli, the main problem with the medieval outlook was its idealism. He thought that many of his Renaissance contemporaries still carried around too much of that medieval idealism, partly because they had not embraced the manly virtues of ancient pre-Christian Rome. The medieval outlook was highly religious. For centuries, the Catholic Church had claimed, and often held, a great deal of authority over political matters, including who would and who would not be the sovereign ruler of a realm. The Church held that it (as the representative of God on earth) was the final authority, not kings and princes. Rulers were expected to support the Church and to acknowledge its power, particularly in religious matters.

Sometimes the Church got involved in political matters, however, especially in Italy. It may seem strange to us now, but during this time, the pope considered himself not only a spiritual leader but also a politically powerful leader. He presided over the tiny Vatican City as he does today, and over a territory called the Papal States, which stretched from one sea to the other across the Italian peninsula. Popes sometimes acted cynically to enhance their own power or that of their relatives. They sometimes interfered in the politics of the region through the making of military alliances and the mustering of troops. The moral authority of the Church was quite low at this point, so much so that the pope could not only sire a son, a direct violation of his vow of celibacy, but also openly promote his son's political fortunes. This and other forms of misbehavior on the part of the Church leaders at this time are partly what inspired the Reformation in which Protestant Christianity was born. Machiavelli gives Church officials little respect, for he writes of them for the most part as purely political players, and not welcome ones at that.

Machiavelli also rejected other aspects of the Church's influence. He knew that the Church's moral teachings permeated his society, that most average people and many a leader at least took them somewhat seriously. But Machiavelli was not even sure that Christianity was the best religion for the common people, and he did not think a leader could be effective if he actually believed and practiced Christian principles.

Another aspect of the medieval period which Machiavelli soundly rejects is its feudal system of overlapping layers of power. Early in *The Prince* he rejects what he calls the "prince-baron" form of rule, which was common during the medieval period. In this system a prince would rule over a given territory, but would have to share his power with hereditary nobility who ruled over smaller sections or fiefdoms. These nobles would have the immediate power over the peasants or serfs who dwelled and worked on their land. They collected the taxes and meted out justice. Under such a system a prince had rather limited authority and had to be ever mindful of the approval or disapproval of the nobles or barons within his realm. The prince also had to share power with the Church and its local representatives—the cardinals, bishops, and priests.

Machiavelli was an early advocate of the idea that man cannot really serve two (or more) masters. He wanted any church to be squarely under the control of the state. He wanted clear lines of authority from the prince to thus reduce the challenges to his authority that could cause political instability and even war. Indeed, Machiavelli saw multiple poles of authority as the greatest political problem facing the Italians, for their peninsula had yet to be united into a country called Italy. Instead, the peninsula was divided into many principalities, a few republics (primarily ruled by oligarchs), and the Papal States. Because of the divisions and the weakness of these still-feudal power arrangements, and frequent civil wars, Italy was a target for invasions from more consolidated and powerful countries such as Spain and France.

Another area in which Machiavelli disagreed with medieval teaching was in the Church's claim that there is a natural law higher than any man-made law. The Church had long taught that divine law (God's law as expressed in scripture) and natural law (God's moral law as it is written on our hearts) were to be considered eternal and to supercede man-made law. The Church could criticize a king's or queen's laws and even urge all Christians to disobey those in authority they considered incompatible with divine or natural law. The Church could even, in extreme cases, deny the legitimacy of a leader whom it considered a threat to the Christian religion, thus in effect urging the overthrow of that individual.

The political consequences of this teaching were and are quite revolutionary. Martin Luther King Jr. made reference to both divine and natural law, for instance, when urging blacks to disobey the (duly promulgated but nonetheless unjust) laws of segregation in the *Letter from a Birmingham Jail.* Machiavelli disliked thoughts about natural law because he strongly favored political stability, which meant always knowing exactly who was in charge and what was expected of the citizens. Because there was perhaps too much of this natural law emphasis in Cicero, an ancient intellectual hero of Renaissance Italy, Machiavelli turned not to him for inspiration but to the ancient Roman historian Titus Livy, who chronicled the times of republican Rome. Even there, Machiavelli selectively drew from the first ten books of Livy's history (the only ones still available for Machiavelli or us) to show how Italy should adopt a practical outlook on politics and life. You will find in Machiavelli's writings, especially in *The Prince* but also surprisingly in *The Discourses,* support for the trend in Europe at that time toward consolidating power even within republican governments.

Machiavelli was born in 1469 in Florence, then an Italian city-state. During his career in public service, which spanned from 1494 to 1512, Florence was a republic, in which citizens participated and elected leaders. Although Florence had enjoyed this form of government for hundreds of years, the powerful Medici family had effectively controlled the regime for quite some time. When the family's influence was temporarily weakened, a Dominican monk, Girolamo Savonarola (whom the Church deemed a heretic), led a revolt to make the republic more democratic—and more Christian. Machiavelli appeared to be a supporter of republican government generally, although he did not think Savonarola was particularly astute. According to Machiavelli, one must always reckon with the Church so long as it remained powerful, but Savonarola challenged the Church and was burned at the stake at the pope's command in 1498.

From 1494 to 1512, Florence's republic was ruled by a Great Council of 3,000 male citizens, of whom the first man was Piero Soderini. After Savonarola's death in 1498, Machiavelli served in the Florentine chancery as well as the Ten of War, a committee which dealt with Florence's military readiness and logistics. As a member of the Ten, Machiavelli organized a citizens' militia, believing that they would fight better than the usual mercenary forces. They did poorly, but the idea still seemed a sound one to Machiavelli. Also as a member of the Ten, Machiavelli served as an ambassador, leading diplomatic missions to other Italian city-states, as well as to France and Germany.

It is safe to say that Machiavelli loved politics. Although he had a wife and children, he enjoyed much more the sophisticated life of the diplomat and the urbane enjoyments of the cities he visited. Machiavelli got the chance to observe the actions of powerful men, including Pope Julius II. He considered himself both a diplomat and an intellectual. Earlier he had received an excellent education in ancient philosophy and history which would have allowed him to carry on many an intriguing conversation. His practical diplomatic experience and his formal education were what he relied upon for his political writings.

Machiavelli's political career, however, was to come to an abrupt end in 1512 when, with the help of the Spanish, the Medici family returned to power. This time they quickly dismantled the fig leaf of republican government. Machiavelli was not to be trusted because he was associated with the earlier government. Because his name was found on a list taken from men accused of plotting against the new government, the Medici's accused Machiavelli of being a conspirator who wished to reinstate the republic. They wanted to send him, and others, a message; they imprisoned and tortured Machiavelli, who was banned from public service. He wisely retreated to outside the city limits of Florence early in 1513. Through all this, Machiavelli no doubt learned a great deal about the effective use of force, because in *The Prince* he recommends these types of tactics himself. Although without this exile Machiavelli would have probably never had time to write his two most important books, *The Prince* and *The Discourses*, he saw living outside the city as a curse. He wrote to his friend Vettori, "So, in the company of these bumpkins, I keep my brain from turning moldy, and put up with the hostility fate has shown me. I am happy for fate to see to what depth I have sunk, for I want to know if she will be ashamed of herself for what she has done."

Scholars argue about which of his books Machiavelli wrote first. Did he write *The Prince* first, and then turn to *The Discourses?* This dispute is important because of the content of the two. *The Prince* seems to advocate one-man rule, or monarchy. The full title of *The Discourses* is *Discourses on the First Ten Books of Titus Livius,* the ancient Roman historian. In this book, Machiavelli seems to argue for the superiority of republican government. Because Machiavelli dedicates *The Prince* to Lorenzo de' Medici, the prince of Florence, in the hopes of being called back to public service, some scholars regard *The Prince* as nothing more than a job application of sorts, a book that tells Lorenzo only what he would want to hear, not whose views are really shared by its wily author. Perhaps Machiavelli did break off in the middle of writing *The Discourses* to write the much briefer *Prince* with the idea of getting it to Lorenzo in a timely manner. There is no doubt that he would have liked Lorenzo to accept it and change his mind about Machiavelli's usefulness to the state (Lorenzo did not). However, if one reads *The Prince* looking for something more than this, there is plenty else to find. It is even possible to see within this book some support for republicanism, and thus to see a positive connection between the two books which at first seem so different.

Machiavelli was finally asked by the Medici government to write a history of Florence, which was hardly the type of job he wanted. After he finished *The History of Florence* in 1525, his fortunes improved; he was allowed back into the city and was given a minor position in the government. But Machiavelli's luck—or fortune as he would call it—was not good. In 1527, when the Medici family was once again overturned and the long-awaited republican government was restored, Machiavelli found himself the outsider again. Having tried hard to associate himself with the Medicis, he was no longer trusted or welcome. He died one month later.

UNDERSTANDING MACHIAVELLI

No philosopher writes in a vacuum, and Machiavelli perhaps least of all. In his letter to his friend and hoped-for benefactor, Francesco Vettori, Machiavelli tells how he conducted his inquiry into politics as a conversation with other great thinkers and leaders. First, he takes off his muddy clothing and puts on regal robes. Then, "Decently dressed, I enter the ancient courts of rulers who have long since died. There I am warmly welcomed, and I feed on the only food I find nourishing, and was born to savor. I am not ashamed to talk to them, and to ask them to explain their actions. And they, out of kindness, answer me."

Machiavelli said that through his writings he was establishing "new modes and orders" or new ways of thinking and acting politically. He studied not only history, but also philosophy, and he openly underscored his differences with philosophers of the past. In his time readers would clearly understand to whom and to what he was referring, but unless the modern reader knows at least generally who these thinkers are (since Machiavelli does not actually name or describe them in any detail), Machiavelli's point may be lost.

Machiavelli intentionally keeps the word *virtue* (*virtú*) on prominent display in his writings. If you have a translation of *The Prince* that is either literal or places the word *virtue* in brackets when the translator has chosen a different, more fluid word, you are fortunate. Machiavelli is not lacking in creativity. He means to use the same word over and over again. The way he uses *virtue* is interesting and extremely important. Prior to the Renaissance, the term might have been used to mean "goodness" through attitudes of mercy, love, charity, nobility, and so on, but Machiavelli defines *virtue* in a way that became popular in the Renaissance: the ability to excel, including the ability to do cruelty and injustice if necessary for success. By using the word in this way, Machiavelli is placing himself at odds with medieval thinkers like Baldassare Castiglione and Christine de Pisan. These authors wrote advice books or "mirrors" for nobility in which they advised themselves and others how to live and rule in accordance with Christian principles. Their idea was that successful leadership had to do with practicing this type of virtue, especially when dealing with those of a lower status. Machiavelli scoffs at this idea throughout the book. He further drives home his point by writing in a manner similar to theirs, for *The Prince* is also an advice book for nobility. The book is an open challenge to the medieval view of what values and behavior philosophers ought to promote.

In *The Prince*, Machiavelli openly challenges the ancient idealist view. He is thinking of Plato, and the ancient Roman historian Cicero, when he writes in Chapter Fifteen that "many authors have constructed imaginary republics and principalities that have never existed in practice and never could; for the gap between how people actually behave and how they ought to behave is so great that anyone who ignores everyday reality in order to live up to an ideal will soon discover he has been taught how to destroy himself, not how to preserve himself." The reference to "imaginary republics" reflects his disdain for ancient idealism. Machiavelli tells us here the reason why he sets his work apart from theirs is he believes their advice is unrealistic and downright dangerous for the few saintly souls who attempt to follow it.

Another area of Machiavelli's *Prince* would not be readily apparent to the modern reader, but is crucial for a full understanding of the book. This area is the political connection between the Medicis and the Church. The man who helped get Machiavelli released from prison was an old friend, Giuliano de' Medici. Giuliano's brother, Giovanni, was elected Pope Leo X in March 1513, and as part of the festivities, the pope ordered Machiavelli and all other prisoners released. Machiavelli thought it best to move to his farmhouse in the country. Although *The Prince* is dedicated to Lorenzo de' Medici, it may have been originally intended for the Medici pope. Machiavelli's friend, Vettori, tried to find Machiavelli a Church position formulating foreign policy for Leo who was hoping to acquire Spanish territory for Giuliano. *The Prince* certainly has plenty of advice that would lend itself to Leo's situation. So, ironically, if *The Prince* is a job application, it may have been an application originally intended for the Church, an institution Machiavelli did not wholeheartedly admire. Although Machiavelli never received a job with the Church, the Medici connection between the leadership of Florence and the leadership of the Church allowed him to remind Lorenzo that, in addition to all his other good fortune, Lorenzo had God on his side, and could confidently proceed to unite all of Italy under one government.

Students are often baffled by the sheer amount of historical detail in *The Prince,* from ancient times and in Machiavelli's time. It is difficult to decipher what is important to remember. Most of his readers would have been familiar with these details although not necessarily with Machiavelli's perspective. The best approach for modern readers is to see Machiavelli's historical analysis for what it was to him: data. He uses history and his recent experience as a data bank to draw support for the political points he is trying to make. It is not unusual for Machiavelli to write about only one aspect of an event, or even to rewrite what actually happened so that it better supports his point of view. Usually, Machiavelli makes a point early in a chapter, and then attempts to give examples that prove his case. The guide to *The Prince* will highlight some individuals and events that were particularly instructive to Machiavelli and thus particularly useful to remember in more detail.

CAREFUL READING

In almost all translations of *The Prince* are words, such as *virtú,* that are unfamiliar to many modern students. Be on the lookout also for such words as *parsimony* and *liberality* that sound old-fashioned. If your translator uses these words and you do not know what Machiavelli meant by them, you will miss the entire argument in Chapter Sixteen. Let us now examine such a case.

Liberality and Parsimony

One way to approach this problem of unusual vocabulary is, of course, to go to a dictionary; but many modern dictionaries may not have all the unusual words you encounter. You may gain some meaning of *liberality* from other words that are in use today and sound like it. The Latin root of *liberality* is *libere,* a root that both *liberty* and *liberal* share, and which indicates "freedom." If you stopped there, however, you might think that Machiavelli is talking about individual freedom or left-leaning politics, but such ideas do not reflect Machiavelli's thinking. The word *parsimony* is also a challenge, because it is difficult to come up with a word in current usage that sounds similar.

To determine what Machiavelli meant by these two words, then, we plunge into the reading without being certain of what he meant. Here is a section from a very literal translation of Chapter Sixteen:[1]

> For, if one wishes to maintain the name of liberal among men, it is necessary that one not omit any quality of sumptuousness—to such an extent, that a prince so disposed will consume all his faculties in such-like works, and he will be finally necessitated, in his wish to maintain the name of liberal, to burden the people extraordinarily, to become exacting, and do all those things that can be done to get money. This will begin to make him hateful to his subjects and, as he becomes poor, none of them will respect him . . .

Upon first reading of such a passage, students are often more confused than ever. This is a time to read slowly and look for what larger point Machiavelli is trying to make. Machiavelli says that to "maintain the name of liberal" the prince must "burden the people extraordinarily" to get money. How does a prince, or any other government, get money from the people? The answer is through taxes, which of course the people find burdensome. This should give us an indication of what Machiavelli means by *liberal:* It involves using a lot of money. Not long after this passage, Machiavelli uses the term *stinginess* as a synonym for *parsimony,* which means "being tight with money."

Machiavelli reasons that if the prince tries to be liberal—that is, free with money, or generous with the people—he will have to overtax those same people to get the money, which will make him hated and disrespected by his subjects. But if he practices parsimony—stinginess—he will actually end up having a reputation for liberality because he will not have to take anything from most of his subjects who are not rich and who are "infinite in number." He will only have to take money from the few—"those to whom he does not give" this generosity of leaving them alone. This point reflects the frequent theme in Machiavelli's *The Prince* that it is best to have the vast majority on the prince's side because of its collective power, even if it means alienating the few who are rich. Those few cannot hurt the prince if the many are on your side. In Machiavelli's day, it was often those least able to avoid it who were oppressed by tax collectors and whose homes might be burned to the ground if they could not pay. Machiavelli tells the prince that the many are easy to please. All he has to do is leave them alone most of the time.

Another Machiavellian trap into which many students fall was probably intentionally laid by him. Machiavelli sometimes seems to use a deceptive or contradictory way of reaching his conclusions. The reader must be aware that Machiavelli may say one thing in one paragraph and say something completely different in the next. Is Machiavelli just a slipshod writer? Does Machiavelli

---

[1] Both sections are from Leo Paul S. de Alvarez's translation of *The Prince.* Irving, TX: University of Dallas Press, 1980, pp. 96–97. Reprinted by permission of Waveland Press, Inc. All rights reserved.

strike you as a man who would not read his writing over and over again to make sure he said what he wanted to say? Below are two examples that explore Machiavelli's unique sense of humor and irony.

Machiavelli's Status

In the letter of dedication to *The Prince,* Machiavelli tries to explain to Prince Lorenzo why he wrote this book and why he is giving it to him. He writes, "I recognize this book is unworthy to be given to Yourself, yet I trust that out of kindness you will accept it, taking account of the fact there is no greater gift that I can present to you than the opportunity to understand, after a few hours of reading, everything I have learned over the course of so many years, and have undergone so many discomforts and dangers to discover."

We know that at or around the same time as Machiavelli wrote *The Prince* he also wrote the *The Discourses,* a larger work with much more information about republican government. He is not telling the whole truth when he says *The Prince* represents everything he has learned, because Lorenzo de' Medici really does not need or probably want to hear about Machiavelli's admiration for republics. The reader should be alerted immediately to the fact that Machiavelli is not above deception when it suits his purposes. Indeed, later philosophers such as Rousseau and Spinoza saw *The Prince* as a subtle argument for republics wrapped in a superficial endorsement of principalities. Modern scholars such as translators Mansfield and Tarcov see much republicanism in *The Prince* and much of a dictatorial nature in *The Discourses.* They conclude that the first book is about founding regimes and the latter about maintaining a lasting republican government.[2]

In the dedicatory letter, Machiavelli offers Lorenzo this explanation of the project:

> I hope it will not be thought presumptuous for someone of humble and lowly status to dare to discuss the behavior of rulers and to make recommendations regarding policy. Just as those who paint landscapes set up their easels down in the valley in order to portray the nature of the mountains and peaks, and climb up into the mountains in order to draw the valleys, similarly in order to properly understand the behavior of the lower classes one needs to be a ruler, and in order to properly understand the behavior of rulers one needs to be a member of the lower classes.

Machiavelli uses a metaphor here to describe his position in relation to Lorenzo's. At first he characteristically depicts himself as humble and of a lowly status; however, if you carefully examine his metaphor, you will find that

---

[2]See their introduction in Niccoló Machiavelli, *Discourses on Livy,* translated by Harvey C. Mansfield and Nathan Tarcov, Chicago: The University of Chicago Press, 1996, especially the section "Republicanism Ancient and Modern," pp. xxvii–xxxiii.

Machiavelli is not as humble as he initially appears. The metaphor he uses is about an artist who must paint in the valley to get a proper perspective of the mountains. Machiavelli is, of course, that painter, who is trying to get a proper perspective on the prince. Think of yourself for a moment as the prince who might be reading this letter. What is Machiavelli saying about your ability to see yourself, or to have the proper perspective on yourself and your actions? Machiavelli seems to be saying that the prince cannot understand himself as well as Machiavelli can understand him. He ends the section by saying that indeed, in order to understand the behavior of the prince, one needs to be of the "lower classes." He also says that the prince will know the lower classes better because of his perspective on the peaks. Perhaps this is somewhat of a compliment, but because Machiavelli goes on to instruct the prince at length about how he should treat the lower classes, one wonders whether Machiavelli meant that, either. Machiavelli believed one thing in common with Plato and Aristotle—that the intellectual who studies politics is better able to decipher the reality than most leaders.

Agathocles' Lack of Virtue

In Chapter Eight, Machiavelli discusses Agathocles, an important military officer in ancient Syracuse. Agathocles had some power, but he wanted all of it. To that end, he made a deal with Hamilcar of Carthage to use Hamilcar's forces in a takeover. Agathocles made sure that he decapitated the state by calling the assembly and senate of Syracuse to a meeting, supposedly to discuss important government policies. He had all the richest and most influential people of Syracuse in one place. He then called in his troops and had them kill anyone who could potentially lead any resistance. The Carthaginians tried to take advantage of their presence in Syracuse to attack and take the place for themselves, but Agathocles counterattacked and in the end they retreated, feeling fortunate to leave Agathocles only in control of Syracuse and not of Carthage itself.

Machiavelli sounds as though he admires Agathocles, and indeed he does in many ways. He says that not much of what he accomplished was because of luck or "help from above," but was rather because of his own skill. Then Machiavelli writes something that puzzles a great many readers:

> One ought not, of course, to call it virtú [virtue or manliness] to massacre one's fellow citizens, to betray one's friends, to break one's word, to be without mercy and without religion. By such means one can acquire power but not glory. If one considers the manly qualities [virtú] Agathocles demonstrated in braving and facing down danger, and the strength of character he showed in surviving and overcoming adversity, then there seems to be no reason why he should be judged less admirable than any of the finest generals. But on the other hand his inhuman cruelty and brutality, and his innumerable wicked actions, mean it would be wrong to praise him as one of the finest men. It is clear, at any rate, that one can

attribute neither to luck nor to virtue [virtú] his accomplishments, which owed nothing to either.

Readers are often convinced by this passage that Machiavelli is, after all, concerned that leaders not be too immoral. He says that he cannot call it virtue when a leader commits massacres, betrayals, and lies and is sacrilegious. It sounds as though Machiavelli is condemning Agathocles for being completely immoral. Indeed, he even says that such a leader cannot be glorious but only powerful.

Again, we have to set this passage in its larger context. In this case, it helps to have read the previous chapter which highlights Duke Cesare Borgia, a Renaissance figure whom Machiavelli admires. Cesare is Machiavelli's ideal. He did everything with *virtú*. Yet, you will find that Cesare was just as cruel as Agathocles, in his own way. Cesare wanted to take over an area in Italy known as the Romagna, a territory adjacent to the Papal States. Cesare was the son of Pope Alexander, which was good fortune indeed. Alexander was interested in helping his son take over this area, which would not only promote Cesare's interests but also Alexander's, because it would effectively add to his power. Cesare thus had the luck, or fortune, to be born the right man. He had the power of the Church on his side. First Alexander bribed powerful people in the area not to resist Cesare. Cesare was then allowed to use French troops borrowed by his father. Cesare was able to enter the land with no resistance. Once there, he found that the place was lawless.

Machiavelli tells us, in order to make the people peaceful and obedient, Cesare hired a man named d'Orco to govern the territory. He told this man to use whatever cruelty necessary to pacify the people immediately. Machiavelli's description is fairly subtle, but he certainly leaves the impression that d'Orco was very cruel. He terrified the people into peace and obedience. Then Cesare used a tricky, but effective, ploy. After d'Orco had achieved what Cesare wanted, Cesare came back and acted surprised and angry with what had been happening. He "punished" his right-hand man by having him killed and cut into pieces in the public square for all to see. The people were both obedient and grateful to Cesare. He then set up regular courts to settle disputes.

Machiavelli says Cesare had so much *virtú* that he would have achieved anything he desired if he had not died suddenly. Machiavelli's unmitigated praise of Cesare should be considered in the context of Machiavelli's criticism of Agathocles. After all, Cesare committed massacres, betrayed his employee d'Orco, lied to him and to the people, and ruled at least initially without mercy and religion. However, Machiavelli thinks that Cesare was glorious and Agathocles was not. What, then, is the difference between Cesare and Agathocles?

Perhaps the key lies in *the way* Cesare carried out his cruelties. He did not do them himself, and indeed convinced the people that he did not know what his governor had been doing. Thus he achieved the effect he wanted, pacification, without the liabilities. If he had done these things himself he would have been hated by the people, as Agathocles probably was. If a leader is hated by the people, he is not glorious. As Machiavelli explains later in the book, it is wise to make the people fear their leader, but not hate him. Hatred means plots, which means the prince must expend much more money and time defending himself from his own people, which of course makes him more vulnerable to foreign enemies. It is simply not in the prince's interest to gain a reputation with the people for being arbitrarily cruel, immoral, and so on.

Machiavelli tempers his criticism of Agathocles by pointing out that he did not sustain his cruelty, and thus he used cruelty well to achieve his purposes. "Those who use cruelty well may indeed find both God and their subjects are prepared to let bygones be bygones, as was the case with Agathocles," he writes. However, he still does not highly praise Agathocles, apparently because he does not think the initial cruelty was accomplished with the ultimate finesse. Finesse is very important to Machiavelli, because it can help the prince achieve more with less actual expenditure of effort and money and with less risk. Chapter 18, which discusses the different varieties of coercion, helps clear up the problem of why Machiavelli admires Cesare more than Agathocles. There, Machiavelli writes: "[Y]ou should seem to be compassionate, trustworthy, sympathetic, honest, religious, and, indeed, be all these things; but at the same time you should be constantly prepared, so that, if these become liabilities, you are trained and ready to become their opposites."

Machiavelli concludes that a ruler cannot always follow the moral rules that others think he should follow, but must often lie and "be uncharitable, inhumane, and irreligious" in order to maintain his power. Machiavelli goes on to make the point about religion more clearly still. The prince must "seem, to those who listen to him and watch him, entirely pious, truthful, reliable, sympathetic, and religious. There is no quality that is more important he should seem to have than this last one. In general, men judge more by sight than by touch." So, Machiavelli thinks that the most important quality the prince must appear to have is religion. He states that the prince can make the people think he is religious because "men judge more by sight than by touch." The few who know the prince is not what he seems to be will never speak out if they know the people are convinced by the prince.

Machiavelli is advocating the cynical use of religion by leaders in order to maintain favorable popular opinion. If most people can be fooled by a simple public gesture, as Machiavelli seems to think, then it will be easy for the leader to make them think he is pious, religious, and good. Such a simple gesture, in our own times, might come from a president who makes sure the cameras are rolling when he goes to church or consults with a minister. Most American presidents have done these things, and it is impossible to tell which of these gestures are sincere and which are public relations ploys, since the public cannot read the president's mind. The clever president, from Machiavelli's perspective, would associate himself with religion in public as much as possible, but not believe in it or act upon it. To do the latter would be to box himself in, to be inflexibly good, which could end up damaging his effectiveness as a leader. At the very least, the reader should come away from Machiavelli's observations a little more likely to look at these gestures with skepticism. Machiavelli's readers should be among the few who judge their leaders by how they actually behave and what they accomplish over time, not by empty gestures.

From this last example of Agathocles' lack of virtue, you can see that sometimes you have to read the chapters before and after the one in question, and sometimes the rest of the book, to understand one passage fully. There is commentary before and after the passage about Agathocles' lack of glory that helps us to understand what Machiavelli really means. You will often find that something Machiavelli says later on the same or similar subject will clarify the puzzling passage. The best way to read books like *The Prince* is more than once so that these associations become clearer still.

GUIDE TO *THE PRINCE*

Machiavelli knows that he is taking a dramatic turn away from the vision of ancient philosophers such as Plato and Aristotle. Be aware of the contrast between the ancients' and Machiavelli's methods and goals. Because of his attitude toward change and this break with the ancient, and also the medieval past, Machiavelli has been called by some observers the first modern philosopher. Machiavelli perhaps would not go so far as to favor change for change's sake, but he does encourage innovation in political matters, and constant adjustment of political actions and institutions to meet changing times. Does the way he thinks seem more familiar to you than Plato or Aristotle?

Be on guard for statements Machiavelli makes that are not to be taken literally. Remember that Machiavelli is a clever author who sometimes purposefully writes in such a way as to make the attentive reader question his motives and compare what he says in one place with what he says in others. The best way to read any of Machiavelli's statements is in the context of the work as a whole.

Letter of Dedication

1. Why does Machiavelli say he is dedicating this book to Prince Lorenzo?
2. How does Machiavelli justify someone as lowly as himself offering advice to Lorenzo? Does Machiavelli actually insult Lorenzo in the process?

Chapter One

What kinds of states or governments are there, according to Machiavelli?

Chapter Two   Machiavelli omits writing about republics in this book because he has written about them elsewhere (in *The Discourses*). In *The Prince*, he seems to be praising principalities, whereas in *The Discourses* he seems to be praising republics. Keep in mind for the rest of your reading of this book that Machiavelli may have purposes other than simply praising virtuous princes and helping Lorenzo. He may still be promoting the idea that the common people's interests should be taken into account, even in principalities.

Why is it so easy to maintain hereditary principalities, according to Machiavelli?

Chapter Three

1. Why do *new* principalities have special difficulties? What do his observations here say about the importance of the people's support for their leader?
2. What is the best way to hurt or frighten people, according to Machiavelli? What should be the prince's purpose in inflicting such injuries?
3. To what "disease" does Machiavelli refer, and what "remedy" does he recommend?
4. Do you agree with Machiavelli that "it is perfectly natural and normal to want to acquire new territory; and whenever men do what will succeed toward this end, they will be praised, or at least not condemned." What is he saying here about the impressions people form of their leaders?

Chapter Four

1. What is the distinction between the "prince-servant" rule and the "prince-baron" rule? Which one does Machiavelli favor? Why?
2. Why would it be easier to invade and occupy the lands of the king of France than the sultan of Turkey?

Chapter Five

1. What are the options open to a prince who takes over a previously self-governing people? Which options does Machiavelli see as most likely to succeed?
2. Why is it so difficult to conquer republics? What does this observation say about Machiavelli's attitude toward the republican form of government?

Chapter Six

1. What makes Moses such a great leader? Does Machiavelli's treatment of Moses, a patriarch of Judaism, Islam, and Christianity, tell us anything about Machiavelli's attitude toward religion generally?
2. Machiavelli mentions the importance of ability (or skill) and fortune (or luck) in political success. Which is more valuable to a leader? Why?

Chapter Seven

1. What did Cesare Borgia do that Machiavelli finds so virtuous and admirable?
2. What does Cesare know about how to avoid being hated by his people? Why do you think the avoidance of hatred is so important to Machiavelli?

Chapter Eight

1. Why are Agathocles' deeds not to be called glorious? What makes Agathocles' actions different from those of Cesare Borgia?
2. What is the difference between cruelties that are done well and those that are done poorly? Can you make an argument that Machiavelli is actually showing some kindness to the people by arguing for cruelty done well?

Chapter Nine

1. On what basis does Machiavelli argue that the objectives or needs of the people are "less immoral" and more easily satisfied than the objectives of the elite?
2. What advice does Machiavelli give about how the prince should treat his people?

Chapter Ten

1. What is even better than having a city that is heavily fortified and prepared for a long siege?
2. What type of preparations and fortifications does Machiavelli recommend for those rulers who must use them?

Chapter Eleven

1. According to Machiavelli, how do ecclesiastical or church rulers maintain their power over the people they rule?
2. Machiavelli states that, because church rulers are governed by a higher power that cannot be understood by human reason, he will say no more about them. Why do you think he includes this statement when he proceeds to write at length about the political exploits of various popes?
3. What qualities does Machiavelli admire in a pope?

Chapter Twelve

1. Why do good laws rely on good armies?
2. Define the following fighting forces—citizen armies, mercenaries, and auxiliaries.
3. What are the strengths and weaknesses of mercenaries and citizen armies? Of these two, which type of army does Machiavelli prefer? Why? Does Machiavelli's preference indicate what he thinks the relationship should be between the prince and his people?

Chapter Thirteen

1. Why does Machiavelli consider auxiliary troops even more dangerous than mercenaries?
2. Machiavelli brings up Cesare Borgia again here, as an example of how to use troops well. Why do you think Borgia's reputation changed when he formed his own citizen army?

Chapter Fourteen

1. Machiavelli suggests that a prince must know military matters well or he will be despised by his troops. What types of training and attitude toward war does Machiavelli recommend for the successful prince?
2. Why do you think Machiavelli recommends not only military preparedness, but also a study of history books?

Chapter Fifteen

1. In this chapter, Machiavelli openly rejects the ancient and medieval approach to political philosophy. What reasons does he give for this rejection?
2. What attitude must the prince take toward morality in order to be successful? Is there any way to defend this stance on the basis of morality—is it necessary for the preservation of the state and thus the people's safety?

Chapter Sixteen

1. Why is it better for both the prince and his people for the prince to be thrifty instead of liberal with his money?
2. Why is an overly generous prince likely to be eventually hated by his people?

Chapter Seventeen

1. Explain Machiavelli's rationale for the observation that it is better to be feared than loved, but that it is never good to be hated. How does the prince become feared by the people without having them hate him?
2. In this and Chapter Sixteen Machiavelli returns to the argument that the interests of the prince and his people coincide, if only the prince sees what is truly in his best interests. Are you persuaded that such a wise principality is possible?

Chapter Eighteen

1. What qualities of the lion and fox should the prince imitate?
2. When the prince is acting like a fox, what kinds of deceptions are allowed? What does his discussion of foxlike deception tell us about his attitude toward morality and religion?
3. Why is it better to control people through the tactics of the fox than the tactics of the lion whenever possible?

Chapter Nineteen

1. What further advice does Machiavelli give a prince about how to avoid being hated by the people?
2. What is the best defense against conspiracies and plots?
3. Explain what Machiavelli means when he says that a prince can be hated for the good things he does as much as for the bad things.

Chapter Twenty

1. Why does Machiavelli insist that it is better for the prince to arm than to disarm his subjects? What kind of subjects would you trust with arms?
2. Near the end of this chapter, how does Machiavelli settle the question of whether or not it is better to build fortresses? Does his conclusion give any indication of what relationship he prefers between the prince and the people?

Chapter Twenty-One

1. Why does Machiavelli advise the prince to always takes sides in a war, instead of remaining neutral?
2. How and why should a prince encourage excellence and unity in his citizens?

Chapter Twenty-Two

What kind of advisers should the prince employ? What kind should he not have?

Chapter Twenty-Three

Why should the prince avoid flatterers at court? What can he do to avoid advisors who simply flatter him?

Chapter Twenty-Four

What (or whom) does Machiavelli blame for the political instability and weakness of Italy?

Chapter Twenty-Five

1. How does Machiavelli characterize the prevailing attitude toward fortune (chance) and God in his day?
2. What attitude does Machiavelli think leaders should have toward fortune?
3. To what is Machiavelli referring when he speaks of "floods" and of building "embankments" or dams?
4. The goddess Fortuna was an ancient Roman deity whom Machiavelli's readers might remember from their education. Toward the end of this chapter Machiavelli states that "fortune is a lady" and in order to control her, the prince must act like a young man who is willing to strike her if

necessary in order to gain control. What political attitude is Machiavelli recommending for the prince through this analogy?

Chapter Twenty-Six

1. In this chapter, Machiavelli returns to Prince Lorenzo's situation and clearly states that he wants Lorenzo to unite Italy into one country (Lorenzo did nothing of the sort). Why does he compare Lorenzo's situation to that of Moses, who freed the Jews from slavery in Egypt?
2. Because Lorenzo is related to the current pope, Leo X, Machiavelli can say that he is favored by God and the Church. Remembering Machiavelli's previous example of Cesare Borgia and Machiavelli's attitude toward the Church generally, how could Lorenzo's connection with the Church help him eventually take over all of Italy?
3. How does Machiavelli appeal to Lorenzo's sense of his own greatness and glory?
4. Does this final chapter help explain why Machiavelli has been such a strong advocate of citizen armies?

BIBLIOGRAPHY

Hans Baron, *The Crisis of the Early Italian Renaissance*, Princeton, NJ: Princeton University Press, 1955.

Jacob Burckhardt, *The Civilization of the Renaissance in Italy*, New York: Oxford University Press, 1937.

Norman Cantor and Peter Klein, eds., *Renaissance Thought: Dante and Machiavelli*, Waltham, MA, Baisdell Pub. Co., 1969.

Paul Oskar Kristeller, *Renaissance Thought: The Classic, Scholastic, and Humanist Strains*, New York: Harper, 1961.

Quentin Skinner, *The Foundations of Modern Political Thought*, New York: Cambridge University Press, 1978.

Quentin Skinner, *Machiavelli*, Oxford: Oxford University Press, 1981.

Leo Strauss, *Thoughts on Machiavelli*, Chicago: University of Chicago Press, 1958.

HOBBES (1588–1679)

BACKGROUND

Thomas Hobbes was born in 1588, during which time his country of England was at war with Spain. His mother was a farmer's daughter. His father, a clergyman, abandoned the family. Hobbes was raised by his uncle and was able to rise from his lowly position because of his brilliance in learning ancient Greek and Latin. He went to Oxford where he became the tutor of William Cavendish, the son of the earl of Devonshire. He remained employed by the Cavendish family for the rest of his life.

Early in his employment, he traveled with the young lord to France and Italy. In Venice he learned of the political struggle the Italian government was having with the Church over which had the ultimate authority. This struggle, in which he naturally sided with the state, may have had a lasting influence over Hobbes's view that the proper relationship was subordination of church to state. Almost a decade later, Hobbes again traveled to Italy and France, where he learned about or was directly influenced by such intellectual giants as Euclid, Galileo, and Descartes. Through Euclid's opus, *Elements*, Hobbes learned the geometrical method of reasoning. This thought left a deep impression on Hobbes, who tried to incorporate it into his political reasoning. He actually met Galileo in Italy, and debated with the great philosopher Descartes and others in Parisian intellectual circles. Thus, as a middle-aged man, he finally acquired an interest not just in learning about philosophy but philosophizing.

In 1640, as tensions between the king's supporters, the royalists, and the parliamentarians escalated, Hobbes fled England for France. Civil war broke out in England in 1643 and led to the victory of the parliamentarians whom Hobbes opposed. In 1640 he wrote *The Elements of Law*, and in 1642 he published *De Cive*, in some ways a more concise draft of his masterpiece, *Leviathan*, published in 1651. Many of Hobbes's books contain similar arguments and conclusions, but Hobbes kept refining them as he continued to write. Although by 1652, the king had not yet been restored, Hobbes decided, nonetheless, to return to England. When Charles II was restored in 1660 by a conflict-weary people, Hobbes received a pension from the new king. He continued to write and debate with mathematicians and ministers until he died at the age of 91, an age especially impressive for the times.

To understand Hobbes's seemingly extreme positions in favor of absolute monarchy, we need to know a little more about the political and religious conflicts of his times. Much has been made of Hobbes's supposedly fearful nature which, according to apocryphal stories, may have even started in his mother's womb. In this view, Hobbes's extreme timidity resulted in his advocacy of a rather rigid conformity. Much more can be explained about his motivations simply by examining the events in England with which he was intimately familiar.

Ever since the notorious Henry VIII (1509–1547),[1] whose trouble getting a divorce from Catherine led him to reject the Catholic Church and establish the Anglican Church, religious controversy had plagued England. The Protestant Reformation added to the tensions, with Puritans dissenting from the established Anglican Church. James I (1603–1625) supported the Church of England. He claimed that he had a divine right to rule—that his authority derived from God's authority. However, by the time James came to the throne, the English parliament increasingly questioned the power of the ruler in part because of the influx of many Puritans into the House of Commons. These dissenters argued against the divine right of kings and they began to complain about controversial issues such as taxation.

Charles I, James's son, gained the throne (1625–1649) as parliament became increasingly more balky. He, too, maintained his divine right to rule, but he soon discovered that parliament was difficult to ignore. He refused to call the parliament between 1629 and 1640, and began a campaign to suppress dissent. When the Scottish (largely Presbyterians) revolted, however, Charles found that he had to call on his parliament to raise taxes. In 1640, the members of parliament convened and demanded concessions from the king, including the execution of some of the king's ministers. By 1642, civil war seemed inevitable and Charles attempted to arrest parliamentary leaders. Meanwhile, dissenting members of parliament, now the majority, began to raise an army. Led by Oliver Cromwell, the "roundheads," as the dissenters were called because of their unstylish haircuts, battled with the supporters of the crown, the royalists. Finally, Charles was executed in 1648, and from 1649 to 1653, England had its commonwealth without a king. From 1653 to 1660, the government changed to a Protectorate which Cromwell ruled through the army.

---

[1]All dates in parentheses in this section refer to the years during which these monarchs ruled.

Hobbes believed that Charles's son, Charles II, was eventually restored to the throne because the English people were weary of conflict and especially weary of Cromwell's puritanical and authoritarian leadership. Charles II was able to come back to England in 1660 without much of a fight, but he did have to make some concessions to parliament. The king's power was balanced with that of parliament's, and some basic individual rights were secured.

Apparently, Hobbes looked upon this recent history of political and religious conflict with horror. He valued peace and thought that most of the matters over which various Christians fought were superficial or nonessential to basic faith. He thought that true knowledge of most religious things was impossible. Hobbes also did not believe people were capable of tolerating different religious opinions. Hence he concluded that any degree of freedom in matters of religion would inevitably lead to disagreement and to conflict. Hobbes thought that the only solution to the threat of civil war emerging from religious disputes was the imposition of religious conformity—strict allegiance, at least outwardly, to whatever church the government established. This is indeed one solution to the problem of religious diversity, but as we will see when we examine Locke's ideas, it is not the only one.

UNDERSTANDING HOBBES

Many students may be reading Hobbes's *Leviathan* or his other works exactly as he wrote them, which may in itself cause problems. Here we quote Hobbes in the original, which is to say, in his original Old English. During the time in which Hobbes wrote his books, English had not been standardized. Readers will therefore be treated to the same word spelled two or even three different ways in the same chapter, capitalizations in the middle of sentences for no apparent reason, and words such as *thy* and *falleth,* which make *Leviathan* sound like the King James version of the Bible. Students who read the original Hobbes should be forewarned and should not allow themselves to be deterred. Old English is still recognizable to us today. Students will probably have no trouble as long as they read slowly and savor the few truly unusual words in context. Old English is often delightful, once readers have gotten into the groove of its patterns.

On the other hand, your version of *Leviathan* may have been edited in such a way that spellings and capitalizations have been standardized, but nothing else has been changed. If so, the reading will be easier, although perhaps less whimsical, and it will be a little more difficult to get the feel of Hobbes as a thinker and a writer.

In either case, readers may encounter words with which they are not acquainted or only vaguely so, because they tend not to be used much anymore, such as *scurrilous, covenant, vain glory,* or *dehortation.* In many cases, you will be able to pick up on the meaning of these words by reading the entire paragraph in which they are contained. In some cases, though, you may have to go to a dictionary, even the *Oxford English Dictionary,* to obtain the precise meaning. This may seem like extra work, but when you consider the cost of remaining confused every time you see the word, the work may seem well worth doing.

Hobbes (like many other philosophers) also uses Latin at certain times, such as *summum bonum,* "greatest good," or *finis ultimus,* "ultimate end." Sometimes you can figure these words out by employing two different techniques—reading in context and looking for familiarity. Remember that Latin is the root language of many English words. *Summum,* for example, sounds like "sum," and *bonum* like "bonus". *Finis* sounds like "finish" and *ultimus* like "ultimate". By using these two techniques you may come very close to the meaning. If you have any doubt, however, use a Latin-English dictionary from the library or ask your professor for a translation.

It may surprise readers that Hobbes quotes the Bible extensively in many of the chapters in *Leviathan* and his other books. This, too, can cause the modern reader some difficulties. The conflicts between royalists and dissenters, which among other things involved religious differences, caused the political turmoil and eventual civil war that influenced Hobbes. Through his political philosophy, he hoped to prevent such violence from ever recurring. We also know that Hobbes was probably not a traditional Christian believer. He wrote extensively about the difference between natural religion, which is what we can *know* about God, as opposed to conventional religion, which is what people *believe.* Hobbes did not trust beliefs, and shrugged off mysticism as so much superstition. He told others not to rely on authorities for their truths but only on their own experience. Given all this, the question for modern readers naturally arises; Why does Hobbes seem to know the Bible so well, and why does he constantly quote it? If Hobbes did not wish to rely on authority, especially religious authority, why does he not shun all biblical proofs?

There are many possible reasons why Hobbes uses the Bible in this way. Often, when readers who are new to Hobbes encounter his quotations, they quickly conclude that he was a devout Christian. They think that, as is the case today, no one would refer to the Bible so much if they did not take it seriously. Indeed, some experts on Hobbes have recently argued that, although Hobbes's Christianity might have been a little quirky, it was still very serious and his biblical proofs were to be taken as an attempt to buttress his philosophical conclusions with religious truths. However, parts of the *Leviathan* and other works by Hobbes make this conclusion problematic. Hobbes argues, for instance, that there is no such thing as immaterial substances, and that it is impossible for one thing to be also two or three, or for one thing to be in different places. The latter would seem to preclude the Christian doctrine of the Trinity of God the Father, Son, and Holy Spirit. Hobbes argued that all we can know about God is that there must be some cause behind all we see in the universe. He then argued that a smart person will not base any of his beliefs on what others say, or on such things as visions, dreams, and prophecy. If these sources are precluded, much of the Christian and other religious belief systems fall away.

If Hobbes could not accept as true the prophecies and stories in the Bible, there could be other reasons why he would still quote the Bible in his books. For one thing, Hobbes wrote at a time during which just about all arguments had to contain biblical backing in order to be taken seriously. Hobbes knew that most of his readers would be Christians, and it was precisely these Christians who were causing the trouble and who needed to be convinced that God did not require them to risk life and limb—and bring on civil war—for religious freedom. Hobbes may have added the biblical proofs to gain the respect and acceptance of those readers who would not accept any conclusion, no matter how logically derived, if it was not consistent with the Bible. Biblical argumentation was the language of the day, so from this perspective, Hobbes had a very good reason for including the Bible even if he did not believe a word of it. Keeping this view as a live possibility allows a reader to see a dual message in Hobbes's writing: (1) a sort of pre-Enlightenment rejection of religious authority in favor of science, and (2) the use of religion as a way of reaching a still highly religiously-charged society.

Hobbes's methodology requires some explanation as it may seem strange to the modern reader that a writer on politics would start with how people's senses work and the interior mechanisms of human thought. This method reflects Hobbes's attempt to be as scientific as possible. For him, this meant two things: His philosophy had to be based on reason, not on religious revelation; and his method had to be as close as possible to the method employed by geometry.

First, the scientific method meant for Hobbes the rejection of all information that was not gained through human senses and reason alone; that is, any knowledge gained from someone else's authority, especially that gained from purportedly supernatural sources, was not to be trusted. For instance, instead of making God and the Bible the test of whether his theories were true, human reason would be the test of what if anything about God and the Bible were true. Hobbes claimed that, consistent with the scientific outlook, he was concerned only with physical things, which were the only things that existed. This is why he started out with an explanation of how our bodies work. At some points in his work, however, he seems to nonetheless move beyond what can be proven or explained by physical observations alone (for instance, about how human beings think), though he does not move in the direction of supernatural explanations. Commentators on this issue have usually concluded that Hobbes's theory is simply not as perfect and seamless as he would have liked it.

Second, Hobbes was impressed with the method of geometry and was convinced that he could bring this same method into the study of human social and political behavior. For Hobbes, using the geometrical method to study politics meant starting out with the basics. If political behavior is human behavior, then we first need to know how human beings work. As in geometry, he would start with simple but unprovable statements which nonetheless seemed to him self-evident. He would then build theorems or simple arguments on the basis of these statements. The proof of whether the basic definitions and the arguments flowing from them were correct was whether the resulting more elaborate theory adequately explained human political behavior. If it did not, then it was time to reexamine the definitions and start again.

Hobbes is trying very hard to build an irrefutable theory of human political behavior. Some of his methods may seem quaint to us today, but if we truly understand his motives for bringing up such subjects as how human beings see, feel, and think, we will be able to appreciate his attempt to put forward a comprehensive theory of politics. Hobbes has to explain how human beings get information about the world around them in order to make the point that no two human beings see the world in exactly the same way. All their information is filtered through the intellectual and emotional differences that result from their physical distinctions. As Hobbes sees it, this basic fact about human nature means that differences in opinion and perspective are inevitable, as is conflict unless artificial uniformity is imposed upon people. Hobbes's proposed absolute sovereignty and authoritarian control is thus one answer to the conflicts caused by human diversity.

Although times have changed a great deal, these two aspects of Hobbes's methodology—the geometric method and the reliance on human reason alone—have carried over, in a general way, into modern social science. Tentative definitions and the theories built upon them are still of the utmost importance. The test of any theory is still how well it explains and predicts human behavior. Arguments that have religious origins are still set aside as being unscientific. Indeed, this aspect of Hobbes's thought was an early example of Enlightenment thought which is generally associated with the eighteenth century. In many ways, we are still living in the world prepared for us by the Enlightenment.

CAREFUL READING

In this section we look at two representative samples from the *Leviathan* in which careful reading is essential. Part of reading carefully is not getting sidetracked from the author's argument by a curious turn of phrase or what seems like extraneous detail. It is especially important for reading Hobbes that the reader always bear in mind where Hobbes is going with his argument. If we stay focused on Hobbes's purpose, most passages can be rather easily untangled.

Absurdities

One of Hobbes's ideas which must be firmly understood in order to grasp his method is the idea of absurdity. Some words, concepts, and phrases made sense to Hobbes; others were simply absurd and had no meaning. Those ideas that Hobbes claimed were absurd reveal much about his purpose. Hobbes argued that there are two kinds of absurd words. One kind is new words that are used but have no definition. The second kind, more difficult to understand still, is discussed next.

> Another, when men make a name of two Names, whose significations are contradictory and inconsistent; as this name, an *incorporeall body,* or (which is all one) an *incorporeall substance,* and a great number more. For whensoever any affirmation is false, the two names of which it is composed, put together and made one, signifie nothing at all. For example, if it be a false affirmation to say a *quadrangle is round,* the word *round quadrangle* signifies nothing; but is a meere sound. So likewise if it be false, to say that vertue can be powred, or blown up and down; the words *In-powred vertue, In-blown vertue,* are as absurd and insignificant, as a *round quadrangle.* (*Leviathan,* Part I, Chapter Four)[2]

Hobbes is attempting to establish through his geometrical method those words and concepts that make sense scientifically and those that do not. This much is obvious. However, it would serve the reader well to ask at what or to whom Hobbes is aiming his criticism. In this paragraph, Hobbes is aiming primarily at Christian thinkers through the types of examples he gives of absurd or insignificant speech. An "incorporeall body" is a body that has no body. A body with no body might be something like a spirit or ghost, something in which Christians believe. Hobbes is simply saying that this is a contradictory term—there can be no body without a body.

Hobbes gives an analogous example of absurdity in the sphere of geometry. A "round quadrangle" is nonsense. Quadrangles by definition have four sides. Thus, if we say "round quadrangle" we are saying nothing, or, as Hobbes puts it, merely making a sound. The same holds true of terms such as "In-powred vertue" or "In-blown vertue." Think about where these terms probably originated. Who or what could put or blow virtue into someone? Although these exact terms are foreign to us, Hobbes elsewhere uses a term that is not so foreign: "inspired." *Inspired* means the same thing as *In-blown,* sharing the same Latin root as *respiration.* Christians use the word *inspired* today much as they might have used *In-blown* back in Hobbes's day. They might say that God inspired this or that thought or action.

Hobbes is taking such terms literally and asking, Is it possible for virtue to be blown or breathed into anyone or anything? Virtue is not a substance, but

---

[2]Hobbes, *Leviathan,* ed. by C. B. MacPherson, Baltimore: Penguin Books, 1968, p. 108. In this chapter, all quotations from *Leviathan* are from this edition.

a state of being. If it is not a substance, then it cannot be blown, breathed, poured, and so forth. Thus such words as *In-blown* and *inspired* have no meaning but are mere sounds.

Hobbes criticizes the language of religion in this way, taking it apart and showing that it makes no sense. In doing so, he is criticizing the scholarship of theologians. He is attempting to place their work firmly outside the realm of science. Hobbes believes that our words need to have a firm basis in experience or else they are capable of being interpreted, reinterpreted, and misinterpreted by all who hear or use them. In matters of religion, this fuzziness of language had, according to Hobbes, been the cause of much disagreement and religious conflict. Often times, Hobbes cloaks his criticism of religious thinking by seeming to aim specifically at Catholic concepts that were generally discredited in England at his time, such as transubstantiation. Yet the passage we have just analyzed does not refer specifically to Catholic concepts, and many of the passages that overtly aim at Catholic ideas could just as easily apply to Christian ideas generally. By seeming to take aim at Catholics, Hobbes may have been attempting to divert attention away from his more general criticism of religion for those who could not or would not follow him down that road.

Authorship of the Laws

Hobbes is not the only philosopher to use the term *authorship* in a way that may puzzle the reader. Usually we think of an author as a person who writes down his ideas, such as the author of this book. Closer to Hobbes's meaning is when we say that so and so owns his actions or is the author of his destiny. To understand his meaning, we will carefully examine a central passage.

> Fourthly, because every Subject is by this Institution Author of all the Actions, and Judgements of the Soveraigne Instituted; it followes that whatsoever he doth, it can be no injury to any of his Subjects; nor ought he to be by any of them accused of Injustice. For he that doth any thing by authority of another, doth therein no injury to him by whose authority he acteth: But by this Institution of a Common-wealth, every particular man is Author of all the Soveraigne doth; and consequently he that complaineth of injury from his Soveraigne, complaineth of that whereof he himselfe is Author; and therefore ought not to accuse any man but himselfe; no nor himselfe of injury; because to do injury to ones selfe, is impossible. It is true that they that have the Soveraigne power, may commit Iniquity; but not Injustice, or Injury in the proper signification. (Part II, Chapter Eighteen)[3]

Again, the most important thing to do when attempting to understand this paragraph is to keep firmly in mind Hobbes's overall purpose. The first paragraph of Chapter Eighteen makes clear that the "Institution" to which Hobbes

---

[3]p. 232.

refers in the first sentence is the social contract or covenant. Hobbes says that through the social contract, every subject is the author of all the actions and judgments of the sovereign. This could not possibly mean that every subject directly makes the laws, since we know what Hobbes would think of that overly democratic idea! Instead it must mean that because every citizen has consented to a social contract to form the sovereign, every citizen also consents to every action of the sovereign. In that sense, every citizen is the author—the ultimate cause—of every decision by the sovereign.

Notice that Hobbes anticipates the difficulty people will have with this view. What if the sovereign does something that hurts his people? For example, let us say that the sovereign decides to raise taxes suddenly, and raises them to the point that businesses go bankrupt and people no longer can afford basic necessities. It would seem that the sovereign is doing something contrary to the will of the people. But if this is so, what would the people be likely to do? If they thought that the sovereign power was created for their benefit, and that the sovereign was now acting contrary to their benefit, they might revolt. But we know that this is exactly what Hobbes is trying to prevent. So, he has to show them how even those actions and judgments of the sovereign that they do not like are actually their own actions and judgments.

This mind-bender is characteristic of Hobbes's social contract philosophy. Think about how he must view that contract. Once made, it is irrevocable. Why would Hobbes think such a notion of the social contract was good for people? We must think back to his description of anarchy as a place in which life is nasty, brutish, and short. Because Hobbes thought the *worst* possible thing for people was anarchy, or civil war, he would say that people should accept any and all abuse from the sovereign rather than revolt. His theory of authorship justifies this level of acceptance.

Finally, Hobbes admits that the sovereign can be iniquitous, but not unjust or injurious. Here again, Hobbes is dealing with the objection that a monarchy or other form of government can do many evil things. Hobbes wants to distinguish here between moral good and evil and just and unjust actions. From reading previous chapters in *Leviathan*, we know that Hobbes thinks moral distinctions are matters of personal opinion. Hobbes says elsewhere, for instance, that one man's tyrant is another man's monarch. Hobbes wishes to focus not on subjective moral judgments—which are what cause conflict—but on the rules set up by the contract, rules that define what is just and unjust. These rules are not subjective in the sense that they are not created or interpreted by individual subjects. Instead, they are created by the sovereign and are only subjective to him. He can change the rules but no one else can. Thus, the subject is free to personally judge the rules, to even find them evil, but at the same time he is constrained from resisting those rules because in the strictest sense they are just. Hobbes here is denying the existence of any natural or transcendent, eternal standard of justice.

The subject is the author of the rules because he supposedly entered the contract in order to secure his life. By obeying the rules, no matter how repugnant, he will live because he will avoid social chaos. Elsewhere in the book, readers will notice that the only instance in which the subject does not have to obey is when the sovereign is no longer able to guarantee the subject's safety or is indeed endangering the subject's life. Even in those instances, Hobbes is careful not to advocate open rebellion.

GUIDE TO *LEVIATHAN*

This guide will cover the first, second, and third parts of *Leviathan,* as well as the review and conclusion—those parts of the work most frequently assigned. There will often be one question per chapter, so read the entire chapter before attempting to answer the question. If there are several questions for a chapter or group of chapters, read the questions first and answer them as they are answered by the text.

Introduction

According to Hobbes, how is the reader to judge whether his theory is accurate? What does the answer say about Hobbes's methodology?

Part I: Of Man   In this section, Hobbes sets up the building blocks of his science of human nature and behavior. Many will wonder why Hobbes has to start out with individual bodily functions such as sight, or why he has to explain how human beings think. For Hobbes it was absolutely essential to construct his observations on the firmest foundations he could possibly erect, using the geometrical method. To explain human political behavior and suggest corrections, one must know about human nature. Hobbes is a materialist, which means he believes that nothing exists or can be thought about that is not physical. So of course he finds that human nature originates in the body.

Chapter One: Of Sense

What is sense? What produces sense? What does this say about how well we can know the world around us through our senses?

Chapter Two: Of Imagination

What is imagination? How does imagination relate to the ideas that "ghostly men" (that is, priests) teach and promote?

Chapter Three: Of the Consequence or Trayne of Imaginations

What distinguishes human beings from all other living creatures?

Chapter Four: Of Speech

1. Hobbes says that the words *true* and *false* are attributes of speech, not of things. Why do you think Hobbes wants to leave truth and falsity at the level of human perception or opinion instead of making them facts?
2. Why are agreed-upon definitions so important for scientific thought?

Chapter Five: Of Reason, and Science
Here Hobbes indicates the significance of some of his previous observations. If we cannot know absolutely the world around us by observation alone because our senses may deceive us, then in order to do science, we must find another way to build knowledge—by proposing definitions and theories which we can agree upon for the moment, and testing them against experience.

Explain what the geometrical/scientific method means to Hobbes. What kinds of errors do we make if we do not adopt the geometrical method?

Chapter Six: Of the Interior Beginnings of Voluntary Motions . . .

1. How do human beings determine what is good and what is bad? If we determine these things subjectively (according to our own personal preferences), how can this aspect of human nature cause conflict?
2. What are the behavioral consequences of human beings having a will or desire that is separate from their ability to reason?

Chapter Seven: Of the Ends, or Resolutions of Discourse

1. Why can there be no absolute knowledge even in science?
2. What is Hobbes's definition of science?

Chapter Eight: Of the Virtues Commonly Called Intellectual . . .

What is the primary passion? What is the relationship between thought and that passion?

Chapter Nine: Of the Several Subjects of Knowledge

Why does Hobbes equate science with philosophy?

Chapter Ten: Of Power, Worth, Dignity, Honour and Worthiness

What is power? In what way does power determine how we honor or dishonor, love or fear someone?

Chapter Eleven: Of the Difference of Manners

1. How does Hobbes disagree with the old philosophers, such as Plato, who thought there was a "greatest good" which, if obtained, would make human beings happy?
2. What is life about, according to Hobbes?

3. Near the end of this chapter, Hobbes distinguishes between natural religion and man-made religion. What is the difference?

Chapter Twelve: Of Religion

1. Do you get a sense here of what Hobbes thinks of most religious believers?
2. According to Hobbes, why did people establish new religions?

Chapter Thirteen: Of the Natural Condition of Mankind . . . This famous chapter describes what Hobbes calls man's natural condition or what we often call the state of nature. Remember that Hobbes knows he has no first-hand knowledge of what men were like before established governments; but he does know what human beings are like when the government is destroyed by civil war. The latter scenario is most likely what Hobbes had in mind when he vividly described man's more beastly qualities.

1. Why are human beings basically equal?
2. Why does competition among human beings occur?
3. What are the three greatest causes of quarrels among human beings?
4. What does Hobbes mean by the "state of war?" When are human beings in that state?
5. What is life like in the state of nature/state of war?
6. What is similar about the state of nature among individuals and the relations among sovereign nations? What is different?
7. Why are human beings in the state of nature interested in peace?
8. What is the law of nature as defined in the final part of this chapter?

Chapter Fourteen: Of the First and Second Natural Laws . . . This equally famous chapter sets up Hobbes's social contract or covenant upon what he considered the firmest of foundations—our desire for self-preservation.

1. What is the right of nature?
2. How does Hobbes now define a law of nature?
3. What are the first and second laws of nature?
4. What right can a man not transfer to a government? How could this exception to the rule be a problem for Hobbes's system?

Chapter Fifteen: Of Other Laws of Nature Here Hobbes lists and describes the rest of the nineteen laws of nature.

1. If you had to explain to someone the central purpose of all these laws, what would it be?
2. Which of these laws would be difficult to enforce in any legal way?

Chapter Sixteen: Of Persons, Authors, and Things Personated

What is the political significance of Hobbes's view that a government is formed with the consent of a majority or plurality?

Part II: Of Commonwealth   In this section of the book, Hobbes builds his political edifice on the foundations of human nature and the social contract laid in the first section. Here he strongly argues for monarchy as opposed to democracy and aristocracy. He establishes the rights and powers of sovereigns, the proper relationship between sovereign and subject, and the ultimate limits of loyalty the subject owes his government.

Chapter Seventeen: Of the Causes, Generation, and Definition of a Commonwealth

1. Why do people make governments?
2. What would Hobbes have to say about the possibility of world government?

Chapter Eighteen: Of the Rights of Sovereigns by Institution

1. What is Hobbes's attitude about changing the government once it has been formed?
2. How does this chapter help you understand what is meant by "absolute" monarchy.

Chapter Nineteen: Of the Severall Kinds of Commonwealth . . .

Hobbes's theory does not prohibit people from establishing a social contract to form a government other than monarchy. They could place sovereignty in a democracy or aristocracy instead. However, here Hobbes makes it clear that monarchy is superior to the other two forms of government. Hobbes thinks the type of government established by the U.S. Constitution is absurd, because, in addition to being too democratic, it divides sovereignty and thus invites conflict and civil war.

1. Explain why Hobbes rejects the terms *tyranny* and *oligarchy*, which Aristotle, among others, employed.
2. What reasons does Hobbes give for preferring monarchy to democracy?

Chapter Twenty: Of Dominion Paternall, and Despotical

How can Hobbes argue that a despotic (tyrannical) government is a product of consent just as much as a commonwealth instituted by the people?

Chapter Twenty-One: Of the Liberty of Subjects

1. How can a person do something freely (with liberty) and, at the same time, out of necessity? What is the political significance of this assertion by Hobbes?
2. What complaint does Hobbes raise concerning Aristotle's theory?
3. Why is compulsory service for soldiers (the draft) during wartime a problem for Hobbes's theory? (Hint: Remember one natural right that people cannot transfer to anyone or anything else.)

Chapter Twenty-Two: Of Systems Subject, Political and Private

What should be the proper relationship between the sovereign and a representative body? Why?

Chapter Twenty-Three: Of the Public Ministers of Sovereign Power

1. From where does the sovereign derive authority?
2. Is this position consistent with what Hobbes has had to say previously regarding sovereign authority?

Chapter Twenty-Four: Of the Nutrition, and Procreation of a Commonwealth

What is your sense, given the contents of this chapter, of what Hobbes's general economic policy would be?

Chapter Twenty-Five: Of Counsel

How does this chapter help to reinforce Hobbes's preference for monarchy over democracy?

Chapter Twenty-Six: Of Civill Lawes

What is the relationship between natural laws and civil laws?

Chapter Twenty-Seven: Of Crimes, Excuses and Extenuations

1. According to Hobbes, what is a sin? Do you think others of his time would disagree with his definition?
2. What are some of the causes of crime that Hobbes mentions?

Chapter Twenty-Eight: Of Punishments and Rewards

1. How does Hobbes differentiate between punishment within civil society and violence in war?
2. What does the term *Leviathan* mean (he gives a description in this chapter)?

Chapter Twenty-Nine: Of Those Things that Weaken, or Tend to the Dissolution of a Commonwealth

What kinds of attitudes, laws, and actions can lead to the weakening or dissolving of a commonwealth?

Chapter Thirty: Of the Office of the Sovereign Representative

1. What does Hobbes think of the common people's ability to learn the value of good government and to obey the commands of the sovereign?
2. What does Hobbes mean when he states that the law of nations (international relations) and the law of nature are the same thing?

Chapter Thirty-One: Of the Kingdom of God by Nature This chapter is especially important because it establishes what Hobbes believes is provable about God by reason alone. The next part of *Leviathan* deals with a Christian commonwealth and as such goes beyond natural or rational religion. Keep this chapter in mind as you read this next part.

1. What is the difference between the natural and the prophetic kingdom of God?
2. What is natural worship? How is this different from customary worship (conventional worship)?
3. What do you think is Hobbes's purpose for emphasizing natural or rational religion?
4. How does Hobbes distinguish himself from Plato at the end of this chapter?

Part III: Of a Christian Commonwealth Hobbes devotes an entire section of his book to a subject he has already more than touched upon: the proper understanding of Christianity and the relationship between the Church and the state. Here he goes much further, though, offering up not his version of "natural religion," but his unique reading of the Christian religion, including his idiosyncratic reading of the Bible. The reader must keep in mind Hobbes's ultimate purpose: to reconcile the spiritual power of the Church to the temporal power of the sovereign. He wishes to show his many Christian readers that they have been mistaken in their belief that true faith demands fighting a sovereign who wishes to impose a different religion. Hobbes will attempt to argue that the Bible, rightly understood, supports the absolute authority of the sovereign even in religious matters, and even if the sovereign is not a Christian. If Hobbes can prove that the Bible does not justify opposition to even a non-Christian sovereign, then he believes he can move people toward lasting political stability and peace.

Chapter Thirty-Two: Of the Principles of Christian Politics

Hobbes claims that miracles no longer happen. If that is so, what is our only source with which to find religious truth, and how will Hobbes use it in this section of his book?

Chapter Thirty-Three: Of the Number, Antiquity, Scope . . . of Holy Scripture

What makes biblical teachings law?

Chapter Thirty-Four: Of the Signification of Spirit, Angel, and Inspiration . . . In Holy Scripture

What point do you think Hobbes is making when he says angels and spirits must be corporeal (have material form)?

Chapter Thirty-Five: Of the Signification in Scripture of Kingdom of God, of Holy . . .

How does Hobbes envision the Kingdom of God?

Chapter Thirty-Six: Of the Word of God, and of Prophets

1. How does Hobbes define prophecy? Can you tell what he thinks of most prophetic claims?
2. How should readers see prophets and prophecy, and why?

Chapter Thirty-Seven: Of Miracles and Their Use

1. What is a miracle, according to Hobbes? Does his teaching here accord with what he said about miracles in Chapter Thirty-Two?
2. Who should be able to say whether something is a miracle? Why is this politically important?

Chapter Thirty-Eight: Of the Signification in Scripture of Eternal Life, Hel[l], Salvation . . . Here Hobbes puts forth his idiosyncratic reading of the Bible on important points of faith.

1. What and where are heaven and hell, according to Hobbes?
2. Why do you think Hobbes puts forth this very materialistic version of central points of Christian faith?

Chapter Thirty-Nine: Of the Signification in Scripture of the Word Church

Who should be the head of the Church, and why?

Chapter Forty: Of the Rights of the Kingdom of God . . . In this chapter Hobbes details the history of the Jews as he sees it. Read it all with one question in mind:

What is the political teaching concerning the relationship between the sovereign and religion that Hobbes wishes to draw out of this history?

Chapter Forty-One: Of the Office of Our Blessed Savior

Christians often call Christ their king. What is the political purpose of Hobbes's teaching that Christ is not king until he comes to reign on earth at some time in the future?

Chapter Forty-Two: Of Power Eccliasticall

By the length of this chapter, Hobbes is showing us the importance of this topic. The power of the Church had to be completely subordinated to the power of the state for unity and thus stability to be maintained.

1. The apostles, who traveled and preached after Jesus died, were obviously not preaching in Christian commonwealths but were often welcome. Would Hobbes have to say their activity was illegal and therefore unjust?
2. If the sovereign commanded his subjects to worship a God other than the Christian God, what would Hobbes say citizens should do? Why?
3. What does Hobbes think of the Catholic belief that the pope has the final word on matters of faith?

Chapter Forty-Three: Of What Is Necessary for a Man's Reception into the Kingdom of Heaven

1. What does Hobbes say is necessary to obtain eternal salvation? What types of things does he omit?
2. By arguing that the only thing Christians must do to follow Christ is to believe internally that he is Christ, what kind of government is Hobbes preparing the Christian to accept?

Review and Conclusion   This long final chapter is truly Hobbes's final word. Here you will find a statement of his purpose and how he hopes his science will be used.

1. What is the use and importance of rhetoric in communicating reason? Is Hobbes's book itself a form of rhetoric?
2. Hobbes adds another law of nature in this chapter. What is it? Why do you think he waited until now to present it? (See Chapter Twenty-One on the subject of running away in battle.)
3. Why should we not distinguish between just and unjust conquest?
4. Where does Hobbes want his doctrine taught, and why?

BIBLIOGRAPHY

Laurie M. Johnson Bagby, *Thucydides, Hobbes, and the Interpretation of Realism,* DeKalb, Northern Illinois University Press, 1991.

Deborah Baumgold, *Hobbes's Political Theory,* Cambridge: Cambridge University Press, 1988.

Glen Burgess, *Absolute Monarchy and the Stuart Constitution,* New Haven: Yale University Press, 1996.

Jean Hampton, *Hobbes and the Social Contract Tradition,* Cambridge: Cambridge University Press, 1986.

Thomas Edmund Jessop, *Thomas Hobbes,* London: Published for the British Council by Longmans, Green, 1961.

David Johnston, *The Rhetoric of Leviathan: Thomas Hobbes and the Politics of Cultural Transformation,* Princeton: Princeton University Press, 1986.

A.P. Martinich, *The Two Gods of Leviathan: Thomas Hobbes on Religion and Politics*, Cambridge: Cambridge University Press, 1992.

Conrad Russell, *The Fall of the British Monarchies*, 1637–1642, London: Oxford University Press, 1991.

Quentin Skinner, *Reason and Rhetoric in the Philosophy of Hobbes*, Cambridge: Cambridge University Press, 1996.

Lawrence Stone, *The Causes of the English Revolution*, New York: Harper & Rowe, 1972.

Leo Strauss, *The Political Philosophy of Hobbes: Its Basis and Genesis*, Chicago: University of Chicago Press, 1952.

Richard Tuck, *Hobbes*, Oxford University Press, 1989.

LIBERALISM

When speaking in terms of political thought, "to advocate individual freedom and popular representation" is the most accurate definition of liberal. It is a definition that adequately encompasses all three authors featured here: Locke, Rousseau, and Mill. Think of another word that comes from the Latin *liber,* meaning "liberty." A classical liberal is someone who values individual liberty and who advocates those governmental constructions that help to guarantee that liberty. Today's liberals and conservatives as well as libertarians all agree on a small but significant number of classical liberal principles and practices, most importantly the words that Thomas Jefferson used with lasting effect in the Declaration of Independence—"the right to life, liberty and the pursuit of happiness"—a close paraphrase of words written by John Locke.

The Bill of Rights in the U.S. Constitution contains core classical liberal rights such as the right to worship freely and without a state-sponsored church, freedom of speech and press, the right to peaceably assemble, the right to due process, and the right to bear arms. Generally in liberal thought the right to own and control one's private property is essential to liberty, and the U.S. Constitution reflects that idea. However, some classical liberal thinkers thought that too much property for some individuals would hamper the freedom of others and that the state should be involved more heavily in regulating private property. A government ceases to be liberal, though, when it goes from regulating private property and taxing with the people's consent, to owning and monopolizing property itself without the people's consent.

Because of the way liberal thinkers view human nature, liberalism as a political philosophy has more in common with realism than with idealism. Liberals start with the assumption that human nature is selfish and individualistic. But unlike the ancient idealists, and like the realists, they wish to construct laws and institutions that work with that human nature, channeling it in positive ways, rather than trying to change human beings' minds and hearts.

LOCKE (1632–1704)

BACKGROUND

John Locke was a member of the early Enlightenment in Europe. His philosophy of natural rights and the social contract inspired later Enlightenment thinkers. Locke was born in 1632 at Wrington, England (near Bristol), the son of a country lawyer. Locke's father had some influence over his future political views. During the English civil war, Locke's father sided with the Puritan dissenters who wished to rid England of Charles I and the Church of England and served as an officer in the Puritan army. Locke's youth coincided with a tumultuous time in England which saw the capture and beheading of Charles I, the formation of several parliamentary governments, the one-man rule of Puritan Oliver Cromwell, and the eventual restoration of Charles's son, Charles II.

Initially, Locke came away from this experience much as Hobbes did: an advocate of absolute monarchy as a solution to political and religious dissent. He even wrote the *Two Tracts* in defense of absolute monarchy. These books closely followed the reasoning of Hobbes on religious matters, but his father's influence and future events influenced him more strongly because Locke later became a forceful advocate for parliamentary supremacy and limited government.

Locke was tutored at home until the age of fourteen, when he went to Westminster School. In 1652 he became a student at Christ Church, Oxford University. There he studied philosophy and natural science. Locke also studied medicine, though he never tried to make a living as a medical doctor. He did, however, in 1666, take a position with Lord Ashley, who was to become the First Earl of Shaftesbury, to provide medical advice and to tutor Lord Ashley's son. Shaftesbury was an important member of the Whig Party in England, which advocated reducing the power of the monarch and increasing that of parliament.

As the Earl of Shaftesbury's political stature increased, so did Locke's. When Shaftesbury became Lord Chancellor and King Charles II's closest advisor in 1672, he used his political influence to have Locke appointed secretary of the Council of Trade and Plantations in 1673. When Shaftesbury lost favor with the king, however, so did Locke. Locke returned to teach at Christ Church, and then lived in France from 1675 to 1680 because of ill health. In 1680, Locke was back in England, once again employed by Shaftesbury. This time his association with the earl got him into serious trouble.

In 1685, Charles's son James II became king. James, a convert to Catholicism, did not impose his religion on England, although he did lift restrictions on the religious freedom of English Catholics and remove a ban on their political appointments. When James's second wife, Mary of Modena, bore him a son, the hopes of many Englishmen that James's Protestant daughters by his first wife would assume the throne were dashed. The English were willing to tolerate a Catholic king, but only for a short while and only if there were a prospect that the ruler would in due course be, and remain, Protestant. They objected to Catholicism not only on religious grounds but also and more importantly on political ones. Most English saw their church, the Church of England, as a guarantee against the meddling of a foreign sovereign (the pope) in their country's political affairs.

Shaftesbury was particularly busy conspiring to exclude James from the throne. Because of his association with the earl, Locke too was suspected of plotting against James and followed Shaftesbury to the United Provinces (to an area later known as Holland) in 1683 to avoid the king's wrath. Shaftesbury died that same year, but Locke began to write numerous political tracts under a false name. He took no chances, denying that he was in fact John Locke even after his name had been removed from a list of plotters wanted for arrest in England. It was during this time that he wrote his politically most influential book, *The Second Treatise of Government,* the authorship of which he denied his entire life, though he later had no need to deny anything.

Change was afoot in England, for in 1688 the parliament brought about the "Glorious Revolution" in which Whigs and Tories alike invited the Protestants William and Mary to take the throne, in effect denying the direct line of hereditary succession. Although Mary was the daughter of James II, and had a right to the throne once the male line died out, her husband Dutchman William of Orange had no such right. However, William refused to be treated as his wife's "usher" and insisted that he be acknowledged as king before he would bring his army to England. Both William and Mary were Protestants. There is some scholarly controversy as to whether *The Second Treatise* influenced the revolution or only justified it after the fact. We do know that Locke's ideas, if not his book, were influential. He actually advised the future King William in Holland during his exile. He also had the honor of escorting Mary to England after the revolution.

To be recognized as king and queen, William and Mary were forced to agree to a more limited, constitutional monarchy with a bill of rights. Parliament emerged more powerful, because the monarchs could not raise taxes without the member's consent. Elections to parliament were to be free, parliament was to meet frequently, and members were to enjoy freedom of speech and debate within parliament. William and Mary also agreed to the Toleration Act. According to this bill, most religions were to be tolerated by the government, but not Catholicism and Unitarianism. Atheists also were not tolerated. Locke's subsequent position on toleration came very close to that expressed in the Toleration Act. Locke felt relatively safe returning to England and assumed a role in the government as commissioner of appeal and adviser to the government on coinage.

The times Locke lived through were tumultuous and full of importance not only for England's future but also for the future history of all constitutional governments, including that of the United States. The idea of self-governance had been slowly emerging in England from at least the thirteenth century with the signing of the Magna Carta, the first agreement restricting the powers of the monarchy. Locke, however, can rightly be called the father of the classical liberal formulation of self-governance as a theoretical idea and not just an accumulation of a series of intermittent contests between monarchs, parliaments, and people. *The Second Treatise,* as well as *A Letter Concerning Toleration* and other works, influenced the American founders. They improved on Locke with a separation of powers (instead of legislative supremacy) and institutionalized checks and balances.

Understanding Locke

Locke is a social contract theorist, as was Hobbes. Locke's social contract is more of a model and commentary on the current situation than a depiction of historical reality. It expresses what he thinks should go into making a government and supporting a government if people behave rationally, thus following their self-interest.

Locke is a philosopher who is easier to understand in relation to previous philosophers, especially Hobbes. It is helpful to note where he disagrees with or moves beyond Hobbes's social contract. For instance, Locke's state of nature is deliberately not as frightful as Hobbes's, because if people are not so frightened in the state of nature, then they will not accept whatever they have to in order to leave that state. Locke's rational human beings would rather live in a state of nature, that is, without government, than to have a government that tyrannizes over them. It is better to have the freedom to defend yourself than to have a government that eliminates this basic right in the supposed name of safety—indeed, what could be less secure?

Hobbes wrote of one natural right—the right to self-preservation, which no government could alter or take away. Locke wrote instead of natural rights, which include the right to self-preservation. The natural rights people have in the state of nature are to be retained by them after they enter into the social contract. These rights include some that Hobbes would have thought far too destabilizing, including the right to own and control one's property, the right to worship freely, and even the right to revolution should the government jeopardize these other rights. Locke believed that, given the freedom to control their own property and enterprises, people would be content to allow others the same rights they enjoyed. Especially in the area of religion, this was a radical departure from Hobbes's ideas. Locke thought that people could, in a sense, accept religious differences, and perhaps even see most differences in theological doctrine and religious practices as not that important.

Locke's attitude toward property reflected a new economic reality. At that time, a new class of merchants was becoming quite wealthy and powerful—a middle class, or bourgeoisie. It was this class that would revolutionize English politics and influence the Glorious Revolution of 1688. This bourgeoisie, or middle class, gained wealth not from the traditional source, land, but through its enterprise. It became possible for a merchant to become very wealthy in a few years if he engaged in the right business at the right time. The old aristocratic class did not welcome this development, for their wealth was inherited, often the by-product of centuries-old grants of land by the king. But with international trade expanding and manufacturing increasing, theirs was not the only or the most profitable way to make money. They retained their titles, but began to lose influence as this new and more populous class demanded more political power.

This major social change influenced Locke's view of property. It is also why he tries so hard to establish an absolute right to property. Locke treats the human individual as property—that is, our bodies are our first and primary property, control over which we cannot give to any other individual or group without leaving ourselves open to destruction. From this right to our own bodies Locke establishes the right to other property through labor. The intermingling of the individual's labor with nature makes what he gets from nature his property. Because man needs basic property to survive, Locke ties the right to property back to the right of self-preservation. He goes beyond rudimentary self-preservation, arguing that through the use of imperishable money, individuals have a right to accumulate as much wealth as they can. Eventually he argues that because this property is the individual's by right, he cannot have it taken away (taxed) by government without his consent.

Keep in mind that Locke believes that a hereditary title should not confer arbitrary power on anyone, and that if anything, political power should be determined by those who contribute the most to the public treasury. Although this may sound reasonable, and is in many ways, critics of Locke have accused him of introducing a crass materialism at the expense of the poor, and the noble aristocratic values of chivalry and virtue. It is probably too harsh to say that Locke invented this new materialism, as it was well underway by the late seventeenth century.

To understand Locke, especially his *Letter Concerning Toleration*, the reader must be aware of the religious context of the times. Recall that Locke's *Second Treatise* was inspired by the controversy over King James's Catholicism. Locke agreed with those who wanted to force James to abdicate; however, his dislike of religious establishment ran deeper than not wanting a Catholic king. Establishment meant a state-sponsored religion, supported by tax dollars, with ministers or priests appointed and paid by the government. Establishment often meant government intolerance and persecution of other religions. England had an established religion, the Church of England.

This church had been created in the sixteenth century by the infamous Henry VIII, whose desire to divorce his wife Catherine because in part she did not give him a surviving male heir brought him into conflict with the pope. When the pope refused to grant him a divorce, Henry's answer was to divorce the Church. Not only did Henry declare himself free of the authority of the pope, but he also declared all England free as well. In the Act of Supremacy, Henry created a separate national church and appointed himself its protector and supreme head. He subsequently went through several more wives in search of an heir, beheading two of them as they fell out of favor. He also persecuted the remaining Catholic clergy and confiscated the property of the Church. Over time, many of the English supported their government's continued suppression of Catholicism as a dangerous religion that fostered divided loyalties.

Locke's view was that no religious establishment, including the Church of England, was just or conducive to true faith. He argued that unless people were given the freedom to worship as they chose without government interference, religious feeling could not be genuine. His concern for toleration did not apply to Catholics, Unitarians, or atheists, however. Atheists in particular could not be trusted because the oaths and promises they made would be valueless if they were not buttressed by a fear of God. But the largest contenders for the attention of the English people were not Catholicism, Unitarianism, or atheism. Various Protestant sects had been gaining ground in England since the Protestant Reformation (sixteenth century). Locke apparently saw no reason not to allow these sects complete freedom and to put them on an even playing field with Anglicanism.

Religion was a tremendously important issue during Locke's day, just as it had been a generation ago in Hobbes's time. Because religious disputes had, in part, led to wars, such issues were critical to Locke's readers. Moreover, the Christian religion, in whatever manifestation, was a more integrated part of people's lives. If literate, a family might have one book such as a Bible or some other piece of Christian literature. School children grew up learning how to read by learning Bible verses and alphabets tied to biblical figures. Because biblical references were commonplace in all kinds of literature and public speech, it was impossible to make a serious political argument without using the language of Christianity, which meant quoting the Bible. Students are apt to come away from reading Locke's *Letter Concerning Toleration* or his *Second Treatise* with the idea that Locke was some sort of biblical scholar, and a deeply religious individual, because he quotes scripture and writes about God. If a writer followed Locke in such extensive biblical quotation today, a student would be justified in these conclusions. During Locke's time, no serious commentator could escape it, regardless if he had strong religious beliefs.

The First Treatise of Government, a shorter work, paved the way for *The Second Treatise*. In *The First Treatise,* Locke tried to disprove Sir Robert Filmer's theory of divine right, that is, that the monarch ruled by the decree of God, that his authority over his people derived from the dominion over nature originally granted by God to the first man, Adam. The monarch's power came from God's will and thus, according to the theory of divine right, must be considered absolute and indisputable. Many rulers, including James I and James II, believed in this theory. Locke tries to destroy it systematically by including lengthy biblical arguments. He provides a very brief summary of this argument at the beginning of *The Second Treatise* and then, after undermining this traditional basis of the king's authority, he constructs a new type of government in which the ultimate authority rests with the people.

CAREFUL READING

Of all the writers studied thus far, you may find Locke the most straightforward. Locke builds his arguments in a fairly logical way, establishing fundamental points and then building upon them. He is also obviously an advocate for a different kind of political system, which is why he felt it necessary to write under another name. Some passages may be difficult because Locke uses an analogy that is unfamiliar today, or because he is trying to make two points at once, one on a literal level and one by way of comparison. At several points in *The Second Treatise,* Locke uses a euphemism which can easily be misunderstood.

Slavery

Locke writes about slavery in several places in *The Second Treatise.*[1] These passages are often seen by students as referring only to the actual practice of

---

[1]All quotations from *The Second Treatise* in this chapter are from John Locke, *Two Treatises of Government,* 6th Edition, Glasgow: W. Paton, 1796. The only change I have made is to replace the old character with the contemporary "*s*".

enslaving individual human beings to a master, the type of slavery practiced on plantations in the South prior to the Civil War. Locke is writing about this type of slavery, but every time he mentions slavery he is also making another, more political, argument. Following are some of the passages in which Locke writes about slavery.

> This freedom from absolute, arbitrary power, is so necessary to, and closely joined with a man's preservation, that he cannot part with it, but by what forfeits his preservation and life together. For a man, not having the power of his own life, cannot, by compact, or his own consent, enslave himself to any one, nor put himself under the absolute, arbitrary power of another, to take away his life when he pleases. No body can give more power than he has himself; and he that cannot take away his own life, cannot give another power over it. Indeed, having by his fault, forfeited his own life, by some act that deserves death; he, to whom he has forfeited it, may (when he has him in his power) delay to take it, and make use of him to his own service, and he does him no injury by it. For, whenever he finds the hardship of his slavery outweigh the value of his life, 'tis in his power, by resisting the will of his master, to draw on himself the death he desires.
>
> This is the perfect condition of slavery, which is nothing else, but the state of war continued, between a lawful conqueror and a captive. For, if once compact enter between them, and make an agreement for a limited power on the one side, and obedience on the other, the state of war and slavery ceases, as long as the compact endures. For, as has been said, no man can, by agreement, pass over to another that which he hath not in himself, a power over his own life.
>
> I confess, we find among the Jews, as well as other nations, that men did sell themselves but it is plain, this was only to drudgery, not to slavery. For it is evident, the person sold, was not under an absolute, arbitrary despotical power. For the master could not have power to kill him, at any time whom at a certain time, he was obliged to let go free out of his service; and the master of such a servant was so far from having an arbitrary power over his life, that he could not at pleasure, so much as maim him, but the loss of an eye, or tooth, set him free, Exod. xxi. (Chapter Four, para. 23, 24)

Locke emphasizes that putting one individual under the absolute power of another is the creation of a state of war between the two. He is clearly trying to define slavery. Locke uses the term *arbitrary* after *absolute*. We know that a person who is arbitrary is someone whose actions are not explained and are most often unpredictable. Locke has now given us a fairly good idea of absolute power.

Locke links absolute power to slavery. To have someone in your absolute power is to enslave him. Slavery is the same as being under someone's absolute and arbitrary power, which includes the power to kill that other person for any reason. Locke argues that no one can give or forfeit to another person his life; no one can willingly enslave himself to another because "a man, not having the power of his own life, cannot, by compact, or his own consent, enslave himself to anyone . . ." Note the crucial point here. Locke is saying that no individual has the right to take his own life. Indeed, a little later Locke says, "[He] that cannot take away his own life, cannot give another power over it." This assertion is a critical component of his case against slavery because, according to Locke's overall philosophy of property, whatever a person has ownership of, he has a right to sell, give away, or even destroy. But even though Locke has earlier written of an individual's body as his own property, and the source of all other property (through the body's labor), he now makes a stunning qualification. Apparently the body is not so much our property that we can dispose of it as we please. He buttresses this point with the idea that God gave human beings life and thus only God has the right to take life away, and with the idea that the desire for life is a sort of natural instinct that no one would give up.

Locke denies that we have the right to commit suicide; but he goes on in the second selection to refer to an instance in which an individual can forfeit his own life, "by some act that deserves death . . ." In other words, if a person has committed a grave crime and is caught, his master or captor can either put him to death or use him as a slave. If he is made a slave under these conditions and he finds the slavery too much to endure, he can always resist the will of his master and thus bring about his own death. This sounds suspiciously like suicide, but Locke makes an important distinction. In a civil society, a society of laws, it is necessary to imprison and perhaps even kill those who have committed crimes. He apparently does not want to apply his condemnation of slavery to these cases. Nonetheless, to make it clear what the relationship is between the prisoner and the jailor, Locke describes their relationship as a state of war between a lawful conqueror and a captive. Does this imply that the prisoner continues to have the right to try to defend himself against his jailor, and even to try to escape?

We can begin to see a clear condemnation of traditional slavery—that is, enslaving those who have committed no crime. Because Locke is not writing a treatise primarily about slavery, however, the reader should wonder what point Locke is trying to make about government here. Locke's insistence that slavery is about arbitrary power should help. What is the opposite of arbitrary power? Locke tells us that once there is a compact between human beings, then there is no more state of war and no more slavery. Because this compact can never include giving another arbitrary power, it must only include giving another limited power for a limited time. Locke makes this point when he draws upon the Bible to talk about what in Locke's time was known as indentured servitude. Locke knows that advocates of slavery and arbitrary power will bring up the slavery mentioned in the Bible as proof that God ordained slavery (that is, divine right of kings). So, he argues that the Jews did not practice slavery, but a sort of contractual arrangement in which people sold themselves to "drudgery" or hard work for a limited time. He also emphasizes the larger context of laws prohibiting ill treatment or murder of servants.

Locke's political message is now clearer. Locke is arguing against the divine right theory in which the king has absolute and arbitrary power over his subjects. Later, Locke makes this analogy clear, using the same idea of slavery in his commentary about the absolute rule of kings. Locke is saying that citizens cannot give the king such arbitrary power over their lives because they do not have the right to take their own lives. When the king has absolute and arbitrary power over his people, he has the power to enslave them, threaten their lives and livelihood, and even kill them. Locke wants to argue that the king has no right to do such things. At the same time he is arguing that any legitimate government rests upon the consent, or contract with, the governed. Further, he is saying that if a king puts himself into a state of war with the people, they have the right to resist, just as a slave has a right to resist his master. Whenever Locke writes about slavery, then, the reader should be aware that Locke is also trying to make points about legitimate government.

Marriage

In Chapter Six, Locke writes about the power of fathers over their children, an argument with implications for monarchy. There, Locke argues that paternal power (the power of fathers) is not exclusive and that it would be better to speak of parental power, because in nature, mothers have just as much, if not more, power over their children. He then qualifies parental power, saying that parents are under an obligation to raise their children (they cannot treat them as slaves) until they reach the age of maturity. Then, parental power ceases because when individuals reach maturity, they also reach the age of consent, and any further dealings with their parents or anyone else must be with their consent. Adopting this line of reasoning, Locke hopes to poke further holes in the theory of divine right of kings. Locke targets the old idea that the king is a sort of father and the subjects are his children.

In Chapter Seven, Locke goes even further by distinguishing between parental and political power. He discusses the relationship between men and women in marriage to prove his case. Locke has just finished talking about the difference between the unions of animals and those of men and women. Unions between men and women typically last longer than those of animals because, reasons Locke, it takes much longer for the human infant to grow into a capable adult. The union or marriage must remain intact as long as there are children to be cared for. This is a sort of naturalistic explanation of what marriage is and what function it serves. Locke then mentions the "wisdom of the great Creator, who having given to man foresight, and an ability to lay up for the future, as well as to supply the present necessity, hath made it necessary, that society of man and wife should be more lasting, than of male and female of other creatures; that so their industry might be encouraged, and their interest better united, to make provision and lay up goods for their common issue, which uncertain mixture, or easy and frequent solutions of conjugal society would mightily disturb" (para. 80). This reference to God should give a careful reader pause. Locke is arguing that a very practical consideration was foremost in God's mind, namely, that God wanted marriage to last because it was more conducive to industry and child rearing ("their common issue"). Notice that he does not acknowledge the New Testament standard for marriage, which is that marriage should last a lifetime. He goes on to strengthen his case for the contractual nature of marriage and warns at the outset that even this relationship falls short of what can properly be called "political society."

> But though these are ties upon mankind, which make the conjugal bonds more firm and lasting in man, than the other species of animals; yet it would give one reason to enquire, why this compact, where procreation and education are secured, and inheritance taken care for, may not be made determinable, either by consent, or at a certain time, or upon certain conditions, as well as any other voluntary compacts, there being no necessity in the nature of the thing, nor to the ends of it, that it should always be for life; I mean, to such as are under no restraint of any positive law, which ordains all such contracts to be perpetual.
>
> But the husband and wife, though they have but one common concern, yet having different understandings, will unavoidably sometimes have different wills too; it therefore being necessary that the last determination, i.e. the rule, should be placed somewhere; it naturally falls to the man's share; as the abler and the stronger. But this reaching but to the things of their common interest and property, leaves the wife in the full and free possession of what by contract is her peculiar right, and gives the husband no more power over her life than she has over his. The power of the husband being so far from that of an absolute monarch, that the wife has in many cases a liberty to separate from him; where natural right, or their contract allows it, whether that contract be made by themselves in the state of nature, or by the customs or laws of the country they live in; and the children upon such separation fall to the father or mother's lot, as such contract does determine. (Chapter One, para. 81, 82)

Locke distinguishes this notion of marriage from political society. Why is this the case, if marriage is to be seen as a contract between two mutually consenting adults? It would seem that both marriage and civil society are contractual arrangements to Locke, but he points to a difference in these paragraphs and in the previous chapter. Locke places upon parents a natural obligation to stay together and care for their children until their children can care for themselves. Although marriage is a voluntary contract between two adults, in a certain way it is also not voluntary. It seems as though Locke wants to impose a strong moral obligation on husband and wife to care for the children, and he seems to want them to be free to separate only after the children are gone. Yet, moral duties or obligations are never as binding in Locke's analysis as are rights. Locke mentions in the last part of the second paragraph an instance in which the wife can separate from the husband before the children are grown, and the children then become the care of one or the other parent, depending on the laws of the land or on their own contract. Locke states that there is "no necessity in the nature of the thing" (marriage) for it to be a life-long commitment, unless husband and wife are under the constraints of "positive law," man-made law, as opposed to the law of nature. Notice that Locke here separates man-made law and the law of nature from God's will, and God's will has already been misrepresented by Locke as desiring "more lasting" commitments, but not permanent ones.

Locke's distinction between marriage ("conjugal society") and civil society comes down to a moral obligation for parents to stay together long enough to raise their minor children. But in political society the government is not a parent of anyone—citizens are not to be considered as children but as adults who can take care of and make decisions for themselves.

Interestingly, Locke seems to backslide on women's equality in the second paragraph of our selection, where he says that because husband and wife have "different understandings," the rule "naturally falls to the man's share; as the abler and the stronger." At first, this assertion may be rather troubling to anyone who is used to thinking of full equality between the sexes. One must keep in mind though the times in which Locke wrote, and one must also read carefully for what Locke actually says. Notice that Locke says they have "different understandings," and "different wills," not unequal intelligence. Locke follows Hobbes and many other philosophers in noticing that every human being sees the world and makes decisions in a different way than others. These inevitable differences of outlook and opinion cause conflict. Locke then says that at some point there must be a decision, a "last determination." Someone has to make a decision, and Locke states that this decision "naturally" falls to the man. The reason he gives for this is also interesting. Locke says that the man is abler and stronger. These are ambiguous words. They could refer only to physical strength. In fact this is the most commonsense way to take Locke's statement. This may also be a difference between conjugal society and civil society. In civil society there is even greater equality among citizens than among spouses in marriage, where moral obligations to children and differences in physical strength are not as relevant as they are in marriage.

Certainly these passages can be interpreted in different ways, but it is useful to note that nowhere does Locke clearly state that men and women are naturally unequal, or have unequal levels of intelligence. Locke, however, was probably more interested in making a larger political point. By comparing the nature of marriage, which he sees as voluntary and contractual but not perfectly so, Locke can contrast it with the perfectly voluntary and contractual nature of civil society while challenging a little the old-fashioned notions of natural superiority and inferiority.

Toleration: Indifferent Things

In A Letter Concerning Toleration,[2] Locke uses the term indifferent in a way that may jar the modern ear. Today we generally use this term to describe a person's attitude, not a thing. When someone asks if we would rather eat steak or seafood, we might answer "I'm indifferent." But this is not exactly Locke's meaning.

> AGAIN: Things in their own nature indifferent, cannot, by any human authority, be made any part of the Worship of God, for this very reason; because they are indifferent. For since indifferent things are not capable, by any virtue of their own, to propitiate the Deity; no human power or authority can confer on them so much dignity and excellency as to enable them to do it. In the common affairs of life, that use of indifferent things which God has not forbidden, is free and lawful: and therefore in those things human authority has place. But it is not so in matters of religion. Things indifferent are not otherwise lawful in the worship of God than as they are instituted by God himself; and as he, by some positive command, has ordained them to be made a part of that Worship which he will vouchsafe to accept of at the hands of poor sinful men. Nor when an incensed Deity shall ask us, "Who has required these, or such like things at our hands?" Will it be enough to answer him, that the Magistrate commanded them. If civil jurisdiction extended thus far, what might not lawfully be introduced into religion? What hodge-podge of ceremonies, what superstitious inventions, built upon the magistrate's authority, might not, against Conscience, be imposed upon the worshippers of God? For the greatest part of these ceremonies and superstitions consists in the religious use of such things as are in their own nature indifferent: nor are they sinful upon any other account, than because God is not the author of them. The sprinkling of water, and the use of bread and wine, are both in their own nature, and in the ordinary occasions of Life, altogether indifferent. Will any man therefore say that these things could have been introduced into religion, and made a part of divine worship, if not by divine institution? If any human authority or civil power could have done this, why might it not also enjoin the eating of fish, the drinking of ale, in the holy banquet, as a part of divine worship? Why not the sprinkling of the blood of beasts in churches, and expiations by water or fire, and abundance more of this kind? . . . We see therefore that indifferent things how much soever they be under the power of the civil magistrate, yet cannot upon that pretence be introduced into religion, and imposed upon religious assemblies; because in the worship of God they wholly cease to be indifferent. (pp. 332–333)

Locke has already said that the government has no right to force certain rites or ceremonies on its citizens. So why does he then go on to write at length about indifferent actions in worship? First we need to figure out what Locke means by "indifferent." We can look at his examples for a clue. Before the selected paragraphs, Locke gives the example of washing an infant as an indif-

---

[2]All quotations from the Letter in this chapter are from John Locke, The Works of John Locke In Four Volumes, 8th Edition, 2nd Volume, London: printed for W. Strahan et al., J. Grosser, publisher, 1777.

ferent thing. He then points out that in worship, this act is called baptism and takes on a unique religious meaning. In this last passage, Locke gives examples such as sprinkling with water (baptism, use of holy water) and the use of bread and wine (Holy Communion). In other words, things that we do in everyday life we also can do while worshiping God, but in the latter case they take on a special religious significance. If these things can take on special religious significance, then, how could Locke refer to them as indifferent?

Locke continuously contrasts what the civil authority's attitude should be toward these matters with the worshiper's attitude. Obviously, a worshiper who believes in the real presence of Christ in the Eucharist or Holy Communion would not be indifferent toward it or see it as simply everyday bread and wine. Locke is clearly not placing the attitude of indifference on the worshiper here, but on the government. In placing the attitude of indifference on the government, Locke is clearly drawing a boundary between religion and government. Locke argues that if government has the power to legislate on indifferent matters of worship then it could enforce a ceremony contrary to God's will and the beliefs of the worshipers, ceremonies such as the sprinkling of animal blood and the sacrificing of dogs.

It would seem that it is for the protection of religion that government should not impose or prohibit certain religious practices on its citizens. Locke even conjures up an image of an angry God who is offended at wrong-headed ceremonies ordered by an interfering government. When Locke says that the government should not legislate about those things that are indifferent, he is not saying that these things are insignificant to worshipers. He is saying that such things should be seen as indifferent by the magistrate or government official; that is, the government should deal with secular matters only, and leave religious matters up to private institutions, for example, churches and families. If the government does not see washing a baby at home as harmful, why should it see baptism as harmful or to be regulated?

Indifference is an attitude after all, and one that the government should have toward religious rites. The reader might ask, and Locke does ask, does this mean that the government cannot prohibit religious practices that run counter to peace and good order? Locke gives examples such as the sacrifice of infants or drunken and sexual orgies. Here, too, the concept of indifferent things comes in handy. Locke replies, "No. These things are not lawful in the ordinary course of life, nor in any private house; and therefore neither are they so in the worship of God, or in any religious Meeting" (p. 334). So, whatever is lawful in ordinary everyday use must also be lawful in worship. Likewise, whatever is considered illegal in everyday use must also be illegal in worship. Locke warns that the government should be careful about such prohibitions. If it wishes to make the religious sacrifice of a calf illegal, it should be prepared to outlaw killing calves—an unattractive proposition for a meat-loving country.

How do we contrast these observations with Locke's insistence that government does not have to tolerate Catholicism, Unitarianism, or atheism? For Locke these two religions and atheism fall into a special category, because he saw them as threats to good order and, in the case of Catholicism, the sovereignty of the government. Locke wrote "That church can have no right to be tolerated by the magistrate, which is constituted upon such a bottom, that all those who enter into it do thereby ipso facto deliver themselves up to the protection and service of another prince" (the pope). Here Locke includes Islam, too, for the same reason (p. 342). In these cases, the government cannot see their ceremonies as things indifferent. For Locke, government must not only be separate from religion but also in some sense superior to it, because government can in fact determine whether a particular religion threatens its existence and deal with it accordingly.

GUIDE TO *THE SECOND TREATISE OF GOVERNMENT*

Locke's thought was a source of great inspiration for the American founders. As you read Locke, you may also want to take a look at the Declaration of Independence and the Constitution to assess the similarities and differences. Locke is a modern political philosopher who, like Machiavelli, rejects the ancient and medieval notion that government should at least ideally be about implanting virtue and uprooting vice. Instead, government is created by human beings to protect their rights, including the right to self-preservation (life), liberty, and property. For Locke, government is the product of a social contract that can be broken if it becomes intolerably oppressive.

Preface (Letter to Reader)

What is Locke's stated purpose?

Chapter One Here Locke summarizes his dispute with the divine right of kings argument that he discussed at length in *The First Treatise of Government*.

1. How does Locke argue that the king cannot trace his authority all the way back to Adam (the first human being in the Bible's Book of Genesis)?
2. How does Locke distinguish political power from the power a father has over his children?

Chapter Two The state of nature is a scenario Locke uses to show what human beings would be like if they had no formal government, and how human beings should think about the formation and purpose of their governments. Here Locke introduces the famous concept of the state of nature.

1. What are the qualities of the state of nature?
2. How do human beings defend their rights (according to the law of nature) in the state of nature? Why is this not the *best* way for our rights to be protected?
3. What does Locke say here about absolute monarchy? Why is it better to be in the state of nature than to be in the hands of such a monarch?

Chapter Three   In this chapter, Locke introduces the state of war, a concept that is crucial to his argument about the limits and purpose of government.

1. What is the state of war? When does it occur?
2. How does the possibility of the state of war encourage people to enter into a social contract or government? How does this discussion of the state of war help us to understand what Locke thinks the role and purpose of government should be?

Chapter Four   Here Locke discusses slavery, which he condemns and equates with the state of war. Keep in mind that Locke's discussion of slavery has more than one dimension. The most important dimension is not immediately obvious—Locke's equation of tyrannical monarchy with slavery. In this chapter we also find a veiled reference, a euphemism expressing the right to revolution: the appeal to heaven.

1. What is Locke's definition of slavery? Why does Locke think most types of slavery are wrong?
2. Other than condemning the actual practice of slavery, what meaning does this discussion have for Locke's condemnation of absolute monarchy?
3. What do you think Locke means here by our "appeal to heaven"? (Hint: This is one of those tricky phrases that is meant to be both literal and figurative.) Of course in a political crisis, people will pray to God. Notice, however, that Locke is not writing a book to endorse the simple hope that God will take care of things. What is he advocating people *do* during such a crisis besides pray? (This phrase is used several times in the treatise, and each time it is associated with very direct political action by the people.)

Chapter Five

1. Why does Locke first discuss our own bodies as our most fundamental property? How does he use the ownership of our own bodies to establish our right to other property?
2. What does Locke mean by the law of nature?
3. What does the law of nature say about the limits of acquiring property in the state of nature? Does this law change when the use of money emerges?
4. Why does Locke compare the lives of Native Americans unfavorably with the lives of even the poorest laborers in England?

Chapter Six

1. What is paternal power? How does Locke criticize it? Remember that this concept was used to justify the divine right of kings theory which endorsed absolute monarchy.
2. How does Locke's rejection of the idea of paternal power in the state of nature possibly affect the issue of women's rights and equality? (This is an issue that Locke probably thought little of, outside of his attempt to denounce the divine right theory, but his arguments do apply to the equality of women.)
3. What gives parents rights over their children? When do children become free?
4. Does this discussion in its entirety give you any idea about what Locke thinks political power should be?

Chapter Seven

1. Locke's discussion of the relationship between men and women is unusual for its time. What is the proper relationship between the two, according to Locke?
2. What does Locke add to his definition of political society here?
3. How can an absolute monarch be said to be in a state of nature with his citizens. How can his subjects be said to be slaves?

Chapter Eight

1. How do human beings enter into civil society? Be sure to catch the details of his account.
2. How does Locke justify having the majority rule at the beginning of this chapter (instead of, for instance, insisting on unanimous approval for every decision)?
3. How does Locke think most *real* governments came to be, as opposed to his description of the social contract?
4. In paragraph 116, Locke argues that we cannot bind future generations to any agreement made by the current generation. Do you think this idea would produce unacceptable political instability? Is it a healthy idea to promote, as Thomas Jefferson apparently thought?
5. Explain Locke's idea of tacit consent. Why does he bring this up?

Chapter Nine This chapter concerns the ends or goals of government. It is no accident that Locke again discusses the state of nature and its "inconveniences" here. If we know why the state of nature is inconvenient, why people would want to leave it, we will also know what Locke thinks the purpose of government is.

1. Why is the state of nature inconvenient? That is, why is it difficult for people living with no government (in anarchy) to solve their own disputes and

protect their own property? (Locke uses the word *wants* here in a way that may be unfamiliar, such as: "First, There wants an established, settled, known law, received and allowed by common consent . . ." This is an old-fashioned way of saying that the state of nature lacks certain things.)

2. What powers must a person give up (hand over to government) in order to leave the state of nature and enter into society or the social contract?
3. Does this chapter help you to understand more clearly what Locke sees as the purpose of government?

Chapter Ten   Readers of *The Second Treatise* often come away thinking that Locke only endorses one form of government as the logical consequence of the social contract, parliamentary democracy. However, Locke makes it clear in this chapter that people can form several types of government freely in a social contract. While Locke may prefer parliamentary democracy, his main task in this book is to proclaim the right to revolution—and hence the underlying popular basis of all types of government as made by the people and capable of being dissolved or changed by them.

1. What types of government can the majority establish? Provide definitions for each type.
2. What is Locke's definition of a commonwealth?

Chapter Eleven   Another common mistake for first-time readers of Locke is to assume that Locke's preferred type of government is identical to the American Constitution. However, you will find if you read carefully in the next few chapters that Locke has not thought of separation of powers and checks and balances in the same way the American founders did. Locke does not create separate branches of government equally capable of checking the others in the way our Supreme Court checks acts of Congress, or like our president vetoes congressional legislation. Instead he makes the legislative power supreme, and the other two powers (executive and judicial) largely subordinate to the legislature. Why he does this is the question you must ask yourself.

1. According to Locke, why does the legislative power have to be the supreme power (supreme over the executive and the judicial powers)?
2. Though supreme over the other powers, what are the limits of the legislative powers? Given that the legislature has limits, where does the supreme power of government really lie in Locke's formulation?
3. Why are issues of taxation and property generally so important to Locke?
4. How does the U.S. government of today measure up to Locke's expectations?

Chapter Twelve

1. Why is the executive power needed?
2. What is the federative power? (Hint: Federations are alliances or collections of sovereign and independent states.)

Chapter Thirteen   Here Locke makes it perfectly clear where the supreme power ultimately lies—with the people through their power to reject their government.

1. Why must the people retain the power of saving themselves from any governmental body? Practically, what would this entail?
2. What should be the relationship between the executive and the legislative power?
3. What limits does Locke place on the executive power in its relations with the legislature? (Remember that monarchs of Locke's day claimed to be able to do all of the things Locke mentions here.)

Chapter Fourteen   Here, Locke seems less restrictive of the executive power because Locke knows that a legislature, especially one large enough to represent the people well, cannot effectively make every decision. There is a practical and important place for executive prerogative.

1. What is prerogative and why must the executive have it?
2. How suspicious does Locke say the people will be of the executive's prerogative power? Is Locke right about this, based on your observations of presidential prerogative as it is exercised today?
3. When and why will the people appeal to heaven? (Remember, this phrase means more than praying, but taking direct action.)

Chapter Sixteen   In this chapter, Locke tackles a subject that seems more suitable to a book on the laws of war—the rights and powers of conquerors and those they conquer. However, always keep in mind that Locke's aim is to strengthen the rights of the people against the threat of tyrannical government. Locke hopes to establish here that even conquerors who have conquered justly cannot do just anything to the people they conquer, especially when it comes to the people's property.

1. What kinds of powers does the conqueror get over those he conquers? What powers can he not rightfully obtain over the conquered?
2. What is Locke's political point in this chapter, especially concerning the people's property rights?

Chapter Eighteen

1. What is a tyranny? Could a democracy become tyrannical?
2. Do you get a sense of how sacred some people thought the king's person (his body) was? How does Locke get around this sense of awe toward the king's person in his discussion of tyrannicide (killing of tyrants)?
3. Is Locke right (as Thomas Jefferson repeated in the Declaration of Independence) that it takes a "long train of abuses" for people to rise up against the government? Does this make Locke's philosophy less dangerous to law and order than it originally appears?

Chapter Nineteen   The practical importance of the question of when government is dissolved is enormous for Locke, for revolution can take place when government is no longer functioning. What Locke is really asking here is when can the people have a revolution, and furthermore, *at what point* in the breakdown of government would it be best for the people to retake their ancient sovereign power and form a new government. It is no wonder that Locke saves this topic for last.

1. Why does Locke distinguish between the dissolution of society and the dissolution of government?
2. When are governments to be considered dissolved, so that *society* can think about creating a new government?
3. What things can the legislature do to lose the people's trust and cause them to revolt?
4. The citizenry would have to be armed in order to present the government with the proper threat against tyranny. How does this relate to the current debate in the United States on gun control and Second Amendment rights?

GUIDE TO *A LETTER CONCERNING TOLERATION*

This letter, originally written while Locke was in exile in Holland in 1685, was first published under a pseudonym by friends, without his consent. Its radical proposals for religious toleration and almost complete religious liberty were not even acceptable to the mainstream Whigs, but only appealed to a smaller segment within that party. It was attacked from many sides as atheistic propaganda. It is, among other things, a work that speaks out against the idea of the official, government-sponsored Anglican Church. Parliament upheld religious conformity and the established church, and severely repressed those known as dissenters or nonconformists, who often faced imprisonment and even death.

Locke's opposition to such policies is straightforward and clear. But there is more to the letter than simply an argument against the Anglican establishment in the seventeenth century, including an argument about the role of government in religious matters generally, the nature of religion itself, and the nature of salvation. Locke reveals his own religious views and criticizes other's views. Readers should be on the alert for these themes because they comprise the more timeless messages. Purportedly, the letter is written to Locke's friend Philip von Limborch, but it was, of course, meant for a much larger audience. Because it is not broken up into sections, the reader must be particularly careful to read the letter and the guide simultaneously in order to catch the natural breakdown of the argument.

Opening Remarks to Philip

1. In the first paragraph Locke quickly turns to his opinions on Christianity, opinions which will be important for understanding the entire letter. What does he think is the mark of the true church?
2. What does he mean by "every one is orthodox to himself?"
3. How does Locke criticize those Christians who see it as their duty to persecute other Christians who do not believe as they do?
4. What point is Locke attempting to make in the second paragraph when he compares concern about competing religious sects (denominations) with concern over moral faults such as adultery and fornication (unmarried sex)?

The Role of Government   Locke starts his section on the role of government, or the commonwealth, with a purposeful statement: "that none may impose either upon himself or others, by the pretences of loyalty and obedience to the prince, or of tenderness and sincerity in the worship of God; I esteem it above all things necessary to distinguish exactly the business of civil government from that of religion, and to settle the just bounds that lie between the one and the other." What follows is a carefully structured discussion that seeks to separate "care of souls" from the "duty of the civil magistrate" or government official.

1. Locke writes that the commonwealth is a society of men constituted for advancing their civil interests. How does Locke define civil interests? What, then, is the duty of the civil magistrate?
2. Locke makes three arguments to back up his conclusion that the civil magistrate does not have the duty of caring for people's souls. In the first argument, why is it that human beings cannot give the government the responsibility for the care of their own salvation?
3. In the second argument, Locke deals with how people actually come to believe in religions. Why is it that the government is ineffective in forcing people to actually believe? What *can* the magistrate do to promote Christianity?
4. In the third argument, Locke states that even if government could get people to actually believe in the established religion it would still not be a good idea to impose one. Why?

What Is a Church?   Locke starts by defining a Church: "A church then I take to be a voluntary society of men, joining themselves together of their own accord, in order to the publick worshipping of God, in such a manner as they judge acceptable to him, and effectual to the salvation of their souls" (321). This may sound like a rather uncontroversial definition of a Church to us, but it would not have been so during Locke's time. For Locke, the Church is not a top-down organization with those at the top leading the rest with their authority, but is a bottom-up organization which the members freely join and then shape. It is less like a family and more like a social contract.

1. How does Locke back up his claim that a church is a free and voluntary society? How does he bring nature into this claim?
2. How should churches make their rules? How does Locke argue against churches that would claim there is only one true way to run a church (with a "bishop, or presbyter, with ruling authority derived from the very Apostles . . . ," that is, Anglicans, Presbyterians, and Catholics)? Locke makes three brief arguments to counter their claims. Notice that Locke is not reluctant to quote the Bible to show that his idea of Christianity differs from theirs. Outline each of his three arguments.

The Purpose of Religious Societies   Locke discusses the "end" or purpose of religious societies (churches), which he deems to be the public worship of God and the acquisition of eternal life.

What is Locke's argument for why churches should not use and do not need to use force in order to make their "ecclesiastical Laws"?

The Church's Duty toward Toleration   Locke starts this section by asking "how far the duty of Toleration extends, and what is required from every one by it." This section is devoted to *churches'* duties concerning toleration.

1. Locke argues, first, that toleration does not mean that churches must keep members who break their rules. Churches can even excommunicate or expel their members without being intolerant. What is Locke's reasoning?
2. Locke contends that no private person can impede or prejudice another person's "civil enjoyments" because of that person's religious views. What type of attitude is Locke advocating we take toward those who do not share our faith?
3. Locke gives an example of two Christian churches in the city of Constantinople who are fighting with each other over which represents the true faith. What is Locke's overall point when he again says "every church is orthodox to it self; to others, erroneous or heretical"? Who does Locke say is the final judge of such matters?
4. In a third argument, Locke discusses the duty of toleration that religious leaders such as bishops, priests, presbyters, and ministers have. What actions must these leaders avoid? What are they obligated to teach their followers?

The Magistrate's Duty toward Toleration   Locke writes, "Let us now consider what is the magistrate's duty in the business of toleration: which is certainly very considerable" (327). The fact that this discussion comes after the analysis of the churches' role may suggest that Locke thinks the attitudes of competing churches is an even greater problem than the attitudes of the civil magistrate, or that the churches' attitudes greatly influence that of magistrates.

1. How does Locke deal with the objection a government official might raise that the people, if left to their own devices, might neglect the care of their souls?

2. Locke uses a series of analogies in this argument concerning health and wealth. Locke says that the government has as little business ensuring a person's health or wealth as it does imposing that person's religion. What larger point is Locke making about the role and limits of government power?

3. Why does Locke not trust the government to make decisions about his health, wealth, or soul?

4. What does Locke mean when he writes, "But to speak the truth, we must acknowledge that the church, if a convention of clergymen, making canons, must be called by that name; is for the most part more apt to be influenced by the court [the government], than the court by the church." Why is he concerned about the church being free from government influence?

5. In his final argument in this section, Locke returns to the theme of freedom of conscience. Why are people's souls still in trouble even if the government happens to be right about the religion it has established for them? (Locke writes, for instance, that "no religion, which I believe not to be true, can be either true or profitable unto me.")

The Magistrate's Attitude toward Worship

1. What does Locke mean by things "indifferent" in worship? Why does Locke consider most ceremonies of religions to be indifferent?

2. Locke states that "In the next place: As the magistrate has no power to impose by his laws the use of any rites and ceremonies in any church, so neither has he any power to forbid the use of such rites and ceremonies as are already received, approved, and practised by any church: because if he did so, he would destroy the church itself; the end of whose institution is only to worship God with freedom, after its own manner" (334). If the government cannot impose or forbid religious ceremonies, how does Locke deal with the objection that the government would then have to allow all sorts of horrors in the name of religion, including infant sacrifice?

3. How does Locke deal with the objection that a government that cannot impose or forbid religious ceremonies must allow "idolotrous" churches, that is, churches that promote worship of idols?

4. Locke gives an example of a pagan (non-Christian) land that is occupied by Christian immigrants who at first are peaceful, until the magistrate of that land becomes a Christian. What is the likely outcome, according to Locke?

5. Locke makes the point that the Jews of the Old Testament had a commonwealth that was a theocracy, that is, ruled by religious leaders and religious law. But Locke argues that "there is absolutely no such thing, under the Gospel, as a Christian commonwealth." How does he make this argument? Why?

The Magistrate's Attitude toward Articles of Faith

1. In this section, Locke focuses on those articles or principles of religion that are matters of belief or understanding, not action or manners. He calls these principles of religion "speculative opinions" or "articles of faith." Locke argues that it is impossible for government to impose articles of faith on any church. Why?
2. Explain the distinction Locke makes here between the power of the magistrate over civil matters and his power over articles of faith.
3. Locke proceeds to the issue of whether government has any right to impose practical articles of religion, that is, those religious rules that "influence the will and manners." Why must government stay out of these matters as well?

Origin and Role of Government   Locke starts this section by saying "But besides their souls, which are immortal, men have also their temporal lives here upon earth; the state whereof being frail and fleeting, and the duration uncertain; they have need of several outward conveniences to the support thereof, which are to be procured or preserved by pains and industry" (339). This statement marks the beginning of a brief general discussion of Locke's political philosophy, which he then ties back into his arguments concerning religion.

1. Why do people enter into a society or social contract with each other, according to Locke? How does this brief discussion of Locke's theory of the social contract help clarify what he thinks are the limits of government power?
2. How does Locke answer the following question: "What if the magistrate should enjoin [require] any thing by his authority that appears unlawful to the conscience of a private person?"
3. Locke insists that if the magistrate tries to compel people to worship contrary to their beliefs, the people are not obligated to follow his orders. Can you see how this very idea could set a society on the path of revolution?
4. When Locke says that God is the only judge between the government and the people when they disagree about the government's religious decrees, he is also referring to the people's right, here on earth, to judge what to do about it. Notice Locke's threat: "the principal and chief care of every one ought to be of his own soul first, and, in the next place, of the publick peace: though yet there are very few will think it is peace there, where they see all laid waste" (341). Do you think Locke is right or irresponsible to make such barely veiled threats?

The Limits of Locke's Toleration   In this section, we find Locke dealing with the thorny question of whether there are churches that should not be tolerated by government because they threaten the very foundation of civil society. He is no doubt thinking primarily of Roman Catholicism here. He gives several examples of sentiments that cannot be tolerated, including "faith is not to be kept with hereticks," "kings excommunicated forfeit their crowns and kingdoms," and "dominion is founded in grace." These are all examples of the old Roman Catholic view that the Church's authority is stronger than that of any governments and that governments' power derives from the will of God as expressed by the Church.

1. Why do churches who hold such views "have no right to be tolerated by the magistrate"?
2. Locke excludes Catholics and Muslims from the right to be tolerated because he says they "deliver themselves up to the protection and service of another prince." What is he talking about? Given his line of reasoning, where would Locke say our ultimate allegiance lies?
3. Locke next tackles atheists, and claims that they, too, do not have a right to be tolerated. Why? In making this argument, what is Locke saying about the relationship between a religious society and law and order?

What Churches *Should* Teach   At the beginning of this brief section, Locke tackles assemblies, or groups, that have raised strong objections to the idea of toleration. It is clear he thinks that most intolerance resides in churches themselves. Here he suggests what they *should* teach their believers in order to produce a more tolerant society.

What does Locke say churches should teach concerning toleration and religious freedom?

Concluding Remarks   In this section, Locke once again addresses the magistrate, or the government, and argues for a policy of toleration.

1. Why does Locke compare the persecution of certain people because of their religion with the persecution of people because of their hair or eye color? What is the similarity he sees between religion and hair color? What will people naturally do if they are persecuted because of such qualities?
2. Locke argues that, under toleration, various churches will keep the peace despite their differences, and even be the main defenders of a tolerant government. Why?
3. Locke reasons that all sects should be permitted to assemble freely, including "Presbyterians, Independents, Anabaptists, Arminians, Quakers, and others . . . Nay, if we may openly speak the Truth, and as becomes one Man to another, neither Pagan, nor Mahometan, nor Jew, ought to be excluded from the civil rights of the commonwealth, because

of his Religion?" Why would Locke include Mahometans (Muslims), which he previously argued were a threat to civil order, but not include Catholics or atheists?

4. Although Locke calls Christianity the "most modest and peaceable religion that ever was," how does he explain why people fought battles over this and other religions? Was it the fault of the religion, or of something else?

5. Locke's final word has to do with the proper roles of government and religion. How does he summarize their division of duties?

Supplement on Heresy and Schism   Locke appended to his letter a short discussion of two terms, heresy and schism. Both are religious concepts relevant to the history of Christianity.

1. Look up *heresy* or *heretic* and *schism.* How are they defined in your dictionary?

2. How can Locke claim in the first paragraph of this section that "men of different religions cannot be hereticks or schismaticks to one another"?

3. Locke claims that there may be different religions even among Christians, and he gives the examples of Papists (Catholics) and Lutherans. Recalling what he has said about heresy and schism, why might Locke here want to call different Christian sects different religions?

4. How does Locke define heresy in the third paragraph of this section? In both examples of heresy, he emphasizes that the issue of heresy arises when one party wants another to believe and express religious opinions "which the Holy Scriptures do not expressly teach." What is Locke saying about the religious quarrels that exist because of opinions not found in the Holy Scriptures?

5. The next paragraph clarifies the trouble Locke has with the idea of heresy. Why should not others be compelled to confess particular religious doctrines of sects such as Lutherans and Calvinists?

6. How does Locke define schism? Why and how does Locke dismiss the idea of schism?

7. In the last two paragraphs, Locke makes it clear that he thinks the entire idea of heresy or schism is wrong. How does Locke express his own religious views about what is truly important to Christian belief?

BIBLIOGRAPHY

Richard Ashcraft, *Revolutionary Politics and Locke's Two Treatises of Government*, Princeton: Princeton University Press, 1986.

Carl L. Becker, *The Heavenly City of the Eighteenth Century Philosophers*, New Haven: Yale University Press, 1932.

John Dunn, *The Political Thought of John Locke,* London: Cambridge University Press, 1969.

Peter Gay, *The Enlightenment,* New York: Knopf, 1969.

Ian Harris, *The Mind of John Locke A Study of Political Theory in Its Intellectual Setting,* London: Cambridge University Press, 1994.

J.G.A. Pocock, *Three British Revolutions: 1641, 1688, 1776,* Princeton, NJ: Princeton University Press, 1980.

Judith N. Shklar, *Men and Citizens, A Study of Rousseau's Social Theory,* London: Cambridge University Press, 1969.

ROUSSEAU (1712–1778)

BACKGROUND

Biographies of Jean-Jacques Rousseau are both interesting and varied. Some, perhaps in a fit of propriety, gloss over youthful immorality and adult irresponsibility. Others delve into Rousseau's psyche and perhaps overemphasize its impact on his philosophy. Some biographers disagree about facts of his early life. Perhaps that is because his life was anything but typical and easy to chart. He was a most unlikely philosopher.

Rousseau was born in heavily Calvinist-Protestant Geneva in 1712. His father was a watchmaker and his mother the daughter of a minister. He never knew his mother, who died shortly after giving birth to him. Rousseau's father, an emotional man by all accounts, was irresponsible and perhaps resentful of the role Jean-Jacques played in his mother's death. Rousseau reports in his autobiographical *Confessions* that his father was fond of telling him about her, tearfully. In 1722, his father was exiled from Geneva after a fight and moved to Lyons, but he did not want his son to follow him. Rousseau lived for a time, still in Geneva, under the care of his grandfather, who was a minister, and women from his mother's side of the family, women who reportedly were very kind to him.

Rousseau was dislodged from this comfortable, largely female nest in 1724 when he was apprenticed to his uncle, a lawyer. His uncle, realizing that Rousseau was not adept at legal work, sent him back home. The next year he was apprenticed to an engraver, certainly a less prestigious profession, but still a potentially stable career. However, according to Rousseau, this man was abusive to him. He ran away in 1728 and wandered for a time on his own in Italy, France, and Switzerland. Thus far he had had little academic preparation. At Turin, he sought help from the Catholic Church and was sent to the house of the widow Baronne de Warens at Annecy. Twelve years his senior, she was to shelter the young man and foster his religious education in order to expedite his conversion to Roman Catholicism. He eventually did convert, for a time, but the price of that conversion was a thorny, emotional attachment to Madame de Warens. She was attractive, intelligent, and not above being tempted by Jean-Jacques and other young men. The flirtation between Rousseau and de Warens escalated for four years before they became sexually involved. The resulting highly charged romantic feelings were to haunt Rousseau for a lifetime. At first, he shared his "maman" with another young man, Claude Anet. Later, Rousseau was her only "petit," but still Rousseau felt a moral conflict about the propriety of their relationship. The new nest Rousseau had chosen was enticing but not comfortable. He did gain, however, a fairly good formal and informal education during these years. Eventually he left, but that was partly because he became intimate with another woman, Madame de Larange.

By 1740 he was on his own, making a living tutoring at Lyon. This career did not last long, however, because Rousseau did not like teaching. He moved to Paris, and there he became secretary of the ambassador to Venice. He resided in Venice for eighteen months, then left that post to return to Paris, where he tried to position himself as an intellectual, in particular as a musicologist. He tried to invent a new system of musical notation and wrote an opera, but both attempts at achieving a career in music failed. He then took a position as secretary to Madame Dupin.

Paris was the center of Enlightenment philosophy, which would lead eventually to the French Revolution and democratic upheavals throughout Europe. Through his association with Madame Dupin, and his attendance at the "salons" of fashionable women in Parisian society, Rousseau eventually met many of the "philosophes" such as Diderot, D'Alembert, and Voltaire. These philosophes were a circle of intellectuals bound together by their faith in reason to solve the inequities and to remedy the injustice they saw in society. Rousseau became a contributor to their publication *Encyclopedie*, and was initiated into this world. At this time Rousseau also become involved with Thérèse Le Vaseur. With Thérèse, Rousseau became a father five times over. They turned each of these children over to an orphanage (at this time, tantamount to a death sentence due to the neglect and abuse at such institutions), because neither parent wanted to care for them. Rousseau simply repeated, in an even more callous manner, his father's disregard for him.

Rousseau's first major recognition as a philosopher came in 1749 when he entered an essay contest sponsored by the Academy of Dijon. The academy's question that year was "Has the reestablishment of the sciences and the arts served to purify or to corrupt manners and morals?" The question referred to the reemphasis in the universities on the liberal arts as an essential part of an education, and the de-emphasis on religion. This question struck Rousseau like a thunderbolt. Supposedly, when he first read it, he had to sit down under a tree, so full of thought was he. His answer, surprisingly, was that the sciences and arts had largely served to corrupt morals. In his essay, Rousseau attempted to prove that the reestablishment of the arts and sciences had corrupted manners and morals. Perhaps he came to this conclusion partly through direct experience. This essay won the prize and was published the next year, making Rousseau an instantaneous philosophic celebrity. His philosophical friends did not like what seemed like a condemnation of their enterprise, yet most continued to socialize and exchange ideas with Rousseau, taking his criticism as a friendly exchange of ideas. Voltaire, however, despised Rousseau for his views, beginning a lifelong mutual animosity. Despite Rousseau's self-proclaimed disgust for the sophisticated lifestyle they all enjoyed, a disgust he immortalized in another essay in 1755, *Discourse on Inequality,* he continued to enjoy that lifestyle for awhile. By this time he had also renounced his Roman Catholicism and returned, at least nominally, to Protestantism so that he could also return to Geneva.

But Rousseau did not stay long in Geneva. Indeed, by now he was ready to retire from the urban life and to try to live according to his publically proclaimed principles. He went to the countryside at Montmorency in 1756 to write a novel, *La Nouvelle Héloise.* There he lived in a relatively rustic setting, enjoying quite a bit of solitude. He took long contemplative walks and became interested in botany. He did, however, frequently entertain nobility who loved the way Rousseau disregarded their rank and treated them as equals (at least in Rousseau's account). They delighted in sitting with him in the open air and hearing his views on society, many of which condemned their very existence. He argued with the philosophe Diderot shortly after moving to Montmorency, just as he had with Voltaire. His new life seemed like a rejection of theirs, as it was. Yet, Rousseau became ever more famous as a leading intellectual.

Publication of his most famous works, *Émile* and *The Social Contract,* in 1762 made Rousseau an enemy of the French government because of their anti-Christian implications. He fled France to avoid arrest and starting in 1765 lived for a year in relative seclusion on the island of Saint Pierre. At this point, Rousseau became somewhat paranoid about persecution. He became suspicious even of friends and thus became more difficult. He enjoyed the simple people of the island, believing them to be uncorrupted by society and modernity. The next year, Rousseau accepted philosopher David Hume's offer of asylum in England. There he began the *Confessions.* Shortly thereafter, he came back to France, living in the country in several provinces, until he felt comfortable returning to Paris in 1770, where he continued to write. In 1778, he accepted the invitation of an aristocrat to visit his estate, where there were no formal gardens but a natural park inspired by Rousseau's love of untouched nature. He died there a few weeks later and was buried on a small island in the middle of a nearby lake. His tombstone stands solitary and isolated on that island.

UNDERSTANDING ROUSSEAU

Although many classify him as an Enlightenment thinker, because in many ways he did advocate Enlightenment ideas, Rousseau is also highly critical of the Enlightenment and modernity in general. Rousseau thinks that civilization corrupts human beings. He equated civilization with vanity and arrogance. The more wealth people accumulate, the more crass materialism impedes individuals from truly experiencing nature and life.

Rousseau paints a picture of a man of his time that could easily be applied to our own time. Human beings attach value to things, think of themselves in terms of wealth and status, and quarrel with others over money and jealous attachments to other human beings. Such people are alive, he might say, but they are not living.

Rousseau not only rejected modern life in the abstract, but more concretely in his own life as well. Over time, Rousseau became less enamored with Enlightenment Paris, with the sophistication of the salons and with the intellectually dishonest arguments of some of the philosophes. He valued the contemplative life, far from the noise of the city and its luxurious attractions. *The Discourse on the Sciences and Arts* and the *Discourse on the Origin of Inequality* strongly reflect this personal and philosophical judgment that modern life is corrupt. If Rousseau's language sometimes seems very strong, it is probably because his level of disgust was particularly strong at the time of writing.

Rousseau's manner of writing is perhaps more artful than any you will encounter in this book other than that of Plato. Keep in mind that Rousseau's respect for rationality is mixed with an equal or greater regard for feeling. Indeed, Rousseau believed that part of what was wrong with modern man is that he had lost touch with his feelings, especially the joy of being alive. Rousseau wanted to communicate with his readers on the level of feeling as well as reason. He wanted his readers to feel indignation over the injustices caused by civilization. He wanted them to try to imagine purer, more innocent feelings of pity and life. Perhaps this is why Rousseau's writing often touches readers at a deeper level, especially when they are reading him in order to examine their own inner lives. Be forewarned that you will not always be getting "cold, hard, rational" argumentation, and often in the first two discourses you will be getting reasoning *about* the importance of emotions.

On the Social Contract presents readers with another problem, especially if they have just finished reading one or both discourses. The author of *On the Social Contract* seems to be of a different mind than the author of the discourses. In the discourses, Rousseau seems to want to critique and dismantle civilization with all of its corrupting socialization. What, then, is he doing building up what seems like the most artificial of civilizations in his social contract? It helps to remember one important fact: Rousseau did not think we could go back. That is, Rousseau did not think it was possible to return to earlier times in which men lived isolated, peaceful lives. We cannot unlearn language; we cannot escape from the need for communities because we have become dependent on civilization and can no longer fend for ourselves.

Given that we cannot return to the state of nature to escape the degradation of modern civilization, the only way to go is forward. Rousseau criticized modernity because it has socialized man badly, to value the wrong things. The good news is that it is possible to use the power of socialization to create a new man, and thus to return as closely as possible to the natural state. Rousseau wished to artificially create the semblance of natural life within society. In doing so, he introduces a theme very much a part of our contemporary intellectual scene: Human beings are mainly shaped by nurture, not nature. The environment in which they grow up can be all-important to how they behave and the values they hold. If this is true, then it behooves our society's institutions, especially our educational institutions, to keep this power of socialization ever in mind and to use it to positively shape citizens' characters.

While the discourses tear down society, the social contract builds it up. What kind of social contract is it? You will find that Rousseau is a bit more blunt than Hobbes and Locke. He points out that the contract is an artificial construct rather than a specific event that occurred at a particular time and place. If the reader is not open to the possibility that the contract is a way of thinking instead of an event, Rousseau's social contract will be hard to understand and difficult to mesh with his call for a mandatory civil religion, censorship, temporary dictatorship, a legislator-founder and a strong government. All of these things seem to the contemporary reader undemocratic—as they are. Remember, he is trying to recapture the *feeling* of freedom that man once had in nature, the feeling that one is not impeded by one's fellow man. Liberal democracy with its majority rule is, for Rousseau, a form of slavery (an indictment echoed later by Karl Marx). Whenever the society's decisions do not represent our wishes we are bound, according to Rousseau, against our will. We cannot feel free under such circumstances. Only if we can all agree will we escape the conviction that we are being compelled or dominated by others.

How can we get unanimous agreement on every issue? Apparently it takes the ingredients some have labeled as "totalitarian," such as public self-examination in order to reconcile one's opinions to those of the majority, and such as indoctrination in a civil religion. But if people were educated and socialized in a different way, would it be so difficult? If people were uninfected with the disease of modernity, if they were simple in nature, tastes, and desires, would this level of agreement be still unattainable? Would such a people desire to, or even be capable of, mounting efforts on which they could be divided? Rousseau thought that a simple people could be easily led, that a simple people could be involved in decision making because they would be able to agree easily on what was the common good.

Many French revolutionaries admired Rousseau's ideas because they saw him as an advocate of democracy. Rousseau's notions of radical equality were reflected in the revolutionaries' decision to mandate the universal title "citizen," given to all, and the revocation of all titles of nobility. Rousseau's disgust for the haughty use of power and accumulation of wealth were played out in the arrest and eventual execution of the king and queen. Rousseau's idea of a unifying civil religion was put into play when the Jacobin party began to strip the Catholic Church of its privileges and property and to proclaim in its place a religion of reason, even erecting a statue of Robespierre's *Supreme Being* at the Cathedral of Notre Dame. Fortunately or not, the radical phase of the revolution was short lived. The radicals were not satisfied with sending nobles and clergy to the guillotine. From the outset they had killed many "citizens" they also perceived as disloyal. As their bloodshed intensified, their utopian revolution began to collapse. What Rousseau would have thought of the revolution—especially the Reign of Terror—is entirely up to speculation as he died in 1788, a year before the fall of the Bastille when the revolution began to intensify.

CAREFUL READING

Rousseau is relatively easy to read in some parts, but in others he becomes quite difficult, often because of the historical or other technical references he makes. Here we will examine three selections that are particularly difficult. These should give the reader an idea of how to proceed.

Qualified Praise of Modern Times

Rousseau's discourses examine human history. In the *Discourse on the Sciences and the Arts*[1] this history is largely factual. Rousseau gives examples of ancient Greece and Rome to illustrate the virtues of earlier, simpler times. He writes of the current advances in the sciences and the arts as if they were a moral disaster. Why, then, at the beginning, does he praise his times in contrast to earlier times? Rousseau gives us a thumbnail sketch of past and present near the beginning of the *Discourse on the Sciences and the Arts,* which is puzzling.

> It is a grand and beautiful sight to see man emerge from obscurity somehow by his own efforts; dissipate, by the light of his reason, the darkness in which nature had enveloped him; rise above himself; soar intellectually into celestial regions; traverse

---

[1]All quotations from this work in this chapter are from Jean-Jacques Rousseau, "Discourse on the Science and Arts (First Discourse) and Polemics" in *The Collected Writings of Rousseau,* Volume 2, edited by Rodger D. Masters and Christopher Kelly, translated by Judith R. Bush, Rodger Masters, and Christopher Kelly, Dartmouth College, Hanover: University Press of New England, 1992.

with Giant steps, like the Sun, the vastness of the Universe; and—what is even grander and more difficult—come back to himself to study man and know his nature, his duties, and his end. All of these marvels have been revived in recent Generations.

Europe had sunk back into the Barbarism of the first ages. The Peoples of that Part of the World which is today so enlightened lived, a few centuries ago, in a condition worse than ignorance. A nondescript scientific jargon, even more despicable than ignorance, had usurped the name of knowledge, and posed an almost invincible obstacle to its return. A revolution was needed to bring men back to common sense; it finally came from the least expected quarter. The stupid Moslem, the eternal scourge of Letters, brought about their rebirth among us. The fall of the Throne of Constantine brought into Italy the debris of ancient Greece. France in turn was enriched by these precious spoils. Soon the sciences followed Letters; the Art of writing was joined the Art of thinking—an order which seems strange but which is perhaps only too natural; and people began to feel the principal advantage of commerce with the muses, that of making men more sociable by inspiring in them the desire to please one another with works worthy of their mutual approval. (pp. 4 and 5)

Just as we will later see Marx and Engels swing through centuries of history in a single paragraph in the *Manifesto,* here Rousseau takes us on a whirlwind trip which may, because of its brief character, leave us confused. The first paragraph sounds like a resounding endorsement of the Enlightenment. It should be a clear indicator that Rousseau is not wholly opposed to the Enlightenment. Notice that Rousseau has man emerging "by his own efforts," in other words, not by God's design. Again, we should wonder about whether Rousseau disliked the Enlightenment if he so admired this view of mankind as self-made or remade in the past few generations.

The second paragraph seems to continue the theme of the first. But to what era is Rousseau referring when he begins by saying "Europe had sunk back into the Barbarism of the first ages." The next sentence does not necessarily answer that question. First, Rousseau indicates that the previous era ended "a few centuries ago." Right away, then, we can identify the time as pre-Renaissance, an identification that is confirmed with the reference a little later to the "fall of the Throne of Constantine" in 1453. Next we must figure out what exactly Rousseau thought was wrong with the medieval era. He says that in that era people lived in a state "more despicable than ignorance." What is a state worse than ignorance? Perhaps having mistaken knowledge? Finally he characterizes the previous era as using a "nondescript scientific jargon" that posed a great obstacle to real knowledge. Here it helps to know something about the way medieval scholars, inevitably Church scholars, wrote. Many indeed seemed to have invented a particular language and systematic way of communicating their ideas that might be called "scientific jargon" by a critic. Rousseau is criticizing the medieval era, with its reliance on the authority of the Church. Given Rousseau's emphasis on feeling free, you can see how he would think of that era as particularly dismal. Rousseau joins with the philosophes in his dislike for the Christian religion, the Catholic Church in particular.

It is to the medieval, Church-centered world of Europe that Rousseau is comparing his own times. By contrast, Enlightenment Europe does not look so bad. He continues on to praise the event which in his view brought the Renaissance to Europe, the capture by the Turks of Constantinople, which caused the inhabitants to scatter into Europe, bringing with them the repository of ancient Greek philosophy—"the debris of ancient Greece." Once we understand that Rousseau is referring to Europe's emergence from the so-called Dark Ages into the Renaissance, it is fairly easy to understand the rest of the paragraph. In the final sentence, Rousseau mentions that the people began to feel the "principal advantage of commerce with the muses" when men desired to please each other with "works worthy of their mutual approval." The phrase "commerce with the muses" might seem to take a strange turn, but the ancient Greek demigods, the Muses, are often still invoked as sources of inspiration and ideas. Renaissance Europe was in a sense having commerce with (engaging with) the source of inspiration and ideas: ancient Greek philosophy. This "commerce" inspired a rebirth in European philosophy, letters, art, and music.

Knowing that Rousseau is praising the Renaissance and Enlightenment in contrast with the medieval era will help explain how he can, later in this essay, criticize the scientific and intellectual efforts of his own day by arguing that "humanity has become corrupted along with the advancement of the sciences and the arts." Europe has been freed from the Dark Ages of the Church but has been enslaved by another form of darkness.

Rousseau's Method

Within the *Discourse on the Origin and Foundations of Inequality among Men*[2] is a useful section at the beginning of the main discourse where Rousseau lays out his purpose and his methods. Here he places himself in relation to his fellow philosophers. Because he is writing about philosophical methods, however, this section is particularly difficult for readers, although the essay itself is generally easy to read and understand.

> The Philosophers who have examined the foundations of society have all felt the necessity of going back to the state of Nature, but none of them has reached it. Some have not hesitated to ascribe to Man in that state the notion of Just and Unjust, without troubling themselves to show that he had to have that notion or even that it was useful to him. Others have spoken of the Natural Right that everyone has to preserve what belongs to him, without explaining what they

---

[2]All quotations from this work are from Jean-Jacques Rousseau, "Discourse on the Origin and Foundations of Inequality among Men" (Second Discourse)" in *The Collected Writings of Rousseau,* Volume 3, edited by Roger Masters and Christopher Kelly, translated by Judith R. Bush, Roger D. Masters, Christopher Kelly, and Terence Marshall, Dartmouth College, Hanover: University Press of New England, 1992.

meant by belonging. Still others, giving the stronger authority over the weaker from the first, have forthwith made Government arise, without thinking of the time that must have elapsed before the meaning of the words "authority" and "government" could exist among Men. All of them, finally, speaking continually of need, avarice, oppression, desires, and pride, have carried over to the state of Nature the ideas they had acquired in society; they spoke about savage man and they described Civil man. It did not even enter the minds of most of our philosophers to doubt that the state of Nature had existed, even though it is evident from reading the Holy Scriptures that the first Man, having received enlightenment and precepts directly from God, was not himself in that state; that giving the Writings of Moses the credence that any Christian Philosopher owes them, it must be denied that even before the Flood Men were ever in the pure state of Nature, unless they fell back into it because of some extraordinary Event: a Paradox that is very embarrassing to defend and altogether impossible to prove.

Let us therefore begin by setting all the facts aside, for they do not affect the question. The Researches which can be undertaken concerning this Subject must not be taken for historical truths, but only for hypothetical and conditional reasonings better suited to clarify the Nature of things than to show their genuine origin, like those our Physicists make every day concerning the formation of the World. (pp. 18–19)

Preceding this selection, Rousseau says that his purpose is to make an account of political history. He says that he wants to mark the moment when "Nature was subjected to the Law"—when natural human beings became civilized under law and government. He insinuates that this progress from nature to civilization has not been positive because it has put the strong under the dominion of the weak and has replaced "real felicity" (happiness) with "a repose in ideas." Interestingly, then, Rousseau thinks an injustice has been done when government impedes the power of the strong over the weak. It will be clear what he means by "strong" as the reader goes further into the discourse.

In the first paragraph of our selection Rousseau starts out by disagreeing with other philosophers who have, like him, relied on an account of the state of nature to explain the "foundations of society." The two most famous of these philosophers who, like Rousseau, have constructed social contracts out of the state of nature, are Hobbes and Locke. Keeping this in mind, it is clear that Rousseau is reacting precisely to their ideas when he criticizes—without naming them—other philosophers. His criticisms are fairly clear. In the second sentence Rousseau criticizes the idea that man can know anything about "Just and Unjust" in the state of nature. Here he actually agrees with Hobbes to an extent. Hobbes thought that man could know what is just or right by nature while in the state of nature, but he could not be expected to act on that knowledge for fear of being taken advantage of by others. Rousseau, however, seems to disagree with the idea that natural man thinks in terms of just or unjust, right or wrong, or that these categories are useful to him. Rousseau disputes a central idea of previous social contract theory, that reason tells man how he can best get along with his fellow human beings, even when he is in a state of nature and unable to comply with the natural law. This sentence suggests that Rousseau does not think natural man is rational. Rousseau directly challenges Locke's notion of property in the next sentence, calling into question whether natural man could even conceive of the idea of property. Then he seems to be criticizing philosophers like Hobbes when he mentions that he does not think it is plausible that natural man could even think in terms of political authority or government.

Rousseau saves the most profound criticism of other social contract thinkers for last. "Finally," he says, "all of them, speaking continually of need, avarice, oppression, desires, and pride, have carried over to the state of Nature the ideas they had acquired in society . . ." In other words, philosophers like Hobbes and Locke did not know what true natural man was. Instead they imagined how socialized man would behave if suddenly he were no longer governed. This criticism, as we have seen from our examination of Hobbes and Locke, is particularly plausible. However, Hobbes and Locke really wanted to do precisely that—show the world what life would be like if human beings *now* were left to their own devices without government. Rousseau simply wants to make a different point. He apparently wants to talk about the very effects of socialization on man. What would man be like if he were not yet socialized into a community?

Near the end of the first selected paragraph, Rousseau mentions the Holy Scriptures as an authority. This allusion seems odd given his reputation for rejecting Christian teachings. But Rousseau brings scripture up as another argument against previous social contract thinkers. Scriptures apparently show that the state of nature never existed in the first place, that from the moment God created Adam and Eve, man was civilized, so to speak. Because neither Hobbes nor Locke (nor Rousseau) felt bound by the literal interpretation of Holy Scriptures, this criticism rings a little hollow, as it should. If we examine the next paragraph in our selection, we will see just how hollow.

In the second selected paragraph, Rousseau deals the reader a particularly tricky hand. He begins by asking us to put aside all the facts, "for they do not affect the question." But, you might object, Rousseau has been arguing with the other philosophers on the basis of what seemed like facts. He even seemed to treat biblical history as an alternative set of facts. Now Rousseau says he wants his readers to understand that he writes not "historical truths, but only . . . hypothetical and conditional reasonings. . . ." He then compares his method with that of the physicists. Turning to a contemporary example, physicists cannot know the "genuine origin" of the physical universe. Physicists these days speculate about a big bang theory. There are multiple versions of the big bang theory, and there are other competing theories of the universe as well. Rousseau's point is that, like physicists, he is attempting to shed light on "the Nature of things" as they are now. He cannot know for certain their true origin or beginning, any more than physicists can be certain about the big bang. But physicists, through their theories, can help us to harness the powers of nature here and now and this is what Rousseau wants to do as well.

Toleration

There are so many examples of paradoxical statements in *On the Social Contract*[3] that it is difficult to choose a representative selection. However, there is one near the end of the essay, in Book IV, Chapter VIII, that certainly calls for careful examination—Rousseau's discussion of civil religion and toleration. Here, Rousseau calls for toleration of the tolerant and intolerance of the intolerant.

> There is, therefore, a purely civil profession of faith, the articles of which are for the sovereign to establish, not exactly as religious dogmas, but as sentiments of sociability without which it is impossible to be a good citizen or a faithful subject. Without being able to obligate anyone to believe them, the sovereign can banish from the State anyone who does not believe them. The sovereign can banish him not for being impious, but for being unsociable; for being incapable of sincerely loving the laws, justice, and of giving his life, if need be, for his duty. If someone who has publicly acknowledged these same dogmas behaves as though he does not believe them, he should be punished with death. He has committed the greatest of crimes: he lied before the laws.
>
> The dogmas of the civil religion ought to be simple, few in number, stated with precision, without explanations or commentaries. The existence of a powerful, intelligent, beneficent, foresighted, and providential divinity; the afterlife; the happiness of the just; the punishment of the wicked; the sanctity of the social contract and the laws. These are the positive dogmas. As for the negative ones, I limit them to a single one: intolerance. It belongs to the cults we have excluded. (pp. 130–131)

For some, civil religion is a sort of paradox in itself. How can one have a "purely civil profession of faith," especially when that faith requires one to believe in a God? Rousseau says that its articles or parts are "not exactly" religious, but rather "sentiments of sociability." Whether he is right about this is up to his reader to decide. He claims that without these sentiments, or feelings, it is impossible to be a good citizen or faithful subject.

In the first paragraph, Rousseau acknowledges that no one can be obligated to believe anything. Sometimes it is very helpful to compare in our minds the arguments of one philosopher with the arguments of others. The idea that we cannot be obliged to believe anything was a common theme in Enlightenment thought. It is in a sense a truism—our minds are always free. But Rousseau does not go the way of Hobbes and tell us it is better for the government to enforce outward religious conformity, even if we do not believe inwardly. Neither does he go the way of Locke, who says that because of this

---

[3]All quotations from *On the Social Contract* are from Jean-Jacques Rousseau, *On the Social Contract,* edited by Roger Masters, translated by Judith R. Masters, New York: St. Martin's Press, 1978.

truism, government should stay out of all religious matters. Instead, Rousseau goes a seemingly more difficult way—the sovereign can banish anyone who cannot believe the articles of faith. Again, he tries to make a distinction between banishing a person for being impious and banishing him for being unsociable. Again, it is up to the reader to decide if this distinction is valid.

Next, Rousseau makes a shocking statement. Anyone who has publicly acknowledged the civil religion and then acts as if he does not believe it should be put to death! Think about the implications of this rule. How would it be carried out? Who would decide if a person is not acting in conformity with the civil religion? Is nonconformity evident if the person does not immediately agree with the general will, a notion of the common good which Rousseau elaborates at length in preceding chapters? Think about the actual experience human beings have with faith—sometimes it is strong, other times weak. Does Rousseau mean to suggest that if we ever waiver in our faith we are liable to be executed? Would not the resulting agreement be based on fear and not on voluntary faith?

In the second paragraph, Rousseau sets forth the dogmas he thinks people must believe to be sociable. People must believe in a good God who is "foresighted" and "providential," and in eternal life, cosmic rewards and punishments, and the holiness or "sanctity" of the social contract and the laws. If our government required such beliefs today, would we call it "tolerant?" Rousseau adds a final, negative dogma: the exclusion of "cults" which are themselves intolerant.

After the selected passages, Rousseau explains what he means by intolerant cults. He begins by saying that we cannot distinguish between civil and theological intolerance. What does he mean by this? Fortunately, he quickly gives us a clue: "It is impossible to live in peace with people whom one believes are damned." Intolerance is defined as a belief that others, who do not share your religion, are condemned by God. He explains that people who believe others to be damned are compelled to convert them to their religion, or torment them out of disgust for their beliefs. Thus, theological intolerance always leads to civil effects. What kind of effects is he really talking about here? Think of the recent history of Europe at his time, battles between Catholics and Protestants over control of the state, for instance. Rousseau concludes that if theological intolerance is allowed, priests become the "true masters," and kings their "officers." This is what he and many other thinkers were trying to avoid: domination of the state by the church.

Rousseau concludes that "one should tolerate all those religions that tolerate others insofar as their dogmas are in no way contrary to the duties of the citizen." While this does not sound like much of a requirement at first, on second glance it is a fairly stringent requirement. First of all, remember Rousseau's definition of intolerance. What religion did not hold the view that it was the one true way, and that other ways were wrong, and that those who were wrong were in eternal danger? Certainly the two main alternatives, Protestantism and Catholicism, shared this condemnation of each other, but Rousseau makes it sound as though he is only referring to Catholicism. He makes reference to Henry IV, King of France from 1589–1610, who renounced his Protestantism and embraced Catholicism in order to attain the kingship. Despite his references to the "pontiff" and Roman Catholicism, Rousseau is actually referring to a more general quality of religion: belief in truth and the consequences of rejecting that truth. In Rousseau's scheme, a person's religion would be tolerated so long as he was able to admit that it was not the best, true, or only way. Although Rousseau's brand of toleration has become more digestible today, it would not have been at his time.

Rousseau is calling for a big change in the mentality of citizens by calling upon them to adopt a nonjudgmental stance toward other religions. This type of toleration might be workable if people did not belong to different sects and if they adhered only to the simple dogmas Rousseau mentions above. Surely Rousseau is straining our credulity on purpose. Perhaps he is asking us to imagine a world in which people share only his simple dogmas of faith, in which there are not theological, doctrinal, or formal divisions around which to compete and shed blood. Perhaps he also believes, ironically along with his nemesis Voltaire, that the simple people cannot get along or be governed without a belief in God and cosmic justice. Are his articles of faith Rousseau's "noble lie"?

GUIDE TO *DISCOURSE ON THE SCIENCES AND THE ARTS*

Rousseau's task in writing the *Discourse on the Sciences and the Arts* was to discuss the question of whether "the restoration of the sciences and arts tended to purify morals." This question was about the value of the Enlightenment's belief in education. Rousseau would answer it with a resounding no.

Foreword   Rousseau wrote a brief foreword to this essay for its inclusion in a collection of his own works that he was preparing.

> Knowing something about his life now, what miseries do you think Rousseau would have avoided had he not written this essay?

Preface   The preface was written after Rousseau's essay won the prize. In it he mentions the "League," a reference to the Holy League, a sixteenth-century Catholic organization created to suppress French Protestantism.

> He writes, "A man who plays the free Thinker and philosopher today would, for the same reason, have been only a fanatic at the time of the League." What is he saying about his fellow intellectuals, namely the philosophes?

Discourse: Introductory Remarks

1. What is Rousseau admitting when he claims that he knows nothing?
2. How does Rousseau regard the scholars to whom he is writing—with contempt or with respect and admiration?
3. Explain Rousseau's analogy comparing his scholarly judges to fair-minded sovereigns.

Part One   The first part of this discourse displays Rousseau's knowledge of history and philosophy, and his admiration for Socrates. Despite his many historical *references* with which many modern readers may not be familiar (in some editions, you can check your editor's notes for explanations for some of these), it is quite possible to follow Rousseau's *argument,* which is really quite simple.

1. Why does Rousseau seem to praise his times in the first two paragraphs? To what era is he comparing his times?
2. Rousseau obviously thinks that sophistication is the result of advances in the arts and sciences. What is the role of such sophistication and refinement in keeping people as slaves?
3. Rousseau compares the civilized men of his day with fieldworkers and athletes and finds them lacking. Why?
4. Rousseau compares the mores (morals) of people of earlier times with people of his day. What is he saying about the role that manners play in breeding true morality?
5. The example of a foreigner visiting Europe is used to illustrate how Rousseau sees the character of his fellow citizens. Explain this example.
6. Next, Rousseau points out that Europe's current troubles are not unique. How does he use ancient and contemporary examples of countries such as Egypt and China to prove this point?
7. What kind of country does Rousseau admire? Why?
8. Socrates is a model for Rousseau. What is it about Socrates' way of thinking that Rousseau admires? If you have read Plato for your course, do you think Rousseau's reading of Socrates is correct?
9. Describe the criticism of ancient Rome that Rousseau puts into the mouth of Fabricius.
10. How does Rousseau conclude this section?

Part Two   In this part, Rousseau explores the impact of the sciences and arts on warlike virtue and morals. He examines the educated elite and finds them, of course, wanting.

1. Explain Rousseau's statement in the first paragraph that the sciences and arts are "generated from our vices . . ." (You will find the answer in the next two paragraphs.)
2. Do you agree with Rousseau's criticism of the arts and sciences, that is, that they do not produce many useful things? Why?

3. What is the general impression Rousseau wants his readers to have of most of his contemporary academics and intellectuals?
4. According to Rousseau, what is the relationship between luxury, wealth, and learning on the one hand and warlike strength on the other?
5. What impression does Rousseau have of the popular culture and tastes of his times?
6. Rousseau mentions the simplicity of the early times. How did men relate to the gods then? How did mankind's relationship to the divine change over time?
7. Rousseau gives several examples to illustrate the point that where arts and sciences are cultivated, the military virtues decline. Do these examples help prove his point? Thinking of our military today, does Rousseau's reflections on the relationship between luxury and military virtue and readiness have any relevance now?
8. Rousseau turns to the detrimental effects of the arts and sciences on morals. He describes the situation as he sees it at schools and universities. What are young people learning and what are they not learning?
9. How does Rousseau criticize the typical art of his time?
10. To what does Rousseau attribute the inequality of his time?
11. Rousseau comments that glory is very badly distributed in his time. Think about our own times. Is glory, or the esteem of the people, given to those who deserve it?
12. Rousseau makes an analogy between natural cures for the poisons of plants and animals and political cures for the poisons of society. What have previous French monarchs done that have reduced the evil effects of the arts and sciences? [Hint: The "great Monarch" and "his august successor" are probably references to Louis XIV and Louis XV, both famous for their patronage of the arts and letters. Louis XV was a particularly notable patron of the sciences.]
13. Rousseau calls his fellow philosophers "charlatans." What does he mean?
14. What has the printing press done for mankind, according to Rousseau?
15. In the last three paragraphs, Rousseau attempts to distinguish between truly great minds, pretenders to intellectual accomplishment, and the rest of the human race. What distinguishes each type from the others? What should each type do, according to Rousseau?

GUIDE TO *DISCOURSE ON THE ORIGIN OF INEQUALITY*

Rousseau wrote the *Discourse on the Origin of Inequality* in 1754 in response to another contest offered by the Academy of Dijon. This time the question was, "What is the origin of inequality among men, and is it authorized by the natural Law?" Although this time Rousseau did not win the prize, this essay develops his idea of the dysfunctional nature of society much further than the first, and introduces some of Rousseau's most famous concepts. It was published in 1755. Although this guide will not cover Rousseau's notes, they are nonetheless profitable to read.

Letter to the Republic of Geneva   Rousseau first writes a letter to his former fellow citizens in Geneva. Even though Geneva had banished his father and barred Rousseau himself from living there because of his seemingly anti-Christian posture, he had apparently come to admire Geneva from afar for its republican form of government, its small size, and its predominant Calvinism. Rousseau finally was welcomed back to Geneva around the time he wrote this letter, in part because Genevans saw it as praising their institutions. Some argue that Rousseau idealizes Geneva. Indeed, we learn more in his letter about the type of government Rousseau wishes existed than we learn about the actual Republic of Geneva, which was in many ways very hierarchical and elitist.

1. Rousseau turns to an imaginary republic, albeit with the suggestion that its qualities are Geneva's as well. Why does Rousseau think a small civil society is better than a large one?
2. Who should be sovereign in Rousseau's ideal city?
3. What is Rousseau's definition of freedom when he says that he would want to live and die free?
4. Why should no one be above or beyond the law? To whom might he be referring?
5. Why would Rousseau rather live in an old than a new republic?
6. What attitude should the citizens of Rousseau's ideal republic take toward war?
7. What relationship should the citizens have to their leaders (magistrates) and vice versa?
8. After telling his fellow citizens of Geneva of their many advantages, about what does he warn them?
9. Rousseau cites an example of a virtuous citizen. He has in mind his father. How does his picture of his father and his early life differ from what we know? Why do you think Rousseau remembers better times?
10. Rousseau refers to the relationship between magistrates and citizens as one of equals on the one hand but superiors and inferiors on the other. In what way are citizens equal to their leaders and in what way are they inferior?
11. What is the role Rousseau sees religious ministers playing in Geneva?
12. Rousseau's commentary on women is famously ambiguous. On the whole, do you think Rousseau is complimenting women with his praise or criticizing them? Explain.
13. In general, what do you think Rousseau admires more than anything else about Geneva?

Preface   Here Rousseau assesses the state of the study of man, critiques previous attempts to find man's true nature, and gives a brief hint as to his own theory of human nature and government.

1. Why is knowing the true nature of man perhaps the most difficult or thorniest task for human beings to undertake?
2. How has the very study of man made it progressively more difficult to really know human nature?
3. In the third paragraph of the preface, what was the first source of inequality?
4. Is Rousseau sure of what he is doing in this essay? Why or why not?
5. Why has there been such disagreement about the definition of natural law according to Rousseau? Where are most philosophers who write about natural law really acquiring their principles, nature or civil society? Explain.
6. Rousseau says that there are "two principles that are prior to reason," from which the rules of natural right flow. What are these two principles? How are these principles different from those philosophers who have established their idea of natural law on a presumption that rational beings alone can know it?
7. What duties do human beings have toward animals, according to Rousseau? Why?
8. At the end of his preface, Rousseau discusses divine will. From what he says here, can you tell what Rousseau thinks is the role of God in human development? Does his inscription at the end of the preface clarify his thoughts on the role of God?

Part One   In this first part, Rousseau establishes the physical and moral superiority of savage man and demonstrates the weakness and depravity of civilized human beings. Part One is easily broken down into several topics.

The Savage's Physical Superiority

1. How does Rousseau envision primitive man physically? How does this man live?
2. To what "supernatural gifts" might he be referring? Why do you think he wants to put these gifts to one side?
3. What advantage does natural man have over the animals when acquiring food?
4. Rousseau makes a veiled reference to abortion and/or child abandonment when he says that in nature physically weak children perish in contrast to his times when "the State, by making Children burdensome to their Fathers, kills them indiscriminately before their birth." How do you think the state might encourage abortions or abandonment, according to

Rousseau? (We will get another chance to answer this question when he mentions the topic again later in the first part.)

5. How does Rousseau explain savage man's relatively safe existence among wild animals?

6. To what does Rousseau attribute many of the illnesses among the people of his times? Do you agree with him that savage man is actually healthier than civilized man?

The Moral Superiority of Savage Man   "I have to this point considered only Physical Man; let us now try to look at him from the Metaphysical and Moral side." Rousseau begins another topic in this essay, as much a commentary on his civilization's immorality as on the innocence of savage man.

1. What, more than anything else, distinguishes man from the rest of the animals, according to Rousseau?

2. What does Rousseau mean by man's perfectibility? How does this quality of human beings make them different from the animals?

3. Why does man's perfectibility also make him more susceptible to becoming an imbecile?

4. Rousseau argues that our reason is led by our passions. In nature, he says, man only desires simple things such as food, sex, and sleep. Can you guess how different civilized man might be in the strength and variety of his desires for these three things?

The Improbability of Civilization   Rousseau begins this section by saying how unlikely man was to ever be removed from his original primitive state.

1. Can you imagine what Rousseau is talking about when he mentions "the sole sentiment of his present existence"? Relate a time when you might have felt this way.

2. Why does Rousseau consider civilized improvements like agriculture to be so improbable?

3. If a primitive man could somehow become a philosopher, what would prevent his knowledge from being passed on to others?

4. Rousseau assumes that savage man led an individualistic, solitary life. Is there any way to argue against this assumption? How would Rousseau answer your argument?

The Improbability of Language

1. Rousseau begins a lengthy discussion of how unlikely it is that language would ever develop. What obstacles does he see standing in the way of savage man inventing language?

2. How does Rousseau's discussion about the improbability of language reflect on the traditional Christian belief that God created man as a civilized human being, charging him with the naming of things?

Pity: The Natural Morality   Here Rousseau introduces an intriguing idea about savage man, given his isolated existence: He naturally pities his fellow man and instinctually wishes to help those in need.

1. How does Rousseau argue that savage man knows no virtue or vice, and that this ignorance actually makes him morally superior to civilized man with all his moral rules?
2. Rousseau argues with Hobbes that man is not naturally evil or vicious. If you have read Hobbes, do you agree or disagree with Rousseau's understanding of him? Why or why not?
3. Rousseau blames reason for stamping out natural pity. How does it do this?
4. Rousseau quotes a great maxim of Jesus Christ. He then contrasts this with a maxim from nature. He says that the latter is less perfect but probably more useful than the first. Again, how does this statement reflect on Rousseau's religious beliefs? Are you beginning to see why he was accused of writing anti-Christian tracts?

Love   Rousseau has some reputation as a romantic, but he does not sound like one here, when it comes to the subject of women. Here he depicts love as one of the most terrible and destructive of passions.

1. What aspect of love is natural and what aspect is artificial, according to Rousseau? Explain.
2. How does Rousseau answer the objection that many male animals fight over females, not just human males?
3. Rousseau claims that in civilized countries laws that enforce sexual restraint (such as marital laws) actually increase the number of abortions. Can you now see more clearly why Rousseau blames the state for increasing the number of abortions?

Inequality

1. To what does Rousseau attribute the inequalities that he sees in his society?
2. What types of inequalities does Rousseau see doing the most harm to people?
3. Why is slavery impossible in the state of nature? What is it about civil society that makes slavery possible?

Concluding Remarks   Rousseau ends the first part by setting forth his agenda for the second part and discussing briefly the method he will employ.

1. What is Rousseau's agenda for the second part of his essay? What will he attempt to show?

2. How does Rousseau deal with the potential accusation that he is dealing with pure conjecture (guessing) in his essay?

3. In the final paragraph Rousseau anticipates some objections to his argument. What are some of these objections? How does Rousseau dismiss them here? [Hint: Rousseau distinguishes between history and philosophy. This distinction is critical to the defense of his stated methods.]

Part Two   In this part, Rousseau gives us human history as he imagines it, always pressing his point that even the smallest of changes leading toward civilization were all very improbable.

Primitive Man, the Savage

1. Rousseau starts with a famous insight into civil society. To what does he attribute the foundation of civil society?

2. Next, Rousseau takes the reader back again to earliest savage man. How did human beings at this time live and relate to one another?

3. How and why did savage man get to the point of making clothing and some tools? How did these inventions help him to think in a more complex manner?

4. What brought human beings together to cooperate at this time?

5. Rousseau writes that if a group of savages planned to catch a deer, but a rabbit ran by one of them while on hunt, that individual would stop cooperating to chase after the rabbit for himself. What is he saying about savage human nature?

Primitive Society

1. How and why did human beings settle into huts or other dwellings? How did this settling down affect their relationships, especially with members of the opposite sex?

2. Why would islanders be the most likely people to have brought language to Europe?

3. What is the origins of nations, according to Rousseau?

4. How does love evolve into jealousy and bloody contests? Besides mates, what other things do primitive people fight over now that they are in society?

5. Rousseau says that because of these conflicts, even primitive societies developed some notions of civility. What does he mean?

Advances in Metallurgy and Agriculture   When men were content to live in huts they still enjoyed quite a bit of independence, writes Rousseau. But two inventions changed this relatively happy state.

1. Why does Rousseau see agriculture as a major step toward the enslavement of mankind instead of as progress?

2. How does Rousseau define justice as it has been invented by human beings?

3. Why does natural physical and mental inequality become more pronounced when people work in agriculture instead of living the solitary lives of the more savage state?

The Fall of Pride

1. How does duplicity (being one thing but seeming another) enter into the human condition?

2. What conditions get people to the point where they are "horrified" by the negative effects of wealth, and hating what affluence has produced in society?

Government and "Justice"

1. Whose idea is it to make a government, and why do they do so?

2. How do people get to the point where they willingly and even proudly accept the "slavery" of government?

3. How does war among nations develop?

4. Rousseau discusses three other accounts of the origins of civil society, and tries to argue that his own explanation is superior. What are the three competing ways of seeing the origin of civil society? What is his argument against each theory? What is the general thrust of his argument?

5. Rousseau speculates that at first government was little more than an agreement among people to act a certain way and follow certain rules. What led people to actually appoint some higher authority ("magistrates") to rule them?

6. Rousseau complains that people who like this form of government call "peace" the worst form of slavery. What does he mean?

7. Rousseau next argues against the idea that civil society is or should be built upon paternal authority. What is his argument against patriarchal government—that is, the king as the ultimate father?

8. Just as other philosophers have discussed the proper extent of government power through a discussion of slavery, so too does Rousseau. Why is slavery so wrong? Why, then, would absolute tyranny also be wrong?

9. Rousseau considers what would be a good contract between the people and its leaders. What is the significance of a contract *between* the people and its leaders as opposed to a contract *among* the people to form a government, as Hobbes and Locke both proposed?

10. Rousseau says this first kind of contract, which he favors, would not be irrevocable. Why not?

11. How did the three types of government—monarchy, aristocracy, and democracy—come into being? Which does Rousseau think best, and why?

12. What drove people to accept hereditary monarchy?

Political and Social Inequality "Political distinctions necessarily bring about Civil distinctions," according to Rousseau. Next, he describes some of the gross inequalities that come from full-fledged civil society.

1. What motivates those who are enslaved by their political and social superiors to try to oppress others supposedly beneath them?
2. Rousseau again identifies the source of almost all other types of inequality as wealth. Explain.
3. Rousseau writes of the progression of inequality and perversion in civil society that there will come a time when people will obey their oppressors' orders, even if it means killing their brother, father, or pregnant wife. Do you think Rousseau is writing about something very unlikely here? Why or why not?
4. Why is complete despotism or tyranny "the extreme point which closes the Circle and touches the point from which we started" (freedom in the state of nature)?

Concluding Remarks Rousseau compares savage man, always at peace and worry-free, with the citizen who is always active, agitated, and tormented.

1. Assess Rousseau's depiction of "savage man." Do you think this depiction is realistic? Why or why not?
2. Assess Rousseau's depiction of civilized man as you now understand it, and as you live the type of life that Rousseau is critiquing. Does Rousseau's criticism ring true? Why or why not?
3. Would you rather be a native Caribbean islander ("the Carib") as Rousseau has described him throughout the discourse, or would you rather continue to live the way you do? Explain.

GUIDE TO *ON THE SOCIAL CONTRACT*

Book I

Introductory Remarks

1. When Rousseau says that he wants government administered in such a way that justice and utility are not opposed to one another, what does he mean?
2. What do you think Rousseau means by "sovereign," and what does it mean to be a member of the sovereign?

Chapter I: Subject of the First Book

1. What do you suppose Rousseau means when he says, "Man was born free, and everywhere he is in chains"?

2. Rousseau uses the words "nature" and "convention" to define the social order. What is the distinction between nature and convention, and is the social order natural or conventional?

Chapter II: Of the First Societies

1. Here Rousseau distinguishes between the society of a family and a political society. What is the main difference? Why do you think Rousseau wants to make this distinction?
2. Rousseau mentions the Dutch scholar of international law, Hugo Grotius, as well as Hobbes, when he discusses the justifications for slavery and absolute government. What positions did they take with which he disagrees?
3. Why does Rousseau disagree with Aristotle over the issue of slavery?
4. In the final part of this chapter, Rousseau jests about the divine right theory (that the king's authority is from God through the first man, Adam). Explain the serious point within the jest.

Chapter III: On the Right of the Strongest

1. Why does Rousseau consider the "right of the strongest" to be a contradiction in terms?
2. Why can force never be the basis of a right?
3. Rousseau mentions that God is responsible for diseases. What is his point?

Chapter IV: On Slavery   Like so many other philosophers, Rousseau chooses to make a point about good government by discussing the institution of slavery. His statements in this chapter are best taken two ways: as a commentary on actual slavery, but also as a commentary on undemocratic government.

1. What is Grotius's position on slavery? How does Rousseau disagree?
2. Explain why a man cannot give himself away to be a slave. How can this principle be applied to the formation of a government?
3. Rousseau tries to prove that the rights of the victor in a war do not include enslaving those he conquers. What is the most important reason why the victor does not have this right?

Chapter V: That It Is Always Necessary to Return to a First Convention

1. Why does Rousseau think it is necessary to return to a first convention, or to examine the original agreement among people to form a government, even if all his prior arguments were proven wrong?
2. Explain Rousseau's statement at the end of this chapter that the law of majority rule presupposes at least one instance of unanimity.

Chapter VI: On the Social Compact We know that in his discourses, Rousseau tries to explain how man could leave the state of nature. Here, Rousseau starts with the assumption that human beings have been pushed to abandon the state of nature. He then tries to imagine what principles would guide them in forming a government, or "association."

1. Rousseau states the fundamental problem or difficulty in these terms: "Find a form of association that defends and protects the person and goods of each associate with all the common force, and by means of which each one, uniting with all, nevertheless obeys only himself and remains as free as before." State this in your own terms. Do you think it is possible for people to be as free in any form of government as they were in Rousseau's state of nature?
2. Rousseau argues that complete alienation to the community brings about equality. Explain how this could be so.
3. If any rights remain with private individuals, what is likely to happen, according to Rousseau?
4. Rousseau brings up a prominent concept in this book, the "general will," which differs from the individual will. Rousseau thinks individual will must conform to general will. What do you think is the general will?
5. How does Rousseau define citizens and subjects? How can an individual be both at the same time?

Chapter VII: On the Sovereign

1. Rousseau claims that in a social contract as he envisions it, a person will have two commitments. What are those two commitments?
2. Do you understand now what he means by a citizen being a member of the sovereign? How can he be a member of the sovereign but also a subject of the sovereign?
3. Why can't the sovereign be subject to itself—that is, bind itself to its own rules?
4. Rousseau argues that when the multitude is united into a body, an attack on one citizen is like an attack on the whole body. Does this statement give you a better idea of the amount of unity Rousseau desires? Under what conditions do you think such unity might be possible?
5. Rousseau mentions that if a citizen refuses to obey the general will, he may be "forced to be free." How can one be free if one is forced to agree?

Chapter VIII: On the Civil State

1. In the first paragraph, Rousseau in effect gives us a definition of justice and morality. Where do justice and morality originate? What are they?
2. What does a man lose when entering into the social contract? What does he gain?

3. Rousseau states that to be driven by one's appetites is a form of slavery, from which man escapes when he enters into society. Does this contradict the picture Rousseau has developed of the state of nature and civil society in his discourses?

Chapter IX: On the Real [Proprietary] Domain

1. How does the creation of the state which has power over all property actually make our property more secure? Notice that Rousseau is forthrightly saying that in civil society the government ultimately owns all property because it has the power to control everything.
2. What should give people the "right of the first occupant" on land?
3. In the second last paragraph in this chapter, Rousseau briefly mentions the possibility of a more communistic arrangement. Regardless of the particular arrangement, what is the fundamental relationship between government and any type of property?

Book II   In this book, Rousseau further explains his view of sovereignty and the general will. Both of these are notoriously slippery concepts in Rousseau's work, so do not be too worried if you did not fully understand them when they appeared in Book I. Even here, it is necessary to read through the entire book to get a clearer picture of what these two words mean.

Chapter I: That Sovereignty Is Inalienable

1. The second paragraph of this chapter contains a great deal of information on sovereignty and the general will. We know the people are sovereign in Rousseau's scheme. In what way is sovereignty an exercise of the general will? Why can sovereignty never be alienated? Explain how power can be transmitted to a person, committee, institution, and so on, but not the [general] will.
2. Why can the general will of the people not bind itself to any future commitment?
3. Rousseau ends this chapter by saying that the commands of the leader can be taken for the general will. How do we know that his commands are accepted as the general will?

Chapter II: That Sovereignty Is Indivisible

1. Why is sovereignty indivisible, according to Rousseau?
2. What mistake have other political theorists made about sovereignty?

Chapter III: Whether the General Will Can Err   Here Rousseau distinguishes between the general will as a pure concept and the general will in practice. As a pure concept, of course, it can never be in error. It is always what it is—a general will toward promoting the common good. However, the more interesting question is how can one obtain the general will in practice with real people?

1. What faults do the people have that may keep them from reasoning well about the general will?
2. What is the difference between the will of all and the general will?
3. Rousseau recommends that there should be no partial society in the state, if the general will is to prevail. Give some examples from our own times of the types of partial societies he had in mind.

Chapter IV: On the Limits of Sovereign Power   What are the limits of government power? How much liberty should individuals have? These are the types of questions Rousseau attempts to answer in this chapter.

1. Who or what judges how much power the government should have over its citizens?
2. Can you now understand how Rousseau can say that by committing ourselves to obedience to the sovereign, we are only working for ourselves and obeying ourselves, and thus we remain free?
3. How does Rousseau answer the question, what is an act of sovereignty?
4. At the end of this chapter, how does Rousseau justify military service?

Chapter V: On the Right of Life and Death   Military service has always been a difficult subject for social contract theorists. Why would a person enter into a contract to save his life and make himself more comfortable only to be obliged to give it up to protect the state? This is the question Rousseau asks at the beginning of this chapter.

1. What is Rousseau's initial answer to this question? Explain the meaning of the rhetorical question he poses concerning a person who jumps out of a window to escape a fire.
2. The second paragraph further answers the question. What is the purpose of the "social treaty"? How does this purpose help explain the fact that sometimes a citizen must be willing to die for his country?
3. How does Rousseau justify the death penalty? Why would anyone enter into a social contract and give government the power of imposing the death penalty on any of its citizens?
4. How are traitors to be treated, and why?
5. How does Rousseau handle the objection that condemning a criminal is a particular act against a particular person, when he had previously said that the sovereign cannot make any laws regarding particular groups or people?

Chapter VI: On Law

1. In the second paragraph, Rousseau notes that all justice comes from God. But why is God's justice not good enough to form societies?

2. In the fifth paragraph, Rousseau finally gives a definition of a law. In your own words, give his definition.
3. In the next paragraph, Rousseau seems to modify, or refine, his notion that the sovereign must treat all members equally and not have different laws for particular people or groups. In what way does he refine his views? Do you think he is still talking about equality here?
4. What is Rousseau's definition of a republic?
5. In the final paragraph, Rousseau identifies some problems with the way the people think. What are these problems and what solution does he just barely indicate in the final sentence?

Chapter VII: On the Legislator   At the beginning of this chapter, Rousseau sounds like only a god could be a good legislator, but he does accept the fact that mere mortals must manage to legislate despite their imperfection. He then goes on to give a legislator, or founder, of a country advice on how to proceed.

1. In the third paragraph, Rousseau describes how the legislator-founder should see the people he is to make into a civil society. What must he do to them and for them?
2. At what point has legislation achieved the highest perfection?
3. Why must a legislator-founder walk away after establishing the founding laws or constitution, instead of continuing to rule?
4. Another difficulty for Rousseau is the way the people think. What is the main problem they have, and how can the legislator use religion to solve the problem?
5. Given what Rousseau says in the final two paragraphs, what is the relationship between religion and politics? Does it seem like Rousseau believes in any religion here, or do all simply serve a political purpose?

Chapter VIII: On the People

1. Why must the legislator start by examining the people's actual circumstances, not just what laws would be good in the abstract?
2. Why is it difficult to give freedom to a people who have never experienced or have long been without it? What must the legislator do, then, to ensure a good founding?

Chapter IX: The People (continued)

1. Here Rousseau tackles the problem of size: How big or small must a well-governed state be? Why does he opt for smaller?
2. What problems with the bureaucracy does he see in the larger state?

Chapter X: The People (continued)

1. What is the best relationship between population size and amount of land?
2. What types of conditions may alter this relationship and argue for more or less land than would first appear necessary?
3. Why is peace a necessary prerequisite for a good founding?

Chapter XI: On the Various Systems of Legislation

1. What are the two principle objects of every founding or system of legislation?
2. Rousseau deals with equality here. What conditions have to be in place for there to be equality among people?
3. Again, Rousseau returns to the unique circumstances of a people who must influence the laws. What sort of circumstances does he mention?

Chapter XII: Classification of the Laws   In this chapter, Rousseau classifies various types of laws, starting with what seems like the most important. But Rousseau has a surprise for us at the end.

1. The first type of law is basically constitutional. The people may always change laws that apply to itself as sovereign. Why must this be the case?
2. Rousseau wishes the second type of law—concerning the relationships of individuals with each other and their relationship to the whole body or the sovereign state—to emphasize independence of individuals in relation to each other but total dependence of all individuals on the state. What is his reasoning?
3. What is the third sort of law? Given what Rousseau has said previously about law-breakers and traitors, how important is this type of law in Rousseau's social contract?
4. Rousseau considers a fourth sort of law to be the most important. What is this law, and why does he think it is supreme and essential to the success of all the other types of law?

Book III   Book III contains several terms that are difficult to understand, and concepts that are contestable enough that scholars have long disagreed about Rousseau's meaning. After carefully reading the entire book you will have a fairly good idea of what Rousseau thinks of various forms of government, and what he thinks is the best form. Armed with this understanding, a second reading may be necessary to clarify some of his specific arguments and ideas.

Chapter I: On Government in General   Rousseau warns his readers to read carefully, because he does not know how to write for those who are not paying attention. Keep this warning very much in mind. His first task is to

define government itself. Establishing what Rousseau means by certain words in this chapter will help immensely with understanding subsequent chapters. You may find a brief answer to the following questions in one place, then an additional answer in another place in this chapter. Simply add to your answer as you see Rousseau return to the question.

1. What is the difference between legislative and executive power?
2. What is the difference between the government and the sovereign?
3. Give Rousseau's specific definition of government.
4. Who are the magistrates, kings, or governors? Who is the prince?
5. What is the relationship between the people and its leaders?
6. Why can the sovereign not govern directly?
7. Why does he say that the more citizens (the larger the sovereign) the less liberty there is?
8. Rousseau does not use the term "ratio" in the precise mathematical sense, but in the general sense of relationship. Under what relationship between the private individual wills and the general will does the government need more force? Under what conditions does the sovereign need more force?
9. Rousseau proceeds more succinctly to give the relationship among the people, the sovereign, and the government. What is their relationship?
10. What is the difference between the state and the government?

Chapter II: On the Principle that Constitutes the Various Forms of Government

1. Why does Rousseau think that the more magistrates there are, the weaker the government will be?
2. Explain the three wills that Rousseau can distinguish in the person of the magistrate. Which will *should* dominate in his decisions, and why? On the other hand, what will predominates *naturally?*
3. Why does Rousseau say that it is not a good idea to have the legislative authority (the citizens) be the magistrates as well?
4. What problems are associated with having too many magistrates?
5. Is it better to have many magistrates, or a few? Explain.

Chapter III: Classification of Governments

1. Provide Rousseau's definitions of democracy, aristocracy, and monarchy.
2. Which types of government are suitable to small, medium and large numbers of citizens? Why?

Chapter IV: On Democracy   Rousseau treats each type of government at more length. Rousseau is creating a type of balance sheet, weighing the pros and cons of each type of government according to what he values, namely liberty and stability.

1. Explain Rousseau's statement that a true democracy cannot exist.
2. What physical and social requirements are there for a democracy to work well?
3. How does Rousseau correct "a famous author" (Aristotle) on the need for virtue in a democracy?

Chapter V: On Aristocracy

1. Rousseau states that in an aristocracy, there are two general wills. To whom do they belong?
2. What are the three sorts of aristocracy. Which one is the best? Why?
3. Does it surprise you to learn that Rousseau thinks aristocracy (the rule of the wise) is the best and most natural form of government? Why or why not?
4. What size requirements are there for the country to be suitable for aristocracy?

Chapter VI: On Monarchy

1. What makes the monarchy different from the other two simple forms of government?
2. What advantages does a monarchy enjoy? What disadvantages are there?
3. How does Rousseau interpret Machiavelli's message in *The Prince?*
4. Why are intermediate layers of authority such as the nobility necessary in a monarchy?
5. Rousseau compares monarchy with a republican government in which the people choose who will be in positions of honor. Which is superior and why?
6. What kind of trouble does the matter of succession cause in a monarchy?
7. What point is Rousseau trying to make about monarchy when he brings in Plato in the second last paragraph?

Chapter VII: On Mixed Government

1. From reading this entire chapter, can you ascertain what is a simple and what is a mixed form of government?
2. How does Rousseau answer the question of whether a simple or a mixed form of government is better?

Chapter VIII: That Not All Forms of Government Are Suited to All Countries

1. What sorts of physical circumstances should be considered when determining what the best government is for any particular people?
2. Why is monarchy suited to wealthy nations, aristocracy to nations of moderate wealth, and democracy to poor nations?

3. What do you think of Rousseau's argument that climate and soil fertility have a lot to do with the character of the people and hence the type of government they should have?

Chapter IX: On the Signs of Good Government   Now Rousseau moves from a more general discussion of government and what conditions call for what kind of government, to a more specific discussion of what in his mind is the mark of a good government. He still denies that he can identify one that is absolutely best under all circumstances, but he nonetheless plunges ahead with the task of evaluating governments.

What is Rousseau's simple answer to the question of how we can know whether a government is well or poorly governed?

Chapter X: On the Abuse of Government and Its Tendency to Degenerate

1. What are the two general ways in which the government tends to degenerate?
2. What two ways can the dissolution of the state come about?
3. Rousseau says that democracy degenerates into ochlocracy (mob rule), aristocracy into oligarchy, monarchy into tyranny. Can you imagine how each change might occur?
4. What is the definition of a tyrant? How does this differ from a despot?

Chapter XI: On the Death of the Body Politic

1. Is the death of the body politic inevitable? Why or why not?
2. What does Rousseau mean by "tacit consent"?

Chapter XII: How the Sovereign Authority Is Maintained

Why does Rousseau admire ancient Rome? Notice that he leaves ancient Athens to one side. Athens' government was a pure democracy that tended to be unstable and actually ruled by demagogues. How do you think Rome would seem better than Athens to Rousseau?

Chapter XIII: Continuation

1. Why does Rousseau think that a good government must include "regular, periodical" assemblies of the people as sovereign?
2. How does Rousseau answer the objection that popular assemblies are difficult to organize on a scale larger than the single town?

Chapter XIV: Continuation

1. What happens to the government and the executive power during the time when the popular assembly is taking place?

2. What is the relationship of the prince to the sovereign during these assemblies? Are you beginning to see clearly the revolutionary nature of Rousseau's thinking?

Chapter XV: On Deputies or Representatives

1. How does Rousseau tie the creation of representatives for the people with money and laziness?
2. If the people have deputies, these deputies cannot be representatives, so what are they?
3. How does Rousseau criticize the English and their parliament?
4. What was the role of slavery in ancient democracies, according to Rousseau? What do you think his conclusion is concerning the possibility of having modern democracies without slavery? How do we reconcile this discussion with his previous condemnation of slavery?
5. If slavery is not the answer, must the democratic city simply remain very small?

Chapter XVI: That the Institution of Government Is Not a Contract

1. After reading this entire chapter, can you determine who is party to the social contract? Why is it important for Rousseau to clarify who the contracting parties are?
2. What is the relationship between the people and their magistrates if it is not a social contract?

Chapter XVII: On the Institution of the Government

Here Rousseau describes how a government might actually come into being.
1. Describe the first two steps in the process of making a government.
2. Why must Rousseau explain that in this process there is first the establishment of a democracy which then decides what form of government it will next establish?
3. What message do you think Rousseau is sending advocates of hereditary monarchy in this discussion and in other chapters you have read so far?

Chapter XVIII: The Means of Preventing Usurpations of the Government

1. How does Rousseau change what would have been the acceptable way to see the relationship between the people and their hereditary monarchy in this chapter?
2. How do periodic assemblies of the sovereign help to prevent usurpations of government (removal of ultimate authority from the sovereign)?
3. What two questions should the sovereign answer every time it assembles? What is the practical importance for the current government of such questions?

Book IV   Rousseau begins his preface to *On the Social Contract* with praise for Geneva; but he ends his book with praise for ancient Roman institutions. His praise of Rome forms his practical suggestions for instituting a good form of government. The question to ask here is not does Rousseau wish to bring back ancient Rome. Clearly he recognizes that no government can be replicated regardless of time and place. Instead, the reader should look for general principles of good government in Rousseau's praise of Rome. His treatment of what he considers to be a good government in the past will further illuminate what Rousseau means by the general will and thus will explain the way he expects it to function.

Chapter I: That the General Will Is Indestructible

The general will is an idea we have already tried to untangle. This chapter makes it clear that the general will is not necessarily a practical reality, but a concept that is more or less achieved in reality according to the situation of the people and the way they are governed.

1. Given what has been said above, in what sense is the general will indestructible?
2. Under what conditions can the general will operate well?
3. Under what conditions is the general will weakened, and under what conditions will it cease to function in any practical sense?
4. How would Rousseau see politics in Washington if he could visit our corridors of power today?

Chapter II: On Voting

1. Why is unanimity a sign of a healthy body politic?
2. What happens to those people who do not agree with the vote to form a social contract? In what way does this preserve the principle that unanimity must exist in the formation of the social contract?
3. On all other votes, Rousseau says that the vote of the majority obligates everyone. How can those who vote in the minority still be free even though their wishes do not prevail?
4. At the end of this chapter, Rousseau discusses what situations call for larger majorities to approve a proposition and what situations call for a smaller majority for a proposition to be acceptable. Explain his reasoning.

Chapter III: On Elections

Why does Rousseau generally favor the method of selecting leaders by lot?

Chapter IV: On the Roman Comitia

The Roman *comitia* were assemblies of various classes of Roman citizens charged with decision-making authority. Here, Rousseau examines this ancient Roman practice at some length. This is a good history lesson, but more importantly, if you are attentive to what Rousseau praises about the comitia, you will see why Rousseau considers ancient Rome an inspiration but not a blueprint for the formation of a good government.

1. Briefly give an account of Rousseau's description of how the comitia came into existence and changed and grew over time, paying special attention to identifying the *curia centuriata,* the *comitia curiata,* and the *comitia tributa.* There is no need to go into excruciating detail. This question requires you to read the entire chapter, then go back to the beginning and answer the following questions.
2. Why do you think Rousseau admires the Roman preference for country living?
3. Rousseau says that no citizen in Rome was denied the right to vote and that the people were truly sovereign by law (*de jure*) and in fact (*de facto*). Based solely on his own description of Roman institutions, is he correct?
4. Toward the end of this chapter, Rousseau says that the *curia centuriata* was the institution in which the Romans' majesty was found and he compares it favorably with the *comitia curiata* and the *comitia tributa.* Explain his choice.
5. Rousseau weighs the value of voice or open voting with voting by secret ballot. After reading his opinion on this matter, how do you think he would evaluate our practice of secret ballot today? Why?
6. At the end of this chapter, Rousseau mentions extraordinary methods used by the Roman republic to obtain the obedience of the populace. What were these methods?

Chapter V: On the Tribunate

1. What was the tribunate in ancient Rome, and what function did it serve that Rousseau so admired?
2. When does the tribunate degenerate into tyranny?
3. What is the best way to prevent abuses of power on the part of the tribunate?

Chapter VI: On Dictatorship

1. Under what circumstances did the Romans elect dictators, and for how long? Do you think this would be a practical solution for times of crisis in today's democracies?
2. What happens to the general will when a dictator rules? What is the dictator's relationship to the sovereign?
3. Why must the dictatorship be limited by law to a brief time?

Chapter VII: On the Censorship

1. What does Rousseau mean by the "censorial tribunal"? What is its role?
2. What is the source of good mores, according to Rousseau?

3. Rousseau insists that good opinions arise from good legislation or a good constitution. How do you think this opinion would fare in our contemporary political culture?

4. Does Rousseau's example of abolishing seconds in dueling give you a better idea of the function of censors? Does censorship necessarily mean what we think of it today—mainly stopping the publication or broadcasting of certain ideas?

Chapter VIII: On Civil Religion   This chapter includes Rousseau's famous attack on Christianity, an attack similar to that of Machiavelli's. He also reveals some of his own ideas about Jesus Christ and the Gospels. His goal, however, is to determine what types of religion are helpful to the body politic and what types are harmful, and he briefly but firmly establishes the benefits of civil religion and its relationship to private religion. Rousseau's definitions of tolerance and intolerance are interesting. They form one side of the controversy we still have today about the meaning of these terms.

1. Rousseau starts out with a sort of history of the relationship between religions and governments. How did people view gods and their relationships to government in pagan cultures?

2. Under what circumstances did people convert to a different pagan religion?

3. How did the teachings of Jesus change the relationship between religion and government?

4. In what way did Christianity cause a permanent conflict over jurisdiction between church and state?

5. How does Rousseau depict Hobbes's view of the proper relationship between religion and government? In what way was Hobbes wrong?

6. Rousseau says there are three types of religion, that of man, that of the citizen, and a third kind. Describe all three. Which does he find most strange? Why?

7. Rousseau seems to praise the religion of man, which is his own understanding of what Jesus really came to teach as opposed to what the Church claimed. But how is even this religion flawed from the point of view of the body politic?

8. Rousseau next launches into a series of criticisms of Christianity, with the general point that this religion is incompatible with effective government. List and explain the reasons why this is the case.

9. Near the end of this chapter, Rousseau puts forth the idea of a civil profession of faith. What is this profession, and why does he think it is necessary?

10. What is Rousseau's definition of intolerance? Could a religion that considers itself to be true and others to be false avoid the charge of intolerance?

11. Do you agree with Rousseau that religious intolerance as he defines it always leads to civil intolerance? What do you think of his opinion that such people must leave the state?

Chapter IX: Conclusion

1. What topics does Rousseau not cover here? Based on what he has said in this book, do you have some idea of what his opinion would be on these subjects?
2. What does Rousseau say he has accomplished in this book? Do you think Rousseau has accomplished this?

BIBLIOGRAPHY

Keith Michael Baker, *Inventing the French Revolution,* New York: Cambridge University Press, 1990.

T.C.W. Blanning, *The Origins of the French Revolutionary Wars,* New York: Longman, 1986.

Rodger D. Masters, *The Political Philosophy of Rousseau,* Princeton: Princeton University Press, 1968.

Jim Miller, *Rousseau: Dreamer of Democracy,* New Haven: Yale University Press, 1984.

Robert Roswell Palmer, *The Twelve Who Ruled,* Princeton: Princeton University Press, 1958.

Robert Roswell Palmer, *The Age of the Democratic Revolution* (Two Volumes), Princeton: Princeton University Press, 1964.

Judith N. Shklar, *Men and Citizens: A Study of Rousseau's Social Theory,* London: Cambridge University Press, 1969.

Tracy B. Strong, *Jean Jacques Rousseau: The Politics of the Ordinary,* Thousand Oaks, CA: Sage Publications, 1994.

MILL (1806–1873)

BACKGROUND

John Stuart Mill was born in 1806 in London to James Mill and Harriet Burrows, and was the eldest of six children. His life was deeply shaped by his father, a philosopher in his own right. James Mill was an advocate of utilitarianism, a philosophy that judges actions, laws, and policies on the basis of how much happiness they produce for how many people. After John Stuart's birth, James Mill met the then-greatest of utilitarian philosophers, Jeremy Bentham, and quickly became his close friend and disciple. Bentham held that human beings were motivated by attraction to pleasure and aversion to pain, and that decisions were right if they produced pleasure and wrong if they produced pain. The aim of government and its laws, then, should be to produce "the greatest happiness for the greatest number."

John Stuart Mill was educated by his father and by Bentham and others to be a great intellectual, and most importantly, a utilitarian like themselves. In his *Autobiography* (1873), Mill complained about this education, one that was so strict and rigorous that he blamed it for causing the nervous breakdown that he suffered when he was twenty. Mill recounts, for instance, "I have no remembrance of the time when I began to learn Greek. I have been told that it was when I was three years old."[1] By 1813 he had read the first six dialogues of Plato. His early memories of learning Greek and also mathematics were not altogether pleasant. At least in hindsight, John Stuart seemed to think that his father was trying to push him into the adult world far too soon. "Of children's books, any more than of playthings, I had scarcely any, except an occasional gift from a relation or acquaintance. . . ."[2] Mill

---

[1] John Stuart Mill, *Autobiography and Other Writings,* edited with an introduction and notes by Jack Stillinger, Boston: Houghton Mifflin Company, 1969, p. 5.
[2] Ibid., p. 7.

explained that, while his father did not exclude such "books of amusement" he "allowed them very sparingly." One gets the impression from Mill's autobiography that his father saw him as more of an educational experiment than as a son. But Mill wrote his autobiography as an adult, at which point he probably could not separate the critical stance he had developed toward his father's type of utilitarianism and his feelings for him and recollections of him as a father.

In 1823, Mill took a position with the examiner's office of the East India Company, and was eventually promoted to the post of chief examiner. He remained employed there until he retired in 1858.

Mill accepted his father's utilitarianism until 1826, even leading the Philosophic Radicals, an organization of young men dedicated to Bentham's utilitarian philosophy. Then he suffered a breakdown which has variously been described as nervous, emotional, or intellectual in nature. In any case, Mill blamed his father's inability to deal with the emotional side of human nature for creating a sterile education which led to his nervous collapse. After this crisis, he turned to the poetry of Coleridge and Wordsworth to discover the human emotions he had so long been trained to suppress. Mill's mature opinion of his father's utilitarianism reflected that of his father's tutelage—it was excessively rationalistic; it did not account for human emotions, rather it treated people dispassionately like numbers or units.

Surprisingly, given his youthful experience, Mill was not to abandon his father's utilitarianism completely, but to modify it in an attempt to make it better and more human. Instead of treating pleasures and pains as equal or to be determined simply by majority opinion, for instance, John Stuart Mill argued that some pleasures were better or more important than others and that the government should promote the pursuit of those more edifying or higher pleasures (such as learning) for the welfare of all.

John Stuart Mill was introduced into Harriet Taylor's intellectual circle when he was twenty-five years old. This woman, who would eventually be John Stuart's wife, was then married to a wealthy merchant whom Mill thought decent but not a match for her intellectual capabilities. Mill was to form a long friendship with her that culminated in marriage. Scholars disagree strongly about the influence this woman had on Mill's life and intellectual development. Some attribute to her Mill's turning away from his father's ultrarationalism; others with the development of Mill's rationalistic side. Some say that she had a profound influence on some of his works (even to the point of coauthoring them), especially on the rights of women. Others regard her influence as peripheral. She certainly had an influence on his views on feminism. His father had held that only middle-class males should vote, but John Stuart was to argue for female suffrage. We know from his autobiography that Mill held Harriet in the highest esteem imaginable, even claiming that she had a great influence on his political philosophy.

When two persons have their thoughts and speculations completely in common; when all subjects of intellectual or moral interest are discussed between them in daily life, and probed to much greater depths than are usually or conveniently sounded in writings intended for general readers; when they set out from the same principles and arrive at their conclusions by processes pursued jointly, it is of little consequence in respect to the question of originality which of them holds the pen; the one who contributes least to the composition may contribute most to the thought; the writings which result are the joint product of both, and it must often be impossible to disentangle their respective parts and affirm that this belongs to one and that to the other."[3]

At first, Mill and Harriet Taylor simply saw a lot of each other, but after two years Harriet told her husband honestly about her feelings for Mill. Eventually John Taylor agreed to tolerate their affair. After this, the two were together frequently and even traveled together. Many scholars maintain that their relationship, while passionate, remained platonic throughout Harriet's first marriage. They maintained a thin public veneer of close friendship to conceal their love in an attempt to conform to social expectations. Then in 1849 John Taylor died, and after the proper period of mourning, Harriet and John Stuart Mill married in 1851.

It would be an understatement to say that their relationship made Mill feel complete. Harriet had the passion and feeling his father could never give him, as well as, in his view, formidable intellectual gifts. A champion of women's equality, Harriet published several works of her own. Mill wrote and published several joint works with her, including "Enfranchisement of Women." When she died in 1858, he was devastated, but he was now motivated by the desire to do what she would have wanted him to do, including continue his philosophical work.

Thus, Mill's father and his wife, more than any others, strongly influenced his life and his works. Despite his strict and sterile upbringing, Mill learned from his father's tutelage and did not wholly reject his father's philosophy. Despite his father's downplaying of the emotional side of his son's nature, John Stuart became a man who could love deeply and feel passionately about the causes he championed.

Mill and Taylor were to be married only eight years. After Harriet's death in 1858, Mill published two of his greatest works, *On Liberty* (1859), which, Mill states in his autobiography, is the result of their collaboration, and *The Subjection of Women* (1869). Both of these works have been included in your guides. Mill published *Utilitarianism* in 1863, a book that represented his critical stance toward Benthamite utilitarianism, which he considered too simple and narrow compared with his own more complex, more humane utilitarianism. Between 1866 and 1868, Mill served as a member of parliament for West-

---

[3]Ibid., p. 145.

minster, where he sponsored legislation to give women the right to vote and to change the laws concerning the property rights of married women. He and others like him pursued parliamentary reform. He died in Avignon, France, in 1873, and was buried next to Harriet. His autobiography was published shortly after his death.

UNDERSTANDING MILL

To understand Mill fully, one has to better understand the utilitarian philosophy that he rebelled against and modified. This philosophy emerged at a time of great change in European history. The economy was rapidly changing toward factory production and creating a more urban population of working poor. A powerful merchant class had emerged as well as a large working class. The old aristocracy was being challenged by the merchant or bourgeois class, whose interests lay in individualism and economic freedom, not in aristocratic monopoly and prescribed privilege. Intellectuals like James Mill and Jeremy Bentham came forward in journalistic and philosophical circles to promote individualism and political reforms.

The great inspiration for *philosophic radicalism* (as their movement came to be called) came from Jeremy Bentham, whose utilitarianism rested on some basic and seemingly commonsense assumptions. Bentham was a firm believer in the power of human reason to break down complex problems into their simpler parts, thus enabling human beings to solve them. For Bentham, it was clear that all human beings are motivated in everything they do to seek pleasure and avoid pain. As noted, Bentham thought that every decision, every act, could and should be measured by how much pleasure or pain it produced. The more pleasure an act produced, the more one could call it "good." If an act produced pain (or the absence of pleasure), it could be called "bad." Pleasurable activities might be bodily, such as eating and drinking, but could also be intellectual or aesthetic, such as viewing works of art or even doing a good deed. Bentham created a fairly complex calculus for choosing among various pleasures, which included considerations such as intensity, duration, certainty, and purity of pleasure, as well as the number of people who could experience the pleasure. The purpose of government was to provide the "greatest happiness for the greatest number" of people. This meant that even though Bentham and other utilitarians were advocates of individualism, this individualism should not be allowed to get in the way of the majority's pursuit of happiness.

Imagine Socrates' response to this utilitarian calculus. He would no doubt argue that there are some pleasures (such as excessive drinking) that, while enjoyable for the moment, can be bad for a person, and that there are some pains (such as surgery) that are really good for a person. Socrates' point was that not everyone knows what will truly make them happy in the long run. Indeed, Bentham's concept of happiness was not as well worked out as it could have been. John Stuart Mill would later criticize Bentham and his father along these lines. He would not argue with Bentham's fundamental assumption that all acts should be measured in terms of pleasure and pain, but he would argue that what is truly pleasurable and what is truly painful are not so easily determined. That meant that such measurements could not be a matter simply of individual preference or opinion but could be submitted to a higher standard of reason and a deeper understanding of human feeling.

Bentham rejected political philosophies based upon nature, such as Locke's theory of natural rights. The rights of a people could not be found in "nature," according to Bentham, but could only be created by government based upon what the people wanted and could agree upon. While an individualist at one level, promoting seemingly hedonistic pleasure-seeking, Bentham thus rejected the earlier liberal notion of individualism in which the protection of individual natural rights was the foremost duty of government. The earlier notion would have demanded the protection of political and religious minorities or even individuals from the tyranny of the majority. Bentham, on the other hand, seemed fairly confident that human beings were enough alike that a formula for providing for the pleasure, and thus the happiness, of the majority would satisfy most of the people most of the time. In this system of thought, the "rights" of minorities would have to be sacrificed if they interfered with the perceived happiness of the majority. This rejection of the idea of individual natural rights is a potential problem for the acceptability of all utilitarian philosophies, including John Stuart Mill's.

At first, Bentham seemed to trust the elites to govern with the common good in mind. However, as these same leaders seemed to continue to largely ignore his proposals, he later advocated political reform as a necessary means to the end of a government dedicated to providing the greatest happiness for the greatest number, not just for the elites. He advocated abolishing the monarchy and the House of Lords as well as extending the suffrage to guarantee that the desires of the majority were heard. He also advocated universal education to help the people identify their interest with the interests of all.

For Bentham, the government most likely to provide the greatest happiness for the greatest number was a government that removed as many obstacles as possible so that the individual could pursue his happiness freely. Bentham advocated the elimination of the common law, which had grown up piecemeal through justices' application of law and precedent to individual cases. The ambiguity of the common law system left, in his opinion, too much room for interpretation and thus for abuse of judicial power. He developed a proposed legal code which would be concrete, uniformly applied, and most of all invulnerable to the biased interpretations of judges.

As he grew older, John Stuart Mill's reaction to Bentham's type of philosophical radicalism was to treat it, not as absolutely incorrect, but as too simple. Man was not just a rational calculator of pleasures and pains, but a being with feelings and aesthetic perceptions which rationalists like Bentham and James Mill had pushed aside in their own lives and thus in their philosophy. Likewise, Mill rejected the simplistic idea that happiness can be pursued and won through a rational calculus. Rather, happiness is most often obtained as a by-product of working toward some other goal, oftentimes a goal greater than that of the individual's self-interest. Indeed, Mill, unlike Bentham, acknowledged that man is not simply a collection of atomistic individuals, but is an individual who is also a social being. Among other things, this meant that there was something intrinsically valuable about participating politically as a citizen, thus being challenged to think about the good of the community. Clearly, Mill thought that some kinds of pleasures were intrinsically more valuable and thus more desirable than others. The standard for Mill was not simply pleasure but the development of our particularly human nature. Thus, those activities that are singularly human activities are more valuable for us and for the good of the community, for instance, than those activities that humans share with animals.

For Mill, Bentham's system did not place enough importance on individual freedom, a value to be balanced against the majority's happiness. Mill argued that the greatest source of human happiness for all human beings is a properly developed human character, and this development requires freedom. In *On Liberty*, Mill argues that individuals must never be forced by society to do anything unless society, through government, is acting to defend itself from the harmful acts of that individual against others. He argues against a paternalistic government that attempts to decide moral matters through the law. Only with a great degree of freedom can human beings adequately explore new and better forms of happiness. True to utilitarian reasoning, however, Mill did not ground the value of freedom in nature or argue that it was a natural right. Mill argued instead that allowing such freedom was valuable because it was in everyone's interest.

Given the times during which he lived and wrote (including his observation of the failed socialist revolution of 1848 in France), it should not come as a surprise that over the course of his career Mill advocated some socialist ideas. He rejected state-run or centralized socialism but was generally in favor of producer cooperatives, or worker-owned and -controlled enterprises. These ideas were widely discussed at this time, a time when Marx and Engels produced the *Communist Manifesto* and promoted their own political theory of class conflict and the inevitability of communism. The working-class people of Mill's time were poor, uneducated, and seemingly trapped in an economic system over which they had no control. Given Mill's interest in promoting the happiness and freedom of the people, it is easy to see how democratic socialism would have seemed to him an attractive option. It is easy to see within Mill's work, two poles that are at least somewhat incompatible: individual freedom and a larger government role in promoting the common happiness.

It might come as a surprise, however, that the mature Mill had doubts about some democratic institutions we generally associate with the defense and maintenance of freedom, such as "one person, one vote." In *Considerations of Representative Government,* Mill proposed the idea of giving every citizen a vote, but giving the educated citizens (not necessarily the same as the rich) additional votes to keep the uneducated majority from overpowering the influence of reason in the democratic process. He also argued that the parliament should not draft legislation directly, but should give this task to legislative commissions whose greater expertise and concentration would produce better proposals. Although he continued to be an advocate for expanding political participation, he understood the perils of democracy quite well and was attempting to avoid them. However, his proposals might seem strangely elitist coming from a philosopher so concerned about the welfare of the individual.

For his time, Mill was a great defender of women's equality and freedom. Notice, however, in *The Subjection of Women,* Mill's reasoning is not always what the contemporary feminist would admire or accept. For instance, Mill argues that women should be allowed to participate in any education and occupation for which they can qualify, but he also says that if women choose the occupation of wife and mother, they must at least when their children are young accept that child-rearing will be their chief occupation. Mill does not argue that women are equally capable of most tasks, only that there is no scientific proof that they are unequal because for all of human history they have not been allowed to participate in public life and in various occupations with men. This argument does not perhaps go far enough for some people today.

The reader is advised not to prematurely categorize Mill. He is not a pure liberal, socialist, or utilitarian thinker. Mill had one of the freest and most wide-ranging minds of his time. He was not attempting to fit his ideas into any particular school of thought or mold. The influence of his early education certainly informed his later thought but just as certainly did not control it. Neither did the influence of his partner, Harriet Taylor. Mill was an independent and creative thinker who, while reacting to the issues of his time, provides us with arguments that are equally prescient today.

CAREFUL READING

Mill's writing is remarkably straightforward in most respects. Nevertheless, from time to time, even this practical utilitarian can become obscure or decide to veil his meaning in oblique references. Below are two examples, one from *On Liberty* and one from *The Subjection of Women.* These passages may give readers of Mill some trouble if they do not read them carefully and thoroughly.

Useful Truth

Utilitarians such as John Stuart Mill are known for measuring everything on the basis of its usefulness for creating the greatest happiness possible, so when readers encounter this passage they may be confused by Mill's insistence that truth is always preferable to opinion. In *The Republic,* Plato offered the idea that sometimes what worked best with the majority of people was a "noble lie," a myth or fiction that would explain their world to them, instill a sense of justice in them, make them respect each other. As long as the noble lie was based on a greater truth, which they could not be expected to comprehend, Plato thought it could be useful. If beliefs are not true or not wholly true but promote good behavior and happiness, why would Mill not welcome them as utilitarian? The following passage finds Mill dealing with this issue and asserting the preeminence of truth.[4]

> The usefulness of an opinion is itself matter of opinion: as disputable, as open to discussion, and requiring discussion as much, as the opinion itself. There is the same need of an infallible judge of opinions to decide an opinion to be noxious, as to decide it to be false, unless the opinion condemned has full opportunity of defending itself. And it will not do to say that the heretic may be allowed to maintain the utility or harmlessness of his opinion, though forbidden to maintain its truth. The truth of an opinion is part of its utility. If we would know whether or not it is desirable that a proposition should be believed, is it possible to exclude the consideration of whether or not it is true? In the opinion, not of bad men, but of the best men, no belief which is contrary to truth can be really useful: and can you prevent such men from urging that plea, when they are charged with culpability for denying some doctrine which they are told is useful, but which they believe to be false? (Chapter Two, para. 10)

First, Mill makes an argument that he has used before and will use again to deal with other questions. For Mill, so much of what human beings have thought across the centuries has turned out to be false or only partially true— that it is almost impossible to be sure that what someone is saying now is absolutely true. So, if someone claims that an opinion is useful to society (perhaps that marriage is generally a good institution), that does not mean that it really is or always will be useful. Remember that the issue here is not truth but usefulness; hence, Mill starts off by sounding very much like a utilitarian, simply claiming what some think is useful to society (whether true or false) may indeed not be useful. Next, Mill buttresses this thought by saying that in order

---

[4]This and all other quotes in this chapter from *On Liberty* are from John Stuart Mill, *On Liberty,* edited by Alburey Castell, New York: Appleton-Century-Crofts, 1947.

to determine that an opinion is socially "noxious" or harmful would require an "infallible judge," just as an infallible judge would be needed to judge whether an opinion was true or false. By emphasizing the need for infallibility as a prerequisite for judging either the social usefulness or the truth of an opinion, Mill is raising the standard for judgment so high that mere mortals cannot attain it. If no human being can be this free of error in their reasoning, then it is not possible for anyone to decide for the rest of society what opinions they should or should not be exposed to. Mill does open the door for judgment if the opinion in question has the opportunity to be fully defended; but to be fully defended, the opinion would have to be fully available to people, so that a decision to withhold it from people could no longer be made.

Next Mill addresses the idea that "heretics," or people with unpopular ideas, might be allowed to argue the usefulness or the harmlessness of their opinions to society, but not their truth. Should such people who are considered "heretics" to society because of their unpopular opinions be allowed to argue that their opinions are useful or not harmful, but not allowed to argue their truth? Think about the position of political minorities. If they are allowed to argue that their beliefs do no harm to society or are somehow useful to society, they are being made to take a subordinate position in society where they have to justify why they should not be censored. Putting people in this position presupposes the infallible judgment that Mill has already argued cannot exist.

Mill states "The truth of an opinion is a part of its utility." This is the heart of his point, for if this is not the case, it will be easy to argue that some false opinions are nonetheless good for society. He grounds this claim in his understanding of the human mind, an understanding with which we can either agree or disagree. Mill does try hard to prove this understanding, but simply asserts it as common sense. He strongly implies that if we want to know whether an opinion is useful or desirable, it is impossible to exclude from our considerations whether that opinion is true or false. When people try to weigh an opinion, they naturally consider whether it is true or false. In the opinion of the "best men," he says, no false belief can really be useful. While this may seem like common sense, Mill does not attempt to prove in any philosophical sense this connection between truth and usefulness. He holds a certain faith in truth, and the reason that discovers it, to always be ultimately what is best for people. He ends this passage wondering whether we can prevent men from making this plea to the superiority of truth, when they are found guilty of denying an opinion or "doctrine" which others find socially useful. That is, can we blame them for claiming that truth is important when they are charged with being "heretics"?

Female Subjects

One task Mill faces in *On the Subjection of Women* is to explain why it is that men have so long dominated women. He gives many reasons, some physical, some having to do with what he perceives to be male nature. In the following passage, Mill discusses some of the reasons peculiar to the relationship between men and women, particularly in marriage, which have motivated women to accept their yoke instead of attempting to throw it off.

> We must consider, too, that the possessors of the power have facilities in this case, greater than in any other, to prevent any uprising against it. Every one of the subjects lives under the very eye, and almost, it may be said, in the hands, of one of the masters—in closer intimacy with him than with any of her fellow-subjects; with no means for combining against him, no power of even locally overmastering him, and, on the other hand, with the strongest motives for seeking his favour and avoiding to give him any offence. In struggles for political emancipation, everybody knows how often its champions are bought off by bribes, or daunted by terrors. In the case of women, each individual of the subject-class is in a chronic state of bribery and intimidation combined. In setting up the standard of resistance, a large number of the leaders, and still more of the followers, must make an almost complete sacrifice of the pleasures or the alleviations of their own individual lot. If ever any system of privilege and enforced subjection had its yoke tightly riveted on the necks of those who are kept down by it, this has. (Chapter One, para. 8)[5]

This passage was at least partly intended to answer questions such as why it seemed that many women were not eager to escape male domination in Mill's time, why many of them tried as hard as they could to please their husbands instead, and why they seemed reluctant to join together to fight for emancipation. Mill claims that in this case of domination, the powerful have greater "facilities" or capabilities for asserting their domination than in any other case. Notice that he uses the word "subjects" to describe women in marriage. He is doing his best to paint the picture as he thinks it really appears—that marriage in his time is truly a sort of slavery. At the same time he is saying that women are subjects who are in a very different type of relationship with their husbands as subjects are with their kings. The relationship of these female subjects is one of great "intimacy" and constant contact. Indeed, Mill does not deny that love enters into such relationships and is part of what holds the system together. Women are more intimate with their husbands than with any of their "fellow subjects," that is, their fellow women with whom they might otherwise join in fighting the system together. Mill uses the word "master" to substitute for husband, again, in order to show us the true situation as he sees it. Women have every reason to try to please their masters and avoid offending them in such circumstances, for each one will benefit from doing so given their situation, even though by doing so they also perpetuate their enslavement.

Mill goes further with the analogy to monarchy when he states that in "struggles for political emancipation," even the champions of freedom are

---

[5]This and all other quotes from *The Subjection of Women* in this chapter are from John Stuart Mill, *The Subjection of Women,* edited by Susan Moller Okin, Indianapolis: Hackett Publishing Company, 1988.

bought off by bribes or intimidated into inaction. Such is even more the case with women in their peculiarly intimate relationship with their "masters." They are constantly being bribed and intimidated. What bribes is Mill talking about? He does not say, leaving it to our imagination. But he is probably referring to the husband's control of all material things—food, housing, clothing, and for the upper classes, the finer things that husbands could provide—as well as the husband's choice of whether to be kind to his wife. These benefits are a "double-edged sword," however, and can be used for intimidation by threatening their withdrawal.

Mill again addresses the question of why women do not join each other in resistance when he says that many would have to risk these individual penalties for the chance of freedom. To start a movement, many women would have to forgo any pleasure or comfort in life in order to make it happen. Mill obviously thinks this is very unlikely, which is why, elsewhere, he states that men must change their minds about the value of women's emancipation (in order for that emancipation to take place). Indeed, his essay is not written primarily for women but for men, to give them the many reasons why it would be in their own and in the collective interest to give women their freedom. Mill ends this passage by emphasizing that the system of male domination of women is very strong, thus leaving the impression that it is insurmountable unless men as well as women change their ways.

GUIDE TO *ON LIBERTY*

On Liberty is a work that largely assumes utilitarianism and does not thoroughly explain that philosophy nor defend against its chief opponent, natural rights philosophy. It is important to keep in mind that this larger philosophical debate lurks in the background, and occasionally, Mill does make reference to this issue. More importantly for understanding this work, sometimes Mill uses the word "rights," but he does so in a very different way from Hobbes or Locke, meshing it with utilitarian thinking. The main theme in this work is individuality, its utility, and hence the need for government to restrict it as little as possible. Take time to number the paragraphs in *On Liberty,* starting with paragraph number one for each chapter. This will help you follow the study guide more effectively.

Chapter I: Introductory

1. What is the subject of *On Liberty?* (para. 1)
2. Mill proceeds to give a sort of "history" of the development of government, which fills the place of a discussion of the "state of nature" in natural rights theories. Give an account of the struggle between liberty and authority as it began in the earliest times and in Mill's time. (para. 2–4)

3. What does Mill mean by the "tyranny of the majority"? (para. 5)
4. Describe what Mill means by "custom," and explain why it is not good enough to make decisions regarding rules in society. (para. 6)
5. What special claim does religion have in promoting "the rights of the individual against society" on the "broad grounds of principle" instead of custom? Why is this claim of religious groups in promoting rights imperfect? (para. 7)
6. In paragraph 8, Mill says that there is "no recognized principle by which the propriety or impropriety of government interference is customarily tested." In the next paragraph, Mill states the principle he wishes to promote. What is Mill's principle? (para. 9)
7. Mill states that he is not going to use reasons grounded in "abstract right" or natural rights philosophy. What reasons does he give for rejecting this philosophy and using only utilitarianism? Very importantly, Mill qualifies the type of utilitarianism he will accept. Given your knowledge of Mill's break with Bentham's utilitarianism, what is the importance of his statement that he will ground utility "on the permanent interests of man as a progressive being"? (para. 11)
8. What areas of human action are generally none of society's business? (para. 12)
9. What is the difference Mill sees between his own utilitarian philosophy and the ancients' political philosophy? (para. 14)

Chapter II: Of the Liberty of Thought and Discussion   At the end of the previous chapter, Mill says that he will break his argument down and first deal with the liberty of thought. He states that it is impossible to detach this liberty from that of speaking and writing. Hence this chapter is a classic defense of freedom of speech and press, though Mill obviously thinks that many people do not know what to do with these freedoms.

1. Why is it important, *especially* in a democratic society, to consider the topic of freedom of thought, speech, and press? (para. 1)
2. Mill quickly turns to his arguments against censorship, either social or legal. His first argument is that the speech to be suppressed may possibly be true. Summarize the objections leveled against this argument and summarize Mill's answer. (para. 3–7)
3. Mill says that some want to censor ideas on the basis that they are not useful or salutary to society. That would seem to be a utilitarian argument of sorts. How does Mill relate a concern for discovering the truth with true usefulness to society? (para. 10)
4. Next, Mill turns to an argument that would be examined carefully by Christians. What impression do you get here of Mill's religious convictions? (para. 11–13)

5. Mill mentions Socrates, Christ (not by name but as the "the event which took place on Calvary," and Marcus Aurelius ("Marcus Antoninus" is Marcus Aurelius). What is his general point? (para. 12–14)

6. Mill brings up an argument by a Dr. Johnson that persecution (including censorship) is an "ordeal through which truth ought to pass . . ." What are Dr. Johnson's reasons, and what is Mill's response? (para. 15–17)

7. Describe how people with socially unacceptable religious beliefs and nonbelievers were persecuted in Mill's time. Why is "social intolerance" especially harmful? (para. 18–20)

8. Mill now turns to the "second division of the argument" which is to assume that all customary opinions are true and to argue why a diversity of opinions is nonetheless valuable to society. What is the key to a "living" truth as opposed to one that has stagnated? (para. 22–23)

9. What is Mill's answer to the objection that the general public cannot really gain from a free and open discussion of all ideas? (para. 24–25)

10. How does a creed decline into a dead series of phrases, according to Mill? Do you find this argument convincing based on your experience with religious, moral, or political creeds? (para. 27–30)

11. In what way does Mill praise Socratic philosophy as better than most of the thought of his own time? (para. 32)

12. Next, Mill turns to "one of the principal causes which make diversity of opinion advantageous," that is, when "the conflicting doctrines, instead of being one true and the other false, share the truth between them . . ." Do you think he is correct in asserting that this is a more common situation than an opinion that is wholly true or false. (para. 33)

13. What credit does Mill give to Rousseau? (para. 34)

14. Why is it beneficial to have at least two parties—a party of stability and a party of reform—competing for power in government? Is Mill's reasoning true today for the competition between the Republican and Democrat parties? (para. 35)

15. Mill deals with the objection that, at least with Christianity, a truth can be found that is not mixed with errors. What is Mill's response? Would this response have helped or hurt Mill's case with more orthodox Christians? (para. 36–38)

16. Mill quickly recapitulates his argument. Then he turns to those people who say that all ideas should be discussed but only in moderation, or without extremism. What is the problem with this seemingly civilized proposal? (para. 43)

Chapter III: Of Individuality, As One of the Elements of Well-Being
Here Mill turns from freedom of thought to freedom of action—whether "men should be free to act upon their opinions . . ." Mill explores both the intrinsic and the utilitarian reasons for promoting individualism as much as

possible. This chapter is a good example of where Mill differed with Bentham and his father on the worth of human development for its own sake, and on areas not easily understood by reason.

1. Very quickly, Mill states the limits of individualism both in expressing opinions and in actions. When can society or government legitimately intervene and stop or punish a person? (para. 1)
2. What kind of person does Mill deem to be a true individual? (para. 2–4)
3. Mill takes another excursion into history in discussing "a time when the element of spontaneity and individuality was in excess . . ." To what time do you think he is referring, and how does that time differ from Mill's own? (para. 6)
4. Next, Mill addresses those who do not want liberty for themselves, attempting to give them reasons why they should allow others to have it. In this connection, he first discusses the role "genius" plays in human progress. What is this role? Would this argument convince those whom he is addressing? (para. 11–12)
5. What are the dangers of the "crowd" or conformism, and what are the benefits of eccentricity? (para. 13–14)
6. Mill describes the social standard of his times this way: "to desire nothing strongly." How does he characterize England under this social standard? What risks is his country taking by upholding this standard? (para. 15–17)
7. What has so far saved Europe from becoming another China, entrenched in custom? Why does Mill fear for Europe nonetheless? (para. 18–19)

Chapter IV: Of the Limits to the Authority of Society Over the Individual   Here Mill delves more deeply into the limits that should be placed on government in the control of individual actions. He makes a useful distinction between being punished by the opinion of others and being punished by government. His question is, "Where does the authority of society begin?"

1. What is Mill's initial answer to the question above and how does he refine it? (para. 2–3)
2. Why is compulsion in education acceptable for instilling the social virtues? (para. 4)
3. Does Mill condemn those who would give advice and try to persuade others whom they think are acting inappropriately? Why or why not? (para. 5)
4. What distinction is Mill trying to make in paragraph 7, and why is it important?
5. How does Mill deal with the objection that there are "private" acts which nonetheless injure others, such as when drinking leads to indebtedness, accidents, or crime? (para. 8–11)

6. Mill says that the strongest argument against public interference in private activities "is that when it does interfere, the odds are that it interferes wrongly, and in the wrong place." (para. 12) He then goes on to give examples of the Muslims (the "Mussulmans"), the Spanish Catholics, the Puritans, fashions in the United States, labor unions or guilds, prohibitions against liquor in "nearly half the United States," "Sabbatarian legislation" (government-ordered shutdown of all businesses, and so on, on Sunday), and laws against the Mormon practice of polygamy. Taking each of these in turn, explain briefly the circumstances and the point of the example. (para. 13–21)

Chapter V: Applications   After summarizing the "maxims" that he has developed in this essay, Mill uses this concluding chapter to refine further his primary principle. He begins by explaining that just because damage to the interests of others can justify the interference of society and government, it does not follow that every time the interests of others are damaged government *should* interfere. It is important to explore the limits of government action even more carefully in order to avoid the possibility of tyranny.

1. Mill's first example of such an area is competition for positions in an "overcrowded profession." (para. 3) Can you understand why some damage to other individuals must be allowed in this area?
2. Mill quickly moves into a discussion of trade, in particular how free of government regulation should it be? What types of restrictions would Mill find acceptable on the sale of poisons or guns, and upon what principle are these restrictions based? (para. 4–5)
3. Drunkenness and idleness were often considered moral sins in Mill's time. What should be the principle of government intrusion into these areas? What do you think of Mill's assertion that it is all right for government to prohibit "offenses against decency"? (para. 6–7)
4. How does Mill defend the freedom to advise or encourage others to do what is considered wrong by society? What is Mill's opinion about outlawing gambling houses? What do you make of his relative silence on "pimping" (trafficking in prostitutes)? (para. 8)
5. How does Mill end up approving higher taxes on alcohol? (para. 9)
6. How does Mill argue against the right to sell oneself as a slave? (para. 11)
7. Mill mentions "third parties" brought into existence through marriage (children). How does (or should) the advent of children change the freedom of both parties in the marriage to get a divorce? (para. 11)
8. What is Mill's position on the freedom of the husband and father to rule over his wife and children? (para. 12)
9. What is society's interest in making sure children receive a proper education? Why does Mill argue for maintaining a diversity of educational

experiences? Is there any reason to think that Mill's scheme for requiring annual public examinations of all children will unduly impose on religious believers a particular way of thinking about religion? (para. 13–14)

10. How could we see Mill's approval of laws restricting marriage to those who can show they have the means to care for children as in agreement with his primary principles of individualism and governmental noninterference? (para. 15)

11. Finally, Mill turns to a "class of questions" having to do with how much government should help others. He lists several objections to this tendency of government. What are his objections? How do you think the government of the United States would measure up to this analysis? (para. 16–20)

12. Explain his praise of Americans in his own time. Would he still praise them for the same abilities today? (para. 21)

13. In paragraph 22, Mill argues for the "greatest dissemination of power consistent with efficiency; but the greatest possible centralization of information, and diffusion of it from the center." What is this design of government attempting to prevent. How could this design be perverted? (para. 22)

GUIDE TO *THE SUBJECTION OF WOMEN*

This essay is divided by Mill into four chapters. It is highly recommended that you number the paragraphs in each chapter so that you will be able to use the questions below more effectively.

Chapter One In this chapter Mill states the problem of inequality and discusses his belief that such inequality is a result of socialization and prejudice, not nature.

1. What is the object of this essay?
2. Why does Mill think it is necessary to answer all the objections to female equality that have ever been stated "by those who take the other side of the question"? (para. 3)
3. How does Mill deal with the fact that the "custom" has always been to treat women as not the equals of men? (para. 4)
4. How does Mill explain how women's "bondage" to men originally came about? (para. 5) How does Mill associate this bondage with actual slavery?
5. Mill admits that women are the physically weaker sex. Why does this not justify them being treated unequally? (para. 7)
6. How does Mill characterize the motivations of men when dominating women? Why is this domination the last of its kind to go? (para. 8)

7. How does Mill answer the argument that male domination of women is natural and therefore not unjust? (para. 9)

8. How does Mill answer the point that women voluntarily accept the rule of men? (para. 10)

9. How does Mill explain the fact that in his time, the main aim of most women was to attract an eligible man? (para. 11)

10. In paragraph 13, how does Mill defend the principle of individual freedom of choice?

11. From your reading of paragraph 15, what kinds of laws concerning women did Mill think unfair and disadvantageous?

12. How does Mill tie women's freedom together with utilitarian interests in prosperity for all in paragraph 17?

13. How much of a person's character does Mill attribute to nature and how much to the person's environment (the influence of her society, her class, and so forth)? (para. 20)

14. According to Mill, how much do men really know about women? Explain. (para. 21)

15. What legislative measures is Mill proposing in paragraph 24 to emancipate women, and why does he think such measures will be good enough? Can you think of an argument by which someone might conclude that women need more help to be truly emancipated?

Chapter Two   Here Mill delves further into women's situation before the law and in society. He discusses what even he still considers to be the legitimate restrictions placed upon women by their special role as child-bearers and rearers.

1. What is the general subject of this chapter? (para. 1)

2. How does Mill characterize the laws concerning women in ancient times? How does he characterize such laws in his own times? Be specific. (para. 1)

3. Why do many men not take advantage of the extent to which the laws allow them to tyrannize over their wives? (para. 2)

4. Toward the end of paragraph 4, Mill discusses a strategy women employ to retaliate against abusive husbands. What is this weapon and why is it not good enough?

5. In what way can a wife have too much power over her husband, even though she is not free? Why is this type of power undesirable? (para. 5)

6. What is the ideal balance of power between a husband and a wife? (para. 8)

7. Do you think that Mill concedes too much to the superiority of the eldest and the provider in paragraph 9, or is he largely correct?

8. How does Mill deal with the chivalrous idea of women as morally better than men in paragraph 10?

9. How does paragraph 12 enhance your understanding of Mill's position on the ideal marriage and family?

10. How does Mill answer the biblical injunction for wives to obey their husbands? (para. 14)
11. How should property be dealt with in marriage? (para. 15)
12. Explain why Mill thinks requiring women to work once married and with children would be a further imposition upon them. How could Mill's discussion of the work involved in child-rearing and household management be employed in an analysis of today's marriages? (para. 16)
13. In paragraph 16, Mill states that "Like a man when he chooses a profession, so, when a woman marries, it may in general be understood that she makes choice of the management of a household . . ." Is this statement consistent with Mill's general teaching on female equality? Why might it seem reasonable to him but be a more controversial statement today?

Chapter Three   In this chapter, Mill addresses many of the stereotypes of women in his times, explaining why they exist and uses these very stereotypes to make his case for emancipating women.

1. In paragraph 1 of this chapter, Mill uses an argument that echoes Plato's in *The Republic*. He argues that even if it is true that, on average, women are less gifted than men, that is no reason to exclude them from various offices and jobs. Provide Mill's explanation. Why do you think Mill feels the need to use this argument?
2. In the same paragraph, how does Mill tie the concept of justice to his utilitarian arguments on women's potential contributions to society?
3. What argument does Mill use for women's suffrage? (para. 2)
4. In paragraphs 4, 5, and 6, how does Mill disagree with the argument that women are not capable of greatness?
5. In paragraphs 7, 8, and 9, Mill discusses some commonly observed attributes of women, probably produced by their peculiar socialization. What are these attributes, and how does Mill make use of them to build his argument?
6. How does Mill turn the stereotype of women as more nervous into a building block of his argument for their emancipation? (para. 11)
7. In paragraph 12, Mill seems to acknowledge that women (at least at the moment) have less intellectual concentration; but how does he turn even this acknowledgment into an advantage for women?
8. In Mill's day there was a line of scientific inquiry that attempted to explain perceived inequalities among races and between the sexes on purely biological differences. How does Mill deal with the observation that men's brains are bigger than women's? (para. 13)
9. How does Mill deal with the statement that "no production in philosophy, science, or art, entitled to the first rank, has been the work of a woman." (para. 16–22)

10. Mill next discusses reasons for women's inferior level of accomplishments related to their current position as managers of the household. List those that would apply only to the upper class. (para. 23)

11. Mill challenges the mixed opinions on women's morality. Explain his argument against these stereotypes. (para. 25–26)

12. Why does Mill call men to help emancipate women? (para. 27)

Chapter Four   In this final chapter, Mill speculates on what advantages society might have from the "changes proposed in our customs and institutions." In this chapter, Mill's utilitarianism is clearly visible. Mill understands that, in a male-dominated society, unless men open their minds to change, it will not likely occur. He also thinks that people generally will only change their minds if it is in their self-interest to do so. Here we find the reasons why men should abandon their prejudices and adopt Mill's point of view.

1. Mill explains how men are socialized from an early age to think that they are superior to women. What benefit would men obtain by changing this socialization? (para. 4–5)

2. In paragraphs 6 and 7, Mill discusses a "second benefit to be expected" from emancipating women—"doubling the mass of mental faculties." At the end of paragraph 7, Mill mentions that freeing women to think of themselves as equals would lead to the "enlargement of the range of their moral sentiments." What prejudice against women, which he has discussed earlier, is he targeting with this statement?

3. Mill attributes the male attitude of chivalry to the influence of women in times past. Explain how women's influence led to chivalry. What ought to replace chivalry, and why? (para. 8–9)

4. Why would Mill like to see women achieve a greater degree of "disinterestedness in the general conduct of life . . ."? (para. 10)

5. Mill argues against the type of charity or philanthropy practiced by women in his time. Why? (para. 11)

6. Explain Mill's statement in paragraph 13 that in his times, "the wife is the auxiliary of common public opinion." Why is this not desirable? (See also para. 14)

7. Describe Mill's ideal marital relationship, based upon your reading of paragraphs 16, 17, and 18. Do you think this relationship would sound appealing to the men whom Mill is trying to reach?

8. What is the "most direct benefit of all" of women's emancipation? (para. 19)

9. In paragraph 21, Mill states that women who want to enter political life, to be members of parliament, for instance, will no doubt either not be married or will be beyond child-rearing age. Why do you think Mill says that this is "common sense"?

10. Assess Mill's entire argument. What are its strengths and weaknesses?

BIBLIOGRAPHY

Wendy Donner, *The Liberal Self: John Stuart Mill's Moral and Political Philosophy,* Ithaca, NY, Cornell University Press, 1991.

Peter J. Glassman, *J.S. Mill: The Evolution of a Genious,* Gainesville: University of Florida Press, 1985.

Joseph Hamburger, *Intellectuals in Politics: John Stuart Mill and the Philosophic Radicals,* New Haven: Yale University Press, 1965.

Michael Laine, ed., *A Cultivated Mind: Essays on J.S. Mill Presented to John M. Robson,* Toronto: University of Toronto Press, 1991.

Bruce Mazlish, *James and John Stuart Mill: Father and Son in the Nineteenth Century,* New York: Basic Books, 1975.

Stephen Priest, *The British Empiricists: Hobbes to Ayer,* London: Penguin Books, 1990.

HISTORY AS PROGRESS

The philosophers we will examine in this section look at history as a story of progress, an upward movement toward a time when people all around the world will live better than they ever have before. These thinkers saw human history as having a beginning, a lengthy middle, and an end. The end they saw was not the end of events, but the end of conflict between different political and economic systems. The middle part of history was full of struggles leading toward this eventual goal. For them, it was humanity itself who drove the struggles, and it was the human condition itself that was leading us toward that happy end.

Kant saw history heading toward a general worldwide liberalism combined with a free trade world economy—an end that he believed would yield "perpetual peace." Marx and Engels saw the end as worldwide communism and, again, lasting peace. These thinkers differ from all our previous philosophers in at least one essential respect—the turning away from the impact of the individual as a source of sociopolitical change to look, instead, at an inevitable course of human history that leads to permanent change.

The philosophers we have discussed thus far put forward arguments that addressed and sought to change human behavior. Through Plato, Socrates argued for people to adjust their souls and allow the rule of reason and pursuit of justice. Hobbes wanted people to see the importance of stable government and reject revolution, which threw society into chaos and bloodshed. Locke urged people to embrace their natural rights and overthrow governments that denied these rights.

Kant and Marx are the first philosophers we have studied who would say they are *not* trying to change people in any way. Instead, they would characterize their work as a task of describing the past and predicting the future. They believed that human beings as a species are more or less programmed to behave in certain ways and that this programming, in relation to situational factors and material forces beyond individual control, has largely determined human history. Each philosopher believes his version of the end of world history is inevitable—a simple prediction of what will happen in the future based on the ineluctable pattern they see in the past.

KANT (1724–1804)

BACKGROUND

At first glance, Kant's life was rather unexceptional. Some writers have even tried to argue that Kant's life is interesting because of the surprising extent to which it is uninteresting! Kant was a brilliant man with humble origins and a rather conventional lifestyle, but it would be a mistake to think of his story or his personality as boring.

Kant was born in Königsberg, in Eastern Prussia (then part of Branden-burg Prussia but now Kaliningrad, Russia) in 1724, during the century of the Enlightenment. He was the son of a harness maker. His first name, Immanuel, comes from the Bible and means "God is with us." His parents practiced Pietism, a religious movement within Protestantism which began in the late seventeenth century and was particularly strong in Königsberg. In Germany, the Pietists split with the Lutheran Church over what they saw as an empha-sis on ritual over spiritual substance, a focus on intellectual understanding of God and church doctrine as opposed to the spiritual nature of religious con-version and the change in living it could bring.

Many Enlightenment thinkers, including Kant, were influenced by this trend in Christianity. However, even though Pietists rejected the perceived rigidity of liturgy in their religious observances, the young Kant disliked the formal church-going forced on him during his college days at the Collegium Fredericianum, a Pietist school (1732–1740). After that, he rarely went to church except when social obligations forced him to do so. Kant did, however, believe in God. In some sense, Kant may have remained a Pietist, part of a movement which took on many expressions, not the least of which was indi-vidual spiritual life divorced from church participation. Kant had little patience with formal religious practices.

At college, Kant studied the classics of philosophy and literature. Then, in 1740, Kant entered the University of Königsberg. It is not clear exactly what course of study he took up, but we know that he studied medicine, physics, and mathematics. His mother had died when he was thirteen, and his father could not afford to pay for Kant's schooling by himself, so Kant worked as a tutor and received help from relatives. His first treatise, written while he was still in school was on physics: *Thoughts on the Correct Evaluation of Life Forces.* It might help some students, worried about their own studies, to hear what happened to Kant's first work. Kant sent copies of it to three prominent scholars. They did not acknowledge receiving it because there was no reason to do so. Another philosopher, d'Alembert, had dealt with the problem six years earlier, but Kant obviously did not know that. His first major effort, then, did not contribute to the advancement of knowledge and revealed his lack of awareness about what was occurring in the larger scholarly community.[1]

In 1747, Kant quit his studies even though he was close to the end, because he could no longer afford the tuition. He became a private tutor to various families in East Prussia. There, he may have had a relationship with one of the women whose children he tutored, Countess Keyserling, who painted the first portrait of Kant. However, nothing resulted from this relationship.[2]

In 1755, a friend helped Kant return to the university and complete what we would now call his doctoral degree. For the next fifteen years, Kant would work at the same university as a lecturer. This post paid less (he received the students' tuition), was much less secure, and had considerably less status than that of professor. He lectured on many fields, including science, mathematics, and philosophy. His early works were on physics and astronomy, including speculation about life on other planets, not on moral philosophy. During this time, he turned down two offers for more secure and prestigious positions as chair of poetry at the University of Königsberg and the University of Jena. This shows, perhaps, how driven Kant already was by his own agenda. He would not be lured by comfort, security, or status into a career path that would take him away from his central interests. Finally in 1770, the University of Königsberg hired Kant as a professor of logic and metaphysics, a career that was to last twenty-seven years.

Kant never married. He never traveled far from Königsberg. Yet again, it would be wrong to say that, apart from his philosophical work, his life was uninteresting. While he had no family, he did have many friends whom he saw regularly. Kant built regular interaction with his friends into his day. His routine is now legendary. He would rise early and begin to think about his agenda for the day. He would then spend an hour or two preparing for his lectures. He lectured in the morning, then wrote until lunch time. Lunch was always an

---

[1]Arsenij Gulyga, *Immanuel Kant: His Life and Thought,* translated by Marijan Despalatovic, Boston: Birkhauser, 1987, p. 12.

[2]Ibid., p. 14.

extensive period of time spent conversing with friends and colleagues. It would be wrong to think that this was mere relaxation or entertainment—Kant was continuing his philosophical activity in a different venue, enjoying his companions' friendship and discussing ideas at the same time. Kant's afternoon and evening were devoted to walking, reading, and contemplation. This cycle was repeated more or less every day and produced an extraordinary degree of scholarly work that resulted, among other things, in these major philosophical tomes: *The Critique of Pure Reason* (1781); *The Critique of Practical Reason* (1788); and *The Critique of Judgment* (1790). There is certainly something to be said for living a well-organized life.

Kant's life was not without some political controversy. As one might imagine, this controversy was in the area of religion. In 1792–1793, his work *Religion within the Bounds of Reason Alone* was submitted to governmental censors, and part of it was found to be too much of an attack on Christian orthodoxy. It was published despite their objections. In 1794, Frederick William II prohibited Kant from ever writing on this topic, and threatened him with unspecified penalties. Kant actually complied with this order, at least until the king died five years later. Meanwhile, he turned his attention to politics. The French Revolution (1789) had spawned wars affecting most of Europe. Whether and how humanity could attain lasting peace occupied many of the great minds of the time. In 1795, Kant published *Perpetual Peace*. In this work he sets out a scenario for the abolition of war on the basis of inevitable political and economic change. He turned back to moral philosophy with *The Metaphysics of Morals* in 1797. Toward the end of his life Kant published *The Conflict of the Faculties,* a summary of his views on the relationship between philosophy and theology. This was the last significant work Kant wrote. His intellectual activity was affected by his growing weakness, and his productivity ceased as he grew older. Kant died in 1804.

UNDERSTANDING KANT

Unlike Marx and Engels, who share to a certain extent Kant's view of human history as driven by forces beyond any individual's control, Kant was an Enlightenment thinker. He lived during the latter part of the era, during which the term was in general use in Europe, and he shared, in a general way, certain social, political, and religious views with the other philosophers of his time.

Kant believed in the Enlightenment, which means he thought society was being irrevocably affected by the spread of knowledge. Scientific knowledge was growing among the intellectual classes of Europe. Kant, and other Enlightenment philosophers, thought there was almost no stopping a trend toward a more republican[3] form of government and a diminishment of auto-cratic hereditary authority.

Kant viewed religion through the lens of the Enlightenment. Although he was not derisive but indeed respectful toward much religious belief, he also thought that religious institutions served as regressive forces in society. Religious belief should not be superstitious, and religious institutions should not be used to legitimize the old power structure. Kant thought that the clergy should facilitate, not impede, progress.

Kant's political works were inspired by specific events of his time as well as general social trends. The French Revolution of 1789 created a French government and army that spread the revolution, and French power, to the rest of Europe. Kant's Prussia, under the leadership of Friedrich Wilhelm II, at first joined with other countries to resist the French onslaught. But Friedrich Wilhelm, although he opposed the spread of French power, did not prevent the spread of Enlightenment thought and allowed it in Prussian universities like Kant's University at Königsberg. Kant disapproved of the excesses of the French Revolution, including the execution of the French king and queen and the subsequent strategy of the French regime to spread revolution by force. However, Kant sympathized with the reasons behind the revolution: the desire to achieve equality among and true representation for citizens. Although he had already aired his views on the Enlightenment of the people and the political process in earlier essays, the treaty between Prussia and France made it politically possible for Kant to publish a vision of universal Enlightenment on a grander scale, *Perpetual Peace*.

In a departure from his usual practice, Kant wrote *Perpetual Peace* for a more popular audience. Indeed the tract might more properly be called a political pamphlet instead of a philosophical treatise. The first edition sold out quickly, and within a year the essay came out in a second edition, translated into English and French. Interpretations varied widely (and still do). Some saw it as a sort of blueprint for world government or an international treaty of peace. Others saw it simply as a moral ideal with little relevance for real life. Still others saw it as a plea for immediate revolutionary action. A quick reading of Kant's essay (which is what most of his readers would have given it) will explain why confusion abounded. Kant was a philosophical genius, but one who had written almost exclusively for an academic audience his entire life. In *Perpetual Peace* he tried to communicate with nonacademics by using the

---

[3]Kant identifies "republican" government with one that provides freedom for its citizens and operates on the basis of their equality, and in which there is a common source of legislation for all. Republican government supposes representation of citizens and thus citizens' consent through their representatives of, among other things, taxation and war. See *Perpetual Peace*, Second Section, First Definitive Article of Perpetual Peace.

form of a treaty or contract among nations—even though he was describing not so much a treaty as underlying developments in national and international politics and economics. Only by not taking the contractual form too literally can the reader begin to glimpse Kant's true meaning.

Kant's message is well worth trying to understand. Indeed, three centuries later, the ideas that Kant puts forth in these political essays seem to some scholars of international relations to be coming true. It will help to review a few concepts of Kant's which contemporary scholars are finding more and more valuable for interpreting events today.

Cosmopolitanism

When Kant uses the word "cosmopolitan" he is not referring to a state of mind. Today, if we use the word at all, we may use it to mean someone who is well traveled, who knows multiple languages, and who appreciates many different cultures. Kant's meaning bears some resemblance to our current usage. For Kant, being cosmopolitan means feeling at home, indeed being at home, anywhere in the world. But the reason for being at home in the world need not be a familiarity with vastly different ways of life. Indeed, one is more at home in a world that very much resembles one's homeland. Kant thought that the world would become more homogeneous as time went by, that governments and economies would resemble each other more and more, so that the laws and practices of foreign countries would be easily recognizable to each others' citizens. At a certain point in the evolution of nations, being cosmopolitan will be easy—it will be as simple as understanding the laws of your own country.

Enlightenment

The concept of Enlightenment, as discussed, is both an intellectual and a popular movement. As an intellectual, Kant is enlightened, but when Kant uses the word "enlightened" he may very well be referring to the average citizen who can become enlightened not in the sense of becoming as learned as Kant, but through understanding his state of equality and natural rights, demanding representation, and rejecting superstition.

Natural Laws

After reading Hobbes and Locke, it may seem fairly clear what the term "natural rights" means. Yet, when we get to Kant, the term undergoes a transformation. In "Idea for a Universal History with a Cosmopolitan Intent," Kant makes natural laws a very important part of his theory. In the first sentence he claims that human actions are "determined in conformity with universal natural laws." What Kant notices is that, although individual human beings have free will (they make choices constantly about what they will do next, and these choices appear to be solely up to them), when you observe the actions of the human race as a whole, free will appears to conform to rules or patterns of behavior. From this larger point of view it would seem that humanity does not have free will but is *determined by human nature, which restricts our choices.* An example of a law of nature or rule of behavior would be that people act mainly in their own self-interests, and that they define that interest in terms of ensuring their security and promoting their prosperity. There are always a few individuals who do not fit this picture. Saints, for example, give their lives for love of God or neighbor; but these few individuals do not disturb the general direction of human behavior.

Philosophers such as Hobbes and Locke agreed that the laws of nature were based upon rational self-interest, but the key for them was that people could understand these laws consciously and act upon them to build a more rational social contract. Thus, for Hobbes or Locke, people could begin to consciously direct their own destiny in a more rational manner. Kant's natural laws are less "rational rules" than they are irrational instincts. They exist and guide human actions even if no one but Kant ever thinks about them or understands their overall effect on the human condition. They are much more akin to the self-interest that guides Adam Smith's "invisible hand" in the economy than Hobbes's or Locke's laws of nature. Kant is saying that regardless of whether anyone but he ever grasps these laws of human nature, they propel the human race toward certain ends. Individual self-interest will ultimately mean human progress in economics, politics, science. This progress will have certain results on the international scene. Eventually we will have world peace, even if no one intended such a result but only intended to pursue their own self-interest. Kant's natural laws are, for want of a better word, deterministic. They propel us forward without our consent. However, at times Kant hedges on this determinism and sounds as though he thinks achieving perpetual peace requires a push.

Scholars

When Kant uses the word "scholars" he may indeed be writing about people like himself, but he may also be using the word more broadly. For purposes of spreading the Enlightenment, a scholar is not necessarily someone with a doctoral degree, but it is someone who is nonetheless studious. A scholar in this broader sense is a citizen who pays attention to politics, who has educated himself well enough on matters of law and current events to speak and write informatively at public events and in popular newspapers and journals. Such scholars can and should carry on their public debates freely; they have an important role to play in the ongoing development of enlightenment in the general population.

CAREFUL READING

Kant is notorious for his difficult writing, which even in English translation sometimes seems to require further translation.[4] Read slowly, make marginal notes, and of course use the guides in this chapter to help you extract Kant's argument. Kant is not a writer who can be skimmed or whose writing in any particular part can be understood if one simply plows ahead. Perhaps more than any of our other philosophers, Kant is one who requires reading more than once. Fortunately, our featured essays are short and you can easily read them twice, even three times. Below are analyses of sections from two of the essays featured in this chapter.

Unsocial Sociability

In the fourth thesis of "Idea for a Universal History with a Cosmopolitan Intent," Kant uses the terms "antagonism" and "unsocial sociability" (or similar words, depending on the translation) to describe human nature. This idea—that human beings are social and unsocial at the same time—can unnerve readers. Below is a passage that appears toward the end of the fourth thesis which sums up Kant's use of these terms.

> Thus, thanks be to nature for the incompatibility, for the distasteful, competitive vanity, for the insatiable desire to possess and also to rule. Without them, all of humanity's excellent natural capacities would have lain eternally dormant. Man wills concord; but nature better knows what is good for the species: she wills discord. He wills to live comfortably and pleasantly; but nature wills that he should be plunged from laziness and inactive comfort into work and hardship, so that he will in turn seek by his own cleverness to pull himself up from them. The natural impulse to do this—the sources of unsociability and of thoroughgoing resistance that give rise to so much evil but also drive men anew toward further exertions of their powers, consequently to diverse development of their natural capacities—indicates the design of a wise creator, not the hand of a malicious spirit who fiddled with the creator's masterful arrangement or enviously spoiled it. (p. 32)

This passage is particularly rich. It is a passage to be mined for all its worth, which is a technique well worth learning. Although your primary objective is, of course, to understand Kant's main point in this particular thesis, it does not hurt to collect all the information you can. In the first part of this passage, Kant does indeed clarify what he means by "unsociable sociability," though he does it by personifying nature, which may at first throw the reader off a little. Kant says "thanks be to nature," almost elevating nature to the level

---

[4]All quotations from Kant's essays in this chapter are from Immanuel Kant, *Perpetual Peace and Other Essays,* translated by Ted Humphrey, Indianapolis, Indiana: Hackett Publishing Company, 1983.

of God. But he thanks nature for all those things we often consider negative features of humanity—incompatibility, vanity, desire for things and power (notice how it helps to "translate" what Kant says into simpler sentences). Without these supposedly negative qualities, humanity's excellent capacities would have "lain dormant," that is, they would never have come out. Ponder that for a moment: Without such negative qualities as vanity or pride and selfishness, our excellent qualities would not have been realized. This statement is characteristic of Kant, who wants to bring supposedly opposite ideas into harmony. How could negative qualities translate into positive qualities and outcomes? The next few sentences describe how. Kant personifies nature as a "she." Whereas man might will peace (that is, consciously want peace), she (man's nature or natural instinct) wills discord. Man wants to rest, but she makes him work hard to pull himself up to a better condition.

Kant then addresses the moral objection: How can he characterize as good those human qualities such as vanity and selfishness that lead to competition and even war? His answer is to acknowledge that they do cause much evil, but they also drive human beings to achieve more than they otherwise would, to develop their natural capacities as much as possible. Without mankind's selfishness and competitiveness, human beings would never have begun the long trek toward civilization, and then toward increasingly better standards of living.

While Kant is making his point about the beneficial affects of mankind's competitiveness, he slips in an indication of his view of God and God's relationship to the world and to mankind in particular. We have already seen that he gives thanks to nature for human nature, which is like thanking nature for itself. He personifies nature, referring to it as a "she." Nature has a will of its own. Immediately we can see that his religious views are unconventional, because he does not tackle the question in the conventional way. Kant does not refer to mankind's negative qualities as "sin." He does not speak of the need for redemption in any sort of Christian or Judeo-Christian scenario. Instead what Christians would call "sin," Kant calls "nature," which would seem to indicate that it is so much a part of what human beings are that it is beyond our ability to remedy. The astute reader might ask: How can human beings sin if they are only acting according to their nature? At the end of the passage, Kant addresses the question of God quite openly. Man's pride and selfishness cause much evil, and yet they indicate "the design of a wise creator, not the hand of a malicious spirit who fiddled with the creator's masterful arrangement . . ." Here is a direct challenge to tradition. What Christians say is sin is actually a part of the creator's master plan, according to Kant. Kant disregards the traditional account of sin in favor of his own view of God as creating, through a process akin to evolution, the evolution of the human species through continual competition, and as we will see, even war. In this treatment of religious questions, Kant reveals just how much he was a philosopher of the

Enlightenment. This insight, and the more obvious point about the positive affects of competition, is well worth remembering.

Right versus Rights

In *Perpetual Peace*, Kant uses the term "right" in at least two different ways. In the first way, "right" means something like good, or what is just. In the second way, "right" comes close to the meaning we give today to rights, as in the right to self-defense or the right to a trial by a jury of one's peers. The trick is sorting out which way Kant is using the term in any given passage. Below is an example of the first, and less familiar, use of "right."

> The homage that every nation pays (at least in words) to the concept of right proves, nonetheless, that there is in man a still greater, though presently dormant, moral aptitude to master the evil principle in himself (a principle he cannot deny) and to hope that others will also overcome it. For otherwise the word *right* would never leave the mouths of those nations that want to make war on one another, unless it were used mockingly, as when that Gallic prince declared, "Nature has given the strong the prerogative of making the weak obey them."
>
> Nations can press for their rights only by waging war and never in a trial before an independent tribunal, but war and its favorable consequence, victory, cannot determine the right. (Second Definitive Article, p. 116)

Kant is clearly using "right" in the first part of this passage in the sense of what is just. Thus it may help to substitute, initially, the word *justice* for *right* here. Prior to this passage, Kant makes the point that previous scholars such as Grotius, Pufendorf, and Vattel have formulated codes of international law or justice which have not been adopted and instead have been used as justifications for war. This is a depressing thought, but then Kant, in a characteristic maneuver, turns this negative observation into a positive one. Kant makes the point that Grotius himself made: the fact that nations nonetheless "pay homage" (or what we might call lip service) to what is right means something. Why do nations pay homage to what is right or just? Kant is once again asking us to think deeply about the supposedly contrary human behavior. References to international law or universal justice, even when used as rhetoric to justify war, are not totally without meaning. Kant reasons that if morality had no meaning, no one would feel the need to justify his or her actions with reference to what is right or good. They would simply proclaim, as did Callicles in Plato's *Gorgias*, that it is a natural law that the strong rule the weak (hence Kant relates a similar, fitting quote from a "Gallic prince"). Kant concludes that the use of the concept of right, even in a rhetorical attempt to justify injustice, is proof of mankind's latent aptitude for morality. As you will see upon reading *Perpetual Peace* in its entirety, Kant does not think this moral aptitude will really be exercised much until at or near the culmination of humanity's political development.

In the final sentence of this selection, Kant uses both meanings of the word *right*. The only way to decipher the meaning of this sentence is to try out both meanings of *right* in your mind and see what makes the most sense at each point. In the first part of the sentence, Kant uses the term "rights." Nations can "press for their rights" through war, he says. This sounds more like "claims" than "justice," doesn't it? But while nations can pursue their rights or claims through war, war cannot determine "right." Does this not have to mean that war cannot by itself determine what is just? Kant is simply repeating the previous sentiment that the use of force (the strong's "right" over the weak) overrides what is right or good, but it is not the measure of what is right or good. Thus, war cannot ever settle the moral question about what is just.

Kant makes the point here and elsewhere that the peace which comes from the settlement of a war is more like a truce or a temporary cessation of hostilities instead of a true peace. True peace must coincide with true justice or right, which cannot be imposed by a victor. It would seem that peace is not determined by whomever is in power but by a more universal and eternal standard discoverable by reason, not by violence.

GUIDE TO "AN ANSWER TO THE QUESTION: WHAT IS ENLIGHTENMENT?" (1784)

Here, as in all of his works, Kant is trying to be systematic. He wants to be sure he makes all of his points in logical order, but today's readers are unaccustomed to his approach. The best way to read Kant is one paragraph at a time. Number the paragraphs in your book to make answering the questions below easier. Make sure you have digested the meaning of one paragraph before moving on to the next. In addition to answering the questions below, it would help to summarize in your notes the central point of each paragraph before moving on.

Paragraph 1

How does Kant define immaturity? What is he saying about what holds most of the people of his time back from their true potential?

Paragraphs 2 and 3

From what you have read in these two paragraphs alone, what do you think Kant means by "enlightenment"?

Paragraph 4

What does Kant think makes enlightenment almost inevitable? Why is the Enlightenment likely to only develop slowly?

Paragraph 5

1. What kind of freedom must a scholar have in order for the Enlightenment to advance?
2. What kind of freedom is not necessary for the Enlightenment, and even harmful to society?
3. Summarize the distinction Kant makes between the public use of reason and the private use of reason.
4. Can you tell what Kant hopes will be the role of religious leaders in bringing about the Enlightenment?

Paragraph 6

Where does the monarch's law-giving authority originate, according to Kant? (Remember that the old way of understanding the monarch's authority was that it came from God. Now, Kant is saying our *rights* come from God, and one of our rights is to govern ourselves.)

Paragraph 7

What is Kant's answer to the question of whether people in his time lived in an enlightened age?

Paragraph 8

What does Kant want princes and monarchs to do regarding religion?

Paragraph 9

Why does Kant say he has focused so much of his attention in this essay on matters of religion?

Paragraph 10

Why does Kant value free thinking so much? What are the political consequences of free thinking?

GUIDE TO "IDEA FOR A UNIVERSAL HISTORY WITH A COSMOPOLITAN INTENT" (1784)

This essay is divided into nine theses or mini-arguments which form part of a larger idea that Kant is trying to develop. He attempts to show how, despite our ignorance of its aims and despite our selfish human nature, human history has been leading the human race in the direction of political freedom and world peace. This guide will be organized primarily around the theses, so there is no need to number paragraphs.

Introductory Remarks

1. In the first paragraph of this essay, what is Kant saying about whether human beings really have free will (the ability to make choices about what direction humanity will take)?
2. What is the difference between looking at individuals' actions and looking at humanity's behavior in the large (as a whole)?

First and Second Theses   In the first thesis, Kant says that all animals, indeed all of nature, seem designed to develop in certain predetermined ways. An acorn, if it survives, will become an oak tree. A human infant, if it survives, will become an adult human being.

Given this, in the second thesis, what is the difference he sees between man and other creatures (especially in the way the two develop toward completion)?

Third Thesis

How do people differ from the animals when it comes to caring for themselves?

Fourth Thesis

Why do humans alone develop society and morals?

Fifth Thesis

What is the greatest challenge or problem for the human species? Why do you think that Kant believes it is the greatest problem? (See also the beginning of the sixth thesis.)

Sixth Thesis

After reading this thesis, do you have an idea of what Kant thinks of human nature?

Seventh Thesis

1. What do you think Kant means by "law governed external relations among nations"? Why can't nations have perfect civil constitutions (with perfect freedom) until there is perfect peace among nations?
2. Many think that Kant would have supported a United Nations–type organization. But Kant is saying in the seventh thesis that there will naturally develop a "federation of nations." In other words, cooperation among nations will be at some point natural, and not a matter of tense and precarious agreements. In the meantime, Kant says we have alliances of nations that serve to make peace for a time. What do you

suppose he means when he refers to this less optimal state as having a "law of equilibrium"?

3. Why does Kant think we have not yet achieved true morality?

Eighth Thesis

1. Kant says that once in place, political or civil freedom is hard to infringe upon or destroy. Why?
2. What is that "universal cosmopolitan state" we are all headed toward as more and more nations enjoy civil freedom?

Ninth Thesis

In this thesis, Kant is justifying his own role. Why do you think he sees his role as predictor of the future as both possible and helpful?

GUIDE TO *PERPETUAL PEACE:* *A PHILOSOPHICAL SKETCH (1795)*

As discussed, the format of this essay was intended by Kant to help communicate to an audience of nonscholars. It resembles a treaty or contract among nations. Thus we have preliminary articles, definitive articles, and supplements, including a "secret article" such as might be in a treaty. The problem is Kant does not think that international peace can come about by simply agreeing to sign a treaty. Quite the contrary, he thinks many changes in the structure of governments, and even in the worldwide economy, are necessary before world peace is a possibility. At the point when these changes are complete, such an international agreement will be easy, and will not need to be in writing to be effective. If we understand that Kant is not really writing a treaty for nations to adopt, but is rather sketching a scenario under which peace will happen in the future, it will be easier to decipher his argument.[5]

To Perpetual Peace (Introductory Remarks)

What worry does Kant express in these opening remarks concerning his own political position upon publishing *Perpetual Peace?* What does he hope will save him?

First Section   In this first section, Kant suggests six "preliminary articles" of perpetual peace. Think of these not as items that warring and squabbling states must embrace to achieve peace. Instead, consider them as the immedi-

---

[5]This guide will not deal with Kant's appendices to *Perpetual Peace*, which are nonetheless instructive, especially on the relationship between politics and morality.

ate conditions of a peace that is well under way. It may even be fruitful to think of this first section as a description of the relations among nations already at or near perpetual peace.

First Preliminary Article   Right away, Kant hits us with a statement that begs a question. A peace treaty that tacitly or secretly reserves issues and will cause future wars is really no peace treaty at all, but a sort of truce.

> Can you imagine what conditions would have to exist among nations for none of them to hold back any issues or points of disagreement that might cause future conflicts?

Second Preliminary Article

> Here Kant must have in mind the partition of Poland, but also the many other agreements monarchs and leaders had made over the centuries to divide or carve up their weaker neighbors' territory. Kant clearly says this is wrong, because a nation is not simply the property of a sovereign. If a nation is not the property of a sovereign, how are we supposed to view it?

Third Preliminary Article

> 1. The United States, and most other nations in the world, have what Kant calls "standing armies" now, that is, armies that are always in existence and ready to fight. Why is it so difficult, in the world in which we live, to conceive of nations abolishing these armies?
> 2. Can you imagine circumstances under which nations could move to a system in which simply calling on citizens to defend their homeland if necessary would be good enough?

Fourth Preliminary Article

> Kant warns against the dangers to peace from nations borrowing from each other (contracting debt) to develop their war machines. Why is this kind of debt so dangerous?

Fifth Preliminary Article

> 1. What is Kant's rationale for why nations should not interfere in each others' internal political conflicts?
> 2. Under what circumstances is coming to the aid of one side no longer an inappropriate intervention in his eyes?

Sixth Preliminary Article

> 1. Here Kant warns of the corrosive effects of such tools of war as spies and assassins. Even in war, he says, there should be some standard of decency

and these tools should not be used. However, he describes war as occurring in a "state of nature." What does this term mean for Kant?

2. What damage do such tools as espionage and assassination do in peacetime?

3. Why do nations now think that they must use these tools in war and in peace. Can you imagine a situation in which nations would not have to resort to these tools?

Final Paragraph of the First Section   In this paragraph Kant focuses on the second preliminary article, suggesting that its implementation cannot be put off forever. He seems to be suggesting, in particular protesting the partition of Poland, that governments should adopt the philosophy of what we would call "national self-determination" right away.

Why do you think Kant distinguishes between the mode of acquisition (which is wrong if forced upon people) and the state of ownership (the current status quo).

Second Section   It is useful to consider the "definitive articles" here not as the immediate conditions of peace or a description of peace, but rather the true causes of peace. Here we see that Kant's understanding of what truly brings peace is not at all naive. Kant understands that real political and economic changes have to take place in order for peace to be anything more than a paper exercise. But Kant also believes these changes are occurring and will (almost) surely be fully accomplished.

Introductory Remarks

What is Kant's description of mankind's "natural state" here?

First Definitive Article

1. Kant lists three qualities that make a state a republic or "republican." What are they? (This is Kant's definition of a republic.)

2. Why is it that republics are prone to peace and nonrepublics are prone to war?

3. Imagine a world of nothing but republican states as Kant would define them. Do you agree with Kant that such a world would finally be at peace?

4. In an attachment to the first definitive article, Kant refines his definition of republic. Describe his new definition.

5. How does Kant distinguish a republic from a democracy? What is wrong with democracy?

6. Why is it more possible to move to a republic government from a monarchy than from an aristocracy or democracy?

Second Definitive Article   In this article, Kant describes a concept that has been a source of much confusion: a federation of nations. First he distinguishes a federation of nations from a nation of nations. A nation of nations would be a world government or an empire.

1. If a federation of nations is not world government, what is it?
2. Why will nations never give up their sovereignty or independence to form a world government?
3. In the paragraph analyzed in the Careful Reading section, Kant mentions famous international lawyers of the past and claims that all the efforts to establish international law have been in vain. Why have they been in vain?
4. Kant describes a "league of peace" instead of a "treaty of peace." This use of the word *league* tells us that Kant's federation of nations is no mere agreement like a treaty, but is much more. We know it is based upon a shared form of government, republicanism. What will make these republics form a "federal association" with each other, and what do you think this association will be, if not a treaty?
5. Do you think this association looks more like NATO or like the European Union?
6. In the last two paragraphs, Kant reiterates why a world government or a "nation of peoples" is not a possibility. Do you think anything less than that (such as a federation as Kant describes it) could bring about lasting peace?

Third Definitive Article

1. Cosmopolitanism is almost synonymous with hospitality, as Kant uses the term. What is Kant's definition of hospitality?
2. At the end of the first paragraph of this article, Kant gives examples of the inhospitableness of coastal and desert-dwelling tribesmen, but he says that in the case of the nomadic desert people, hospitality ("the privilege of aliens to enter") is extended to the extent that it makes commerce possible. How can this limited hospitality (allowing commerce among peoples) bring us closer and closer to true hospitality or a cosmopolitan world?
3. How does Kant view the European countries' domination of native peoples in America, Africa, and elsewhere?
4. What do you think of Kant's opinion, expressed in the final paragraph of this article, that there is a sort of community among the peoples of the earth which makes injustices in one part of the world felt in all other parts? Is this true today? If not, why not? If so, what is the practical effect of such feelings?

First Supplement: "On the Guarantee of Perpetual Peace"   In the first of two supplements, Kant gives the reader the underlying, theoretical reasons why perpetual peace is very likely our future. Here it would help to remember what he said in his earlier essay, "Idea for a Universal History with a Cosmopolitan Intent." Both in "Idea" and here Kant argues that forces inherent in human nature and humanity's situation are driving us forward toward a day in which peace is not merely a temporary truce but a permanent reality.

1. In the first paragraph of this supplement, Kant has a debate of sorts with himself about whether to call the forces that are driving history "nature" or "providence" (God's will). Why does Kant, by the end of the paragraph, conclude that it is better to think in terms of nature? (It might help your understanding to look up the Greek myth of Icarus, if you do not already know it.)

2. In the third paragraph, Kant describes how nature has placed human beings in the right position to achieve peace. What are the three things nature has done that will lead to peace?

3. At the end of the third paragraph, Kant links trade with the development of peaceful relations among nations. Why do you think he links the two?

4. In the fourth paragraph, Kant details the effect war has on spreading people around the globe. From reading this paragraph, what do you think is Kant's attitude toward war in general?

5. In the fifth paragraph, Kant explains what he means when he says nature wills something (like war) to happen. He explains that nature does not make such things a duty for men to obey. Instead, she does them herself. Explain in your own words what you think Kant means here.

Three Phenomena That Will Contribute to Eventual Peace   At the end of the first supplement, Kant enumerates three phenomena that will contribute to the eventual peace of the world: the development of republican governments, the continuing existence of national differences in culture and religion, and the effects of international trade.

Republican Governments

1. Why does the threat of war lead people to submit to government and laws?

2. Kant states that forming a republican constitution is a difficult task. Some people even say that to form one requires a nation of angels. But he goes on to explain why a republican constitution is quite possible, even with a nation of devils. Explain Kant's reasons for this confident statement.

3. Kant goes on to point out that our sense of morality is not what causes republican constitutions or, generally, law-governed relations among human beings. Rather a people's morality can only develop under the right type of government (and maybe the right international situation). Do you agree? Explain.

National Differences

1. Why is a state of war among nations preferable to the rule of one nation over all others?

2. How does nature intervene to prevent any one nation from dominating all others? (Nature's ability to prevent empire would also apply to any sort of world government.)
3. What kind of peace must develop among nations if empire or world government are not possibilities?

Effects of International Trade

Why is international trade perhaps the most effective means of bringing and preserving peace? Do you see this happening in our world today? Explain.

Second Supplement: "Secret Article for Perpetual Peace"   In this supplement, Kant tries to spell out his role in the enlightenment of mankind, and the role of other philosophers like him. As amusing as this section may seem (and we cannot possibly know if Kant's tongue was planted in his cheek or how far), it does address an important question that could not be ignored: Do ideas lead this movement or do they simply reflect the trends of the day?

1. What is the "secret article"?
2. How does the nation consult the advise of philosophers? How can Kant say that such a process is secret?
3. What should be the relationship between the philosopher and the jurist or representative? (If you sense ambiguity in what Kant has to say about this, you are right.)
4. Why shouldn't kings be philosophers or philosophers kings?
5. Do you agree or disagree with Kant's final statement that philosophers as a class are incapable of plotting (sedition), forming cliques, or inventing propaganda. What type of people would they have to be in order to live up to this description?

BIBLIOGRAPHY

William A. Galston, *Kant and the Problem of History,* Chicago: University of Chicago Press, 1975.

Arsenij V. Gulyga, *Immanuel Kant: His Life and Thought,* Boston: Birkhauser, 1987.

Susan Shell, *The Rights of Reason: A Study of Kant's Philosophy and Politics,* Toronto: University of Toronto Press, 1980.

Susan Shell, *The Embodiment of Reason: Kant on Spirit, Generation, and Community.* Chicago: University of Chicago Press, 1996.

Yirmiahu Yovel, *Kant and the Philosophy of History,* Princeton, NJ: Princeton University Press, 1980.

Marx (1818–1883) and Engels (1820–1895)

Background

Why do we still study Marx and Engels? After all, the Berlin Wall came down in 1989 and communism in Eastern Europe and the former Soviet Union has collapsed under its own weight. Chinese communism seems to be slowly evolving toward a system mixed with capitalism. Other communist regimes, Cuba for example, are not doing well, and it seems only a matter of time before they, too, succumb to democracy and capitalism. Understandably, many students wonder why they must still study an ideology that appears to have no future.

There is the historical significance, of course. To understand many of the enormous political upheavals and wars of our recent past, one needs to be aware of the source of the greatest ideological divide of the twentieth century. Although few enthusiastic communists remain intent on bringing the world the Marx and Engels communism, many still see the world through the Marxist lens. Soviet-style communism may indeed be on the wane, but socialism appears to have a future. Analysis of social conditions based on economic class has a future through analyses of the relations between rich and poor countries and between the rich and poor in the advanced capitalist countries. The Marxist way of thinking is alive and well and deserves a great deal of study. It is always best to go back to the original source of any political theory in order to understand its fundamentals.

Karl Marx and Friedrich Engels might seem an unlikely pair to become revolutionaries. Marx was born in 1818 in the town of Trier, Prussia (Germany was not yet a united country). He was part of a large, ethnically Jewish family. Both his mother and father came from families in which the men had been rabbis. His father, however, rejected that role and his religious heritage. He converted to Lutheranism and became a lawyer. This decision may have had more to do with practical matters than spiritual. Jews were discriminated against in German society, excluded from certain careers, and socially ostracized. By converting to Christianity, Marx's father opened up a more promising future for himself and his family. Although he was baptized in the Lutheran Church in 1824, Marx was raised without religion and perhaps learned the lesson that serious religion was more of an impediment to progress than a help in life. Marx's father was greatly influenced by the Enlightenment views that had spread to Prussia. A neighbor of the Marx's, Baron von Westphalen was, despite his position, an advocate of what Marx and Engels call in the *Communist Manifesto* "utopian socialism." He, too, influenced the young Karl, who was to become engaged to the baron's daughter, Jenny.

Mainly because of his father's wishes, Marx pursued an advanced education in law. He went to the University of Bonn in 1835, but he found his studies too formal and confining. He became bored quickly and spent more time socializing, drinking, and writing poetry than studying. His father transferred him to the University of Berlin. Perhaps his engagement to Jenny also motivated Marx to take college more seriously. This time, he was at a place that suited his temperament better, and he delved into a discipline that fascinated him more—philosophy. He eventually received his doctoral degree in 1841 from the University of Jena.

It was at the University of Berlin that Marx soaked up G.F.W. Hegel's philosophy of *dialectical history*. He associated with a group of students who idolized Hegel, the recently deceased professor of philosophy, and who were using his theory to formulate their own political ideas. As with any great thinker, Hegel influenced people across the political spectrum from left to right. Needless to say, Marx soon identified with the left-wing Young Hegelians who used Hegel's ideas to criticize religion and the conservative Prussian government. When he graduated, Marx was unable to obtain a university teaching position with his Ph.D. because of his radical views on politics and religion, which the government did not want to support. He became an editor of a left-wing newspaper instead, a move that would make him much more of a threat. During this time, influenced by his own social observations and by his contact with other activists and intellectuals, Marx began to put his uniquely materialistic spin on Hegel's theory of history.

In 1843, Marx married Jenny, resigned from his editorship to protest the government's censorship, and he moved to Paris. Paris was a hotbed of European radicalism, an environment that quickly turned Marx into a committed communist. Influenced especially by Ludwig Feuerbach's theory of *psychological alienation* as the root of religion, Marx began to formulate his materialistic political and economic theory in earnest.

Marx had briefly met Friedrich Engels, but he did not really know him well or appreciate his work until 1844. Impressed with some of Engels's scholarship,

Marx collaborated with Engels to write a political satire, "The Holy Family," in 1845. By then they were in England and the publication marked the beginning of a lifelong partnership. Engels was a member of a wealthy family that owned factories in the German Rhineland as well as in England. Unlike Marx, he did not receive any university education because he wished to go directly into the family business. This move, at age 16, did not stop his self-education, however, because he had an extraordinary mind. By the young age of 18 he was already considered an intellectual and a social critic by those who encountered him, and his influence was spreading.

Although his family did not approve of his growing absorption with left-wing politics, which was often critical of the family's own way of doing business, they never disowned him. Indeed, Engels continued to work for his family's firm until retirement. His wealth allowed him to grow in knowledge and engage in scholarship critical of the government and economic injustices. It also allowed him to support Marx and his family much of the time when Marx could not provide for them without giving up his revolutionary activity. Even so, three of Marx's six children did not live to see adulthood because of the hard life they lived. It may seem strange and even hypocritical to think of Engels, certainly a member of the rich class by anyone's estimation, keeping his wealth and at the same time professing to be a friend of the working class. However, Engels apparently thought that the greater good was served by his not being poor.

Marx died in 1883, but Engels lived until 1895. In these remaining years, Engels became Marx's literary executor, deciding when and how Marx's work would be presented. Through his own writings, and his presentation of Marx's writings, Engels had an enormous influence on how Marxism was to be perceived. This was especially the case with Engels's treatment of dialectical materialism as an all-encompassing way to understand just about everything in human experience. It is likely that Marx would never have agreed with this attachment to a single explanatory idea. Engels also went beyond Marx in his analysis of the plight of women. In *The Origin of the Family, Private Property and the State,* he claimed that original family life was communistic, but with the invention of private property came monogamous marriage and patriarchal family structures, all of which have contributed to women's subordinate and oppressed position. This thesis, and others like it, have had an important influence on modern feminist theory.

A look into the way the working people lived might explain why there was so much talk of socialism, and so much social unrest, in the capitals of Europe at this time. We now know that capitalism has changed in a great many ways and has created more material abundance for more average people than any other economic system. We also know that governments have adapted to the needs of the poor and working class in ways that have softened the impact of the capitalist system. Capitalism with all its faults appears to have worked better than the experience of communism. To Marx and Engels, however, none of this seemed possible.

Factory labor drew people out of the countryside and into the cities where they were more likely to experience extreme poverty than prosperity. Factory labor was long, hard, and dangerous. There were no workplace health and safety laws, and no limits on child labor which was widespread. Women also worked long hours in factories. Many were paid barely enough to keep themselves fed and the rent paid, if they were lucky. Prostitution abounded. People died young.

Capitalism appeared to be a trap in which the poor had to work simply to survive. There was no welfare safety net, no unemployment insurance, no medical care for the poor. Under these conditions, Marx and Engels, and many others, saw the working class as virtual slaves. In their view, factory owners treated workers as though they were no more than parts of a machine. This perception is part of what Marx and Engels came to mean by "alienation" or "estrangement." They thought that these conditions would become so intolerable that the workers would finally achieve "class consciousness" and undertake the final revolution into communism.

As mentioned, capitalism developed in ways Marx and Engels did not expect. A larger and larger middle class developed that had no stake in revolution and a big stake in political stability. On the other hand, the communist regimes that were created and inspired by Marxism did not conform to Marx and Engels's expectations either—not in how they came into being nor in how they developed. Marx and Engels predicted that the communist revolution would only occur in countries that had already gone through an advanced form of capitalism—countries such as England where they wrote the *Communist Manifesto*. But communist revolutions took place in largely agricultural, peasant societies such as Russia and China. Instead of living more abundantly and feeling more valued, people in communist countries lived under totalitarian dictatorships. Under the Soviet leader Joseph Stalin, for example, millions of people were murdered or starved to death during Stalin's drive to consolidate his power. Estimates of the death toll under Stalin range between 20 and 50 million lives, with the latter end of that range based on recent access to more complete records after the collapse of Soviet communism. Chinese leader Mao Zedong's bizarre social experiment, the Cultural Revolution, was designed to make the Chinese more ideologically pure and did so at the expense of more millions of murdered and imprisoned people. To this day, China's strictly enforced one-child policy forces women to undergo unwanted abortions or go to great lengths to conceal the presence of second children. Pol Pot's takeover of Cambodia in the late 1970s left another 2 million dead in the name of remaking Cambodia into a communist model. The horrors that many millions have experienced in the twentieth century in the name of communism are certainly not what Marx and Engels had in mind when they thought about the end of capitalism. One question to keep in mind as you read Marx and Engels is what, if anything, within their thought could allow such ruthless misuse of their theory?

UNDERSTANDING MARX AND ENGELS

The ideas of Marx and Engels did not occur in a vacuum. Criticism and calls for drastic change in the political and economic system of Europe were ongoing at the time they developed their particular version of socialist theory. At the time, there were many brands of socialism, but except for the Marx and Engels brand, they all had one thing in common: persuasion and choice. Other socialist thinkers, such as Marx's old mentor Baron Von Westphalen, promoted socialist ideas on the basis of reason. They thought that their task was to show how the world would be a much better place if people stopped acting unreasonably (self-ishly) and began to live according to reason (sharing and cooperating). Some of these socialist thinkers were inspired by Christianity, others by the philosophies of the Enlightenment. Some were liberal reformers, others utopians. But all of them were wrong, according to Marx and Engels. They labeled their competitors unscientific and put their theory forward as the scientific alternative.

What did it mean to Marx and Engels to be scientific? Fundamentally, they believed that they were rejecting wishful thinking and using provable facts. First, they claimed to have produced systematic descriptions of human behavior throughout history and in the capitalism of the present. They claimed to have discerned laws of human behavior visible in history. Second, they claimed, on the basis of these laws, that they could predict with some degree of accuracy what would happen in the future. These two claims not only help explain why Marx and Engels thought they were scientific in their approach, but also why their theory has been more attractive and lasting than the other theories with which they contended. The other theories tried to get people to change their attitudes and actions toward their fellow human beings. Marx and Engels showed how human beings would eventually change through the operation of historical forces beyond their control. Like Kant, they thought that a better future was assured, despite the worst that so-called human nature had to offer. That is a very attractive theme and hopeful promise.

Marx and Engels gave themselves quite a task: to examine all of human history with a view to finding within that history a behavioral pattern that could then be projected into the future. Marx and Engels wrote so much in order to achieve their goal that it is impossible for most undergraduate students to read even a fraction of their total output. This makes it difficult to see the general outlines of their theory without a little help. A tour of these guides will make any reading more intelligible.

Remember that Marx was greatly influenced by the thought of Hegel. Hegel's view was that human reason or spirit—collectively expressed in human actions, particularly the actions of entire societies or civilizations—is what moved history forward. Hegel thought that all human beings had a desire for recognition by their fellow human beings. Indeed, he thought that without recognition from others of our basic humanity and equality as humans, we could not feel fully human and thus not fully free. Hegel expressed this basic insight in sometimes mystical ways. He would write that the Spirit was emerging through history, becoming more and more conscious of itself. What he probably meant by this was that human beings, struggling for recognition throughout history, were becoming more and more aware of who they were and what they wanted from each other and from their government. The first society, Hegel wrote, was a slave society. But the slaves were not recognized as human beings. Something within them rebelled against this treatment, and eventually caused them to overthrow the system. Over time, through innumerable struggles between those who would dominate and those who were dominated, better and better governmental arrangements were formed with more and more equality. This process—*the dialectic*—has somewhat unfortunately been given the shorthand expression *thesis, antithesis, synthesis.* Hegel thought that within any given society (thesis), there lay a contradiction by which all members were unequally recognized (antithesis), and that this contradiction led to rebellion and a new agreement among members of society (synthesis). The new agreement still had contradictions, however, and so the conflict continued. At the end of history, these struggles for recognition and equality would cease because the government made by mankind at that point would reflect these values. At the end of history, people will have arrived at the optimal form of government to fit their nature.

Marx took Hegel's dialectic as his reference, but found the terms *reason* and *spirit* far too vague and mystical. Marx believed that something much more concrete shaped and motivated human behavior: things. Specifically, Marx claimed that at any given time and place, a certain level of technology existed with which to produce things. Marx call this technology—the spear and fishing pole, the ox and plow, the steam engine and assembly line—the "mode of production." The mode of production greatly influenced what kind of economic and thus social relationships formed among people. Generally speaking, those who owned or controlled the mode of production became the ruling class, and those who labored for them were the ruled. Over time, the mode of production would be made obsolete as new technology was invented in the never-ending quest to improve production and prosperity. This would change the social relations, too. New economic classes would emerge and demand more political power. Rather than a struggle for recognition of human equality, *the dialectic of Marx and Engels was about the struggle for ownership of the means of production and the political power that flowed from that ownership.*

Marx and Engels called the mode of production the "base." The base largely determined the "superstructure" of any given society. The superstructure included the form of government, the culture, the religion, and the political philosophy of the times. By this formulation of base and superstructure, Marx and Engels claimed that such things as government, culture, religion, and political philosophy tended to support the power of the ruling class. That is not to say that members of that class got together and consciously created all of these things in order to keep their power, but rather that because they were in charge they naturally encouraged those institutions and ideas that were compatible with their own position in society. A couple of examples will suffice to show how this line of reasoning works. Both will come from the Marx and Engels analysis of capitalist society, because that was their main subject.

The predominant religion of Europe was Judeo-Christianity. As you will see if you read "On the Jewish Question," Marx had a critical view of Judaism very early in his career. In that piece, he clearly ties Judaism with the greed of capitalism in a way that seems blatantly anti-Semitic. Christianity for Marx was a sort of ideology that allowed the masses of poor human beings to continue to accept their lot in life. If they were suffering abuse from their bosses and landlords, the Christian message encouraged them to bear these indignities and wait for their reward in heaven. By focusing on heaven instead of earth, people were encouraged not to see the injustices done to them as ultimately important, or to think that injustices would be punished in the next life by God.

Marx and Engels thought that Christianity was compatible with capitalism and that it tended to support the power of the rich. In order to see their exploitation, people would have to abandon their religious beliefs—only then would they be outraged enough to revolt. Marx and Engels thought that the very deprivation and suffering caused by capitalism would eventually be enough to draw people away from faith. Once true justice among people was established on earth there would be no need for Christianity or any other religion—none of which were ultimately true.

Another useful example involves political philosophy. What would Marx and Engels have to say about the political philosophy that undergirds the U.S. government? You will get a taste of their critique of classical liberalism in the *Communist Manifesto.* In general, Marx and Engels thought that classical liberal ideas such as the vote, individual rights, and constitutional government were a sham. Looking at our own society, they would likely say that while the U.S. constitution gives every adult citizen the right to vote, this is not a true democracy but rather a system of veiled exploitation. They would focus their attention on who runs for office and where they obtain their power. If only the rich or those supported by the rich can run for office then the people have no real choice—they can vote for one representative of the rich or the other. A true Marxist would see very little difference between today's Democrats and Republicans. Both, they would say, are in the pockets of corporations, lobbies, and wealthy individuals with greedy interests of their own. Before we dismiss Marx and Engels as being too conspiratorially minded, we should look at contemporary controversies over campaign finance reform.

Likewise, Marx and Engels would claim that the rights represented in the Constitution sound good on paper but are not equal in practice. Does the poor person really have the same free speech rights as the rich person? The rich person has far greater ability to make his or her voice heard, especially with today's mass communications technology. A person can take out ads in newspapers, on radio and television, for instance. The education gap between the poor and the rich leaves the former much less equipped to exercise all of their rights. In general, Marx and Engels thought that wealth determined who really had rights in a liberal society. That is why they called for the abolition of democracy as we know it: They did not think there was any way to make it truly democratic. Instead, true equality comes from communal property and truly puts people on an equal footing.

Students are sometimes surprised at how utopian Marx and Engels sound when they write about the communist future. This is certainly the case in the essay "Alienated Labor," in which they depict labor in communist society as completely satisfying and selfless. How do we get from the greed and depravity of all other epochs of human history to a completely different society at the end of history? This strikes students as just as utopian as any of the contemporaries of Marx and Engels, as more of a norm or set of values to strive for than a statement of actual fact. How could Marx and Engels predict such a future, in which people work for the love of working, in which people no longer compete for money or material goods, in which the individual finds ultimate fulfillment as part of a larger team?

The answer has to do with their environmentalism—not the kind to preserve the environment—but the kind that stresses the importance of the human environment for shaping human nature. Marx and Engels claimed that what we call permanent human nature (self-interest, for instance, or the religious instinct) is simply a by-product of the social conditions of any given time. We are, in other words, what we are taught to be by our education and by the behavior of others around us. Our education and the models we have in our society are strongly influenced by the mode of production, the economy, and the power relationships that these create.

While this brand of environmentalism may sound depressing at first, for Marx and Engels it offered the greatest hope for mankind. Change in human nature need not occur because we choose to make it occur; it can happen as a by-product of a change in the mode of production, economy, and power relationships. Marx and Engels attempt to show how the communist revolution is inevitable because of the unbearable stress that capitalism places on human beings. If this is so, then under new arrangements in which property is owned by no one and no one has more power than another, human nature will conform to the new circumstances. Marx and Engels realized that this would not happen overnight, which is why they discuss in the *Communist Manifesto* and elsewhere a transition phase, the "dictatorship of the proletariat." During this phase, accommodations have to be made with the "bourgeois right," or the capitalist way of looking at the world. People will have to be paid different wages for different amounts and quality of work, for instance. Eventually, though, through the equalizing of property and through the socializing effects of public education, a new type of human being will emerge.

Before we dismiss this type of environmentalism as more utopianism, remember that our society, especially its psychologists and social scientists, has largely accepted the idea that environment—especially in childhood—shapes human attitudes and behaviors. That is why our society places so much emphasis on shaping the environment of children through programs such as Head Start, Parents as Teachers, and Drug Awareness and Resistance Education (DARE). What would people be like if they had been raised in an environment where selfishness had no place? We do not know because none of the communist experiments of the twentieth century ever managed to change the environment to that extent.

CAREFUL READING

Marx and Engels are among the most difficult political thinkers to read because of the terminology they choose. Like many of our contemporary philosophers, for better or worse, they have created a language of their own to deal with the unique concepts that they have discovered or invented. Critics call this use of language an abuse—or jargon. Until the reader understands certain key words in the jargon of Marx and Engels, he or she will be lost. This section will attempt to train the reader to untangle the meaning of these and others that will be encountered in the writings of Marx and Engels. Keep in mind as you read these works the essential questions—"What are Marx and Engels trying to get across in general?" What is the bottom line? This will keep you from getting bogged down in the sometimes tortured language.

The Revolutionary Bourgeoisie

In the *Communist Manifesto*[1] there is an examination of the role and revolutionary character of the bourgeoisie, which, of course, are the rich capitalists.

---

[1]The edition used is that which appears in Karl Marx and Friedrich Engels, *Basic Writings on Politics and Philosophy*, edited by Lewis S. Feuer, Garden City, New York: Anchor Books, Doubleday & Company, Inc., 1959.

How could they also be seen as revolutionaries? Marx and Engels condense a considerable amount of thought on this topic into a few paragraphs, using colorful and sometimes figurative language. The question is, what is it that the bourgeois have done that is so revolutionary and so necessary for the oncoming communist revolution? Below we find the most crucial paragraphs for answering this question:

> The bourgeoisie, historically, has played a most revolutionary part.
>
> The bourgeoisie, wherever it has got the upper hand, has put an end to all feudal, patriarchal, idyllic relations. It has pitilessly torn asunder the motley feudal ties that bound man to his "natural superiors," and has left remaining no other nexus between man and man than naked self-interest, than callous "cash payment." It has drowned the most heavenly ecstasies of religious fervor, of chivalrous enthusiasm, of Philistine sentimentalism, in the icy water of egotistical calculation. It has resolved personal worth into exchange value, and in place of the numberless indefeasible chartered freedoms, has set up that single, unconscionable freedom—free trade. In one word, for exploitation, veiled by religious and political illusions, it has substituted naked, shameless, direct, brutal exploitation.
>
> The bourgeoisie has stripped of its halo every occupation hitherto honored and looked up to with reverent awe. It has converted the physician, the lawyer, the priest, the poet, the man of science, into its paid wage laborers. The bourgeoisie has torn away from the family its sentimental veil, and has reduced the family relation to a mere money relation. (from Part I)

What do Marx and Engels mean by the bourgeoisie playing "a most revolutionary part"? After all, we have learned that Marx and Engels thought the bourgeoisie, the rich, was the oppressor class, determined to maintain the status quo. However, remember that Marx and Engels take a very broad view of history. They see the capitalist era as one of several, each of which have swept away existing social arrangements and replaced them with new ones. Their description of the effects of the bourgeoisie on society is supposed to help us understand in what sense the bourgeoisie are revolutionaries.

In the second paragraph, Marx and Engels compare the effects of bourgeois or capitalist society with feudal or medieval times. Here, if you encounter some unfamiliar words, the best you can do is look them up. There you will find that "patriarchy" has to do with rule of the father, and you will remember that divine right theory, which justified the rule of kings, was based on a patriarchal theory. You will find that "idyllic" has to do with rustic, pastoral life, with the connotation of pleasant, peaceful, and simple times. From this comparison alone, you might conclude that Marx and Engels are looking back to feudal times with longing, but this would be a mistake.

Even though they make feudal times sound better, there are clues within the text that lead you to see the simplicity of these times as illusion. Notice that they put "natural superiors" in quotation marks, a method to indicate that one should doubt the truth or sincerity of that claim. In feudal times, nobility was considered naturally superior to the common classes. Commoners were supposed to show them respect and not question their wisdom. The feudal community of natural superiors and natural inferiors has been replaced with "naked self-interest," and "callous 'cash payment'." This sentence is key. In capitalism, there is no feeling of community, there is simply payment for services. Payment is the only "nexus" or relationship between man and man. So, there is no longer any illusion about one's boss being worthy of that role because he is naturally superior and wise. The worker knows there is no difference among people, except a difference in property.

Marx and Engels go on in this second paragraph to describe the many illusions of the feudal period which kept people happier with their lives than they can possibly be in capitalism. Notice that in a capitalist society, people lose their religious faith or fervor, their sense of chivalry, and their philistine sentimentalism. What do Marx and Engels mean by chivalry and "Philistine sentimentalism." If you have seen a movie about medieval times, chances are you have seen chivalry. It was the code of conduct of the knight or noble gentleman, and it included the proper way to treat women and those people who were one's natural inferiors—with kindness, and a sense of protection. "Philistine" sentimentalism is uncultured or simple sentimentalism or emotion. In this context, Marx and Engels are probably talking about the Christian and chivalric morals of the times, which were unexamined and thought to be very simple. All of this, they say, has been plunged into the "icy water of egotistical calculation." The picture is beginning to fall into place. It is not that Marx and Engels are believers in chivalry or Christian morality. Rather they are describing a process in which people have been forcibly stripped of their illusions, their ability to justify their existence based upon beliefs about their place in society, their religious faith, their moral code. Capitalism makes it impossible to hang on to these illusions, which in the past gave people quite a bit of psychological comfort.

The rest of the paragraph only helps us understand this process better. Human value is "exchange value," that is, in capitalism we become what we are worth on the market—the price of our labor. Marx and Engels make reference to "the numberless indefeasible chartered freedoms," which are the freedoms of the feudal era. "Indefeasible" has the same meaning as the more familiar "unalienable." An indefeasible freedom is one that cannot be abolished or made void. A chartered freedom is one that is granted, in this case, by the sovereign or lord of the realm. These medieval freedoms, varying according to social rank, are replaced in capitalism by one "unconscionable freedom—free trade." This is now simple enough to understand, as is the last sentence, which nicely summarizes the point—that exploitation veiled by illusions in feudal society has been replaced by direct exploitation.

After taking time to understand the second paragraph thoroughly, the rest comes easier. Capitalism has taken away all respect for our "natural superiors," including those mentioned in the third paragraph—doctors, lawyers, priests, poets, scientists. It has done this by equalizing all people as "wage laborers." Later, they mention that capitalism has changed the family, too. No longer are sentimental feelings about the family possible, when all members are seen as makers of money or consumers of resources. They will say more about the family later in the *Manifesto*.

Soon after the selected passage, Marx and Engels compare the industry of feudal with capitalist times. This is important for understanding the revolutionary character of the bourgeoisie. Compared with the capitalists, the feudal nobles were apparently lazy. Here they seem to praise capitalism for its achievements. This praise should be taken seriously, and it should be remembered that nowhere do Marx and Engels suggest doing away with the capitalists' factories and other machinery of production. Marx and Engels thought that this machinery, which in itself was very revolutionary, could only be properly used for the benefit of all mankind if it were not owned by the rich but shared by all. The machinery could mass produce; now all that was needed was for it to produce for the masses, instead of the profits of a narrow few. Marx and Engels further discuss the revolutionary nature of the bourgeoisie, still comparing it with other times. Unlike past eras, in which "[c]onservation of the old modes of production" was in the interest of the richer classes, the capitalists are the first wealthy class to obtain wealth "by constantly revolutionizing the instruments of production, and with them the whole relations of society." Think about capitalism in our own day. Is there a lot of "revolutionizing" going on? Are not companies always changing their products, improving them, altering the way they are produced to maximize efficiency and profits? They have to do this in order to remain competitive with other capitalist enterprises. This is what Marx and Engels mean by "revolutionizing." As you can see, they thought that this revolutionizing led to constant instability in social relations. Again, think of the situation today. When a company changes the technology it uses to produce something, it may have to fire old workers and hire new ones with different skills. If a company invests in computerization, it may need fewer workers to do the same amount of work, and so lay off or let go some of its employees. Even today, workers may often feel at the mercy of their employers, changing jobs and even skills many times within the course of a lifetime. Marx and Engels are pointing out that all of this constant change can be very socially destructive. They finish by using another strong comparison with feudal illusions. When they say "[a]ll that is solid melts into air" they are not saying that feudal beliefs were solid, but that they seemed solid.

On the basis of this condemnation of capitalism, the reader might think there is nothing good that comes out of this mode of production. However, it is precisely the lack of illusions, the naked misery that Marx and Engels thought was the inevitable product of capitalism, that was necessary for class consciousness to emerge in the people. Unless they were driven to abandon their romantic illusions, they would never see that they were an exploited class, and they would never get angry enough to revolt and change their situation. In this sense, also, the bourgeoisie are a revolutionary class—they are more or less compelled by the logic of profits to create the conditions for revolution, and thus for their own destruction.

Alienation

The term "alienated" appears throughout Marx's essay entitled, "Alienated Labor" (some translators use the term "estranged" instead).[2] We use this term today to mean a certain attitude toward others. It indicates "not identifying" with others, or feeling like an outcast. This meaning is not wholly different from what Marx is trying to get across. However, Marx's meaning is more specific and has to do with the effects on people of the capitalist mode of production. The following passage from the beginning of "Alienated Labor" contains this concept and a few others than can bedevil the reader:
We proceed from a *present* fact of political economy.

> The worker becomes poorer the more wealth he produces, the more his production increases in power and extent. The worker becomes a cheaper commodity the more commodities he produces. The *increase in value* of the world of things is directly proportional to the *decrease in value* of the human world. Labor not only produces commodities. It also produces itself and the worker as a *commodity,* and indeed in the same proportion as it produces commodities in general.
>
> This fact simply indicates that the object which labor produces, its product, stands opposed to it as an *alien thing*, as a *power independent* of the producer. The product of labor is labor embodied and made objective in a thing. It is the *objectification* of labor. The realization of labor is its objectification. In the viewpoint of political economy this realization of labor appears as the *diminution* of the worker, the objectification as the *loss of and subservience to the object,* and the appropriation as *alienation [Entfremdung]*, as externalization [*Entausserung*].
>
> So much does the realization of labor appear as diminution that the worker is diminished to the point of starvation. So much does objectification appear as loss of the object that the worker is robbed of the most essential objects not only of life but also of work. Indeed, work itself becomes a thing of which he can take possession only with the greatest of effort and with the most unpredictable interruptions. So much does the appropriation of the object appear as alienation that the more objects the worker produces, the fewer he can own and the more he falls under the domination of his product, capital. (pp. 59–60)

Keeping in mind Marx's agenda—the criticism of capitalism and the promotion of communism—will help a great deal in understanding this and other

---

[2]Selections from this essay will be taken from the translation of Loyd D. Easton and Kurt H. Guddat as it appears in *Karl Marx, Selected Writings,* edited by Lawrence H. Simon, Indianapolis, Indiana: Hackett Publishing Company, 1994, pp. 58–68.

passages in "Alienated Labor." With this much insight alone, you can no doubt get the drift of what Marx is saying here about what labor is like under capitalism. However, the specifics are less clear, partly because of the rather alien terminology! The first term that we encounter is "political economy." Take a moment to think about this term. In what way would the economy be political for Marx? Of course, the economy influences politics, and politics is an attempt to maintain the status quo of the economy for the benefit of the rich. So, for Marx, politics and economics are very much intertwined and a person cannot understand one without the other. Capitalism is political economy, and only under communism will people experience economy without politics.

Then Marx introduces some paradoxes which he has observed in capitalism. "The worker becomes poorer the more wealth he produces," for instance. Here he is trying to describe the illogic he sees in capitalism, but even more, he is trying to show the human impact of capitalism. In capitalism, the increase in the value of things causes a decrease in the value of the human world. What exactly does this mean? We know that capitalism is always about producing more and better things and making more money. Is not Marx saying that as capitalists pursue more money and make more "value" for themselves, they decrease the value or diminish the worth of human beings? In other words, life itself is diminished by the pursuit of profits. Indeed, Marx wants to make this perfectly clear, because he goes on to indicate that capitalism makes the worker and his or her labor into commodities—things to be bought and sold. Apparently this is not what Marx thinks life should be about, and we begin to get a glimpse of his own opinion on how we should see other human beings and ourselves.

Marx then goes on to refine what he is saying about people and their labor being commodities under capitalism. He says that in the capitalist system the products of labor stand opposed to labor as an "alien thing, as a power independent of the producer." Again, we have to stand back and think about how capitalism operates. Marx says that the person who labors under capitalism produces something that is alien to himself, something that is other than himself. How could it be different, the reader might ask. What we produce is not who we are, right? Well, we have to consider the possibility that Marx would not agree. In fact, Marx might say that we are thinking like products of a capitalist environment. Indeed what we produce, according to Marx, is a large part of who we are. That is what makes capitalism so terrible for Marx. Capitalism (political economy) takes our identity from us by alienating us from our labor and the products of our labor. How does it do this? The latter part of the third paragraph gives us a clue. Here he says that the "realization of labor is its objectification." This in itself is not bad, because Marx thought that the realization or end of all kinds of labor was a certain objectification, that is, the ability to stand back and see who you are and what you can do from the finished product of your labor. However, in capitalism "this realization of labor appears as the *diminution* of the worker, the objectification as *the loss of and subservience to the object,* and the appropriation as *alienation . . ."* Capitalism results in the diminution of the worker (of his worth, importance). The objectification of his labor does not allow him to step back and see himself in what he has produced. Rather, when he steps back he sees that his product is lost—that it is not his and that indeed he is subservient to or the slave of that product, which provides wealth and power for the capitalist. The worker feels simply like a cog in the capitalist machine, alienated not only from the product of his labor but also from other human beings.

The final paragraph helps to emphasize and further clarify the effect that Marx is describing here. Indeed, the worker has so little control over what or how he produces that he may be diminished to the point of starvation. He is told what to make, how to make it, how long to work, and at the end of the day, the factory owner takes almost all of the profits of his labor and gives him back only enough to hopefully survive. The worker has no choices if he wants to survive; he has become completely dehumanized. Marx is trying to communicate what he sees as a great injustice, albeit in a language that at times seems too obscure.

This selection from "Alienated Labor" should give you a better picture of what Marx wants, not just what he is criticizing. If capitalism is about alienation, then communism for Marx must be about the reunification of human beings with their labor and the products of their labor. "Alienated Labor" will give you a clear sense of just how important human labor was to Marx. Remember, Marx was very much a materialist. There was nothing more to human life than the sum total of a person's actions in this world. So what we produce in the world in a material sense, and how we interact with each other in the process, was hugely important for Marx. As you will see, people could find ultimate happiness and fulfillment in their labor, but only if it was done under communist conditions.

Who's Who?

In the "Critique of the Gotha Program,"[3] as in some other works by Marx, it can sometimes be difficult to figure out whether Marx is explaining his opinion or describing the opinion of someone else. This is especially the case at the beginning of the "Critique." Two worker's parties in Germany, the Social Democratic Worker's Party (SDAP) and the General Union of German Workers (ADAV), had decided to merge. They met at Gotha in 1875 and hammered out a compromise platform for socialist activity in Germany. The ADAV was a

---

[3]All quotations from this work are from Karl Marx, *Critique of the Gotha Program,* New York: International Publishers, 1938. (Volume XI of the Marxist Library)

socialist party which had rejected Marx's way, instead siding with the liberal-socialist ideas of Ferdinand Lassalle, another of the Young Hegelians. Lassalle's ideas were completely unacceptable to Marx, who wrote this detailed critique of their statement. By reading the "Critique" we get a clearer picture of why Marx rejected the route of liberal and socialist reforms and instead remained committed to communist revolution. Because most of the confusion is produced at the very beginning of the essay, let us examine Marx's critique of the first paragraph of the Gotha statement. Marx starts out by quoting the statement itself.

> 1. "Labour is the source of all wealth and all culture, *and since* useful labour is only possible in society and through society, the proceeds of labour belong undiminished with equal right to all members of society."
>
> *First part of the paragraph:* "Labour is the source of all wealth and all culture."
>
> Labour is *not the source* of all wealth. *Nature* is just as much the source of use values (and it is surely of such that material wealth consists!) as labour, which itself is only the manifestation of a natural force, human labour power. That phrase is to be found in all children's primers and is correct in so far as it is *implied* that labour proceeds with the appropriate subjects instruments. But a socialist programme cannot allow such bourgeois phrases to cause the *conditions* to be ignored that alone give them meaning. And in so far as man from the beginning behaves towards nature, the primary source of all instruments and subjects of labour, as her owner, treats her as belonging to him, his labour becomes the source of use values, therefore also of wealth. The bourgeois have very good grounds for fancifully ascribing *supernatural creative power* to labour, since it follows precisely from the fact that labour depends on nature, that the man who possesses no other property than his labour power must, in all conditions of society and culture, be the slave of other men who have made themselves the owners of the material conditions of labour. He can only work with their permission, hence live only with their permission.
>
> Let us now leave the sentence as it stands, or rather limps. What would one have expected as conclusion? Obviously this:
>
> "Since labour is the source of all wealth, in society also no one can appropriate wealth except as the product of labour. Therefore, if he himself does not work, he lives by the labour of others and also acquires his culture at the expense of the labour of others."
>
> Instead of this, by means of the words *"and since"* a second proposition is added in order to draw a conclusion from this and not from the first one. (pp. 3–4)

First, Marx quotes from the Gotha Program. In one sentence the program makes a very powerful statement that must be broken down to be thoroughly understood. Only if we thoroughly understand what the authors wanted to say in this sentence will we really understand Marx's critique. Labor, according to the program, is the source of all wealth. Of course the authors are attempting to criticize the existing capitalist economy, so most capitalists would not look at wealth in this way. They might say that capital is the source of wealth, or that their own genius is the source of wealth, not mere labor. So by saying that labor is the source of wealth, the authors of the Gotha Program are locating the true ownership of wealth in those who labor, not those who own or those who plan. They then go on to say that labor is also the source of all culture. In their opinion, perhaps, it is those who actually produce the cultural products—the manifestations of culture such as buildings, music, food—not just those who conceive of them, who are to be credited with creating the culture. Labor is possible only in and through society, according to the authors. They see labor not as an individual act for individuals, but a social activity for the survival and well-being of society as a whole. They see human beings as social beings, not as isolated individuals who make a social contract for the protection of their individual safety and rights. They conclude that because labor is a social activity, the proceeds of labor belong equally to all members of society. This conclusion does not necessarily follow their premises. However, it does state clearly what the authors think should happen to property—it should be equally divided among all people. Now let us look at Marx's critique.

Marx takes the sentence apart for purposes of proving each part wrong. Obviously, there are many areas in which the authors of the Gotha Program and Marx would agree in general. Remember, however, that Marx thought his theory scientific and superior to all others. He is trying to establish his theory as better than that of the Gotha Program. It is for this reason that he takes on each premise and the conclusion.

Marx disputes the idea that labor is the only source of wealth. Nature, he says, is just as much a source of wealth as labor. Human labor is actually just another "manifestation of a natural force." This would indicate that Marx sees man as a part of nature, not standing over and apart from it. Marx identifies the Gotha Program's description of labor as the only source of wealth with the bourgeois view. It is in bourgeois children's primers. If you remember what Locke had to say about labor as the source of value, Marx's opposition to this idea becomes clearer. Locke used this idea to reject the idea of communal property. Locke says that once a man mixes his labor with something in nature, it becomes his (private) property. That is why, in Marx's view, a socialist program cannot accept such "bourgeois phrases" unless it discusses the conditions under which labor is either the source of private property or communal property.

After contrasting the bourgeois way of viewing labor and value with the communist way, the next sentence is a little easier to understand. Marx is characterizing the capitalist way of viewing value and ownership when he describes man behaving toward nature "as an owner." If he looks at it this way, then he becomes the owner when he mixes his labor with nature—his labor creates the wealth. But if we look at nature, which we are given in common even according to Locke, as the source of wealth, too, there is a source of wealth independent from the individual's labor. Another way of looking at nature is not as owner of it, but as user or borrower of its resources. In the rest of that paragraph, Marx discusses the bourgeois' reasons for viewing labor as the source of wealth. Those who accumulate more property establish sole ownership over it;

then they can use their wealth to exploit those who continue to only have their labor to sell. In effect, those who own property can make "slaves" out of those who do not. The bourgeois have the power of life or death over the laborers, because they can decide whether they will work and thus whether they will eat.

Next, Marx makes a transition to a suggested conclusion which is different from what the sentence from the Gotha Program suggests. Notice that in this suggested conclusion, Marx is accepting the program's flawed statement that labor is the source of all wealth. Thus he is arguing that, even given that premise, different and more appropriate conclusions can be drawn. Marx's conclusions are aimed squarely at the bourgeois. If a person does not work (which must mean by manual labor), then he "lives by the labour of others" and obtains his culture from those others whom he exploits.

Marx's final sentence suggests that the second proposition in the Gotha Program's sentence is either misleading or unnecessary, and that more direct conclusions could have been drawn by simply sticking with the first proposition. Ask yourself in what way Marx's conclusion is different from the Gotha Program's conclusion. Is he making a different point entirely, or is it simply his emphasis which is different? Why do you think Marx wants to make a much stronger statement about the role of the bourgeoisie in exploiting the laboring class?

GUIDE TO THE *COMMUNIST MANIFESTO*

Marx and Engels wrote the *Communist Manifesto* as a commission from the Communist League, a German worker's party headquartered in London, in 1847. The term *manifesto* was frequently used in England to mean "party platform." Here the Communist League sets out its (largely Marx's and Engels's) understanding of the historical movement toward communism, how the league's platform differs from other socialist parties and philosophies, and what the communist revolution will entail. Unlike many other works of Marx and Engels, this pamphlet is not meant as a scholarly proof of their arguments but rather an ideological rallying cry. True to their expectations, it has been the most widely read. Its comparably simple language and brief exposition make it a good place to start. Even if you have read the *Manifesto* already, do not skip it this time—you will see things you did not see before.

Introductory Remarks and Part I: Bourgeoisie and Proletarians

1. Why do Marx and Engels refer to communism as a "specter"? What is the purpose of writing this pamphlet?
2. How do Marx and Engels generally see history?
3. What is unique about modern bourgeois society? Why is it this, the capitalist era, that will bring about the ultimate class struggle and revolution?

4. Marx and Engels thought that all societies would have to go through advanced capitalism first before experiencing the communist revolution. In this sense, capitalism was essential to the development of communism. How does capitalism prepare the way for communism?
5. How do Marx and Engels depict work under capitalism?
6. How will the proletarians achieve class consciousness (the awareness of their plight as a class and the desire to change it)? What are the steps the proletariat will take?
7. What is the role of the "bourgeois ideologists"? How would Marx and Engels fit here?

Part II: Proletarians and Communists

1. How are the communists distinguished from the other working-class parties, and how do they see their role in bringing about change?
2. In this part, Marx and Engels take on Lockean liberal ideas such as individual liberty and the right to private property. Keeping in mind that they are addressing classical liberalism, what do they say about each of the following issues:

   —private property
   —wage labor
   —individuality and freedom
   —incentive to work
   —high, bourgeois culture
   —the bourgeois family
   —the proletarian family
   —marriage, as it relates to women
   —national independence (sovereignty)
   —the "eternal truths" of bourgeois philosophy

3. What is the "dictatorship of the proletariat" like? How do Marx and Engels describe the final stage of full communism?

Part III: Socialist and Communist Literature   Here Marx and Engels hope to distinguish their (and the Communist League's) brand of communism from other socialist and communist ideas which were popular at the time. Notice they put the various socialisms into three broad classes: reactionary socialism, conservative or bourgeois socialism, and critical-utopian socialism and communism.

Reactionary Socialism

1. The first example of reactionary socialism is feudal socialism. Feudal socialism emerged as a reaction to the new bourgeoisie. This class got its power from its own industry, not from inherited wealth and land. Do you get a sense of when these advocates of dying feudalism could be called socialists?

2. Marx and Engels briefly discuss "Clerical Socialism" under the category of feudal socialism. What is clerical socialism and how do Marx and Engels criticize it?

3. Next Marx and Engels discuss "Petty-Bourgeoisie Socialism." Who were the petty-bourgeoisie?

4. What were their socialist themes?

5. Why will the petty bourgeoisie eventually disappear?

6. What was the influence of French thought on German socialism? What opinion do Marx and Engels express of the quality of German socialist literature?

7. Marx and Engels imply that German socialism arrived on the scene too soon, and was aimed at the wrong target. How so?

8. How do Marx and Engels tie the petty-bourgeoisie (the "Philistine") together with German or true socialism?

Conservative, or Bourgeois, Socialism

1. Marx and Engels do not deal with separate schools of thought in this category, but lump many people together. What kind of people fall under the category of conservative socialism? What do you think they all have in common?

2. How do Marx and Engels see the conservative socialist's attitude toward the proletariat?

3. What is the attitude of Marx and Engels toward the conservative socialists' tendency to push for reforms instead of revolution?

Critical-Utopian Socialism and Communism

1. Marx and Engels list socialist thinkers Saint-Simon, Fourier, and Owen in this section. What do they all have in common?

2. Marx and Engels contrast the development of actual conditions for the emancipation of the proletariat (the capitalist era must come before communism) with the "new social science" advocated by critical utopian socialists and communists. What is this social science in contrast with what Marx and Engels are doing in their "scientific" scholarship?

3. What about this type of socialist literature is good and useful?

4. From their description of critical-utopian ideas at the end of this section, do you get an idea of what Marx and Engels mean when they call such ideas "fantastic"?

Part IV: Position of the Communists in Relation to the Various Existing Opposition Parties

1. How do the communists fight for the immediate or short-term interests of the working class?

2. How do the communists represent the future or long-term goals of the communist movement?

3. Why do the communists pay the most attention to Germany at the moment?
4. What assumption lies beneath the closing slogan, "Working Men of All Countries, Unite!"

GUIDE TO "ALIENATED LABOR"

Marx wrote "Alienated Labor" as part of a larger work, which came to be known as *Economic and Philosophic Manuscripts*, in 1844. It is one of his most famous and well-read essays because in it he describes very succinctly what he thought was wrong with labor under capitalism, and what labor should be like. It may come as a surprise to you that, far from disliking labor and wanting future communists to do as little of it as possible, Marx thought labor should and would be their greatest delight. For this to happen, property had to be abolished. Labor under capitalism was "alienated," according to Marx. But under communism this would no longer be the case, and people would find great joy in working as hard as they could.

Critique of Political Economy   As we know, political economy is synonymous with capitalism, for Marx. Thus, in this first part of the essay, Marx provides a criticism of the capitalist way of thinking.

1. What effects does capitalist political economy have on the workers?
2. Describing how capitalists think about the emergence of capitalism out of feudalism, Marx writes, "Competition, freedom of craft, and division of landed property were developed and conceived only as accidental, deliberate, forced consequences of monopoly, the guild, and feudal property, rather than necessary, inevitable, natural consequences." What is he trying to say about the way capitalists see what they have done as opposed to the way Marx sees what they have done? (Clue: Look at the opposed adjectives describing "consequences.")

Introduction to the Concept of Alienation

1. Marx begins this section by listing "private property, greed, division of labor, capital and landownership, and the connection of exchange with competition," and linking them all to the money-system. Speculate on why Marx would find all of these aspects of capitalism alienating, and why would he reject the use of money as a part of the process of alienation.
2. In the next paragraph, Marx criticizes those philosophers who theorize from a "fictitious primordial state." What philosophers might he be writing about, and how does he criticize their approach?
3. What does Marx really mean when he says the worker becomes a "commodity"? What does he mean by the "objectification" of labor?

4. A little later, Marx writes that "the worker is related to the *product of his labor* as to an *alien* object." Does this help clarify what Marx means by the objectification of labor?

Closer Consideration of Objectification and Alienation   Marx writes, "Let us now consider more closely the *objectification,* the worker's production and with it the *alienation* and *loss* of the object, his product." He will explain in more detail what he has just introduced.

1. Marx writes that under capitalism, the worker is like a slave to what he produces. In what sense can a human being be said to be a slave to an object?
2. Marx describes quite effectively the paradox of the worker in the capitalist system, including the contrast between capitalists' "palaces" and workers' "hovels." Describe some other paradoxes Marx sees for the worker.

Alienation of the Production Process   Marx begins this section by writing "Up to now we have considered the alienation, the externalization of the worker only from one side . . ." Here Marx will show that the capitalist mode of production is itself alienating to the worker.

1. Why is labor itself external to the laborer under capitalism?
2. Marx describes a situation in which the worker is only happy when he is not working, in which he sees work as only a means to an end (leisure, food, and so on). Even though times have greatly changed since Marx's day, does Marx's description of the worker's attitude resemble the attitude of today's worker? Explain why or why not.
3. Marx says that eating, drinking, and procreation are human functions, but if they are made into a human being's "sole ends," then they are merely animal functions. Do you agree with him? Is he describing a defect of the capitalist way of life that still exists today?

Alienation from our Species   In this section, Marx defines human beings as "species-beings," by which he means social beings. Here he describes what he thinks the human species is really like.

1. Marx describes man as a species as, like the animals, living by "inorganic nature." Then, he says that man differs as a species from other animals because "the realm of inorganic nature by which he lives is more universal." These passages will make a lot more sense if we remember that "organic" for Marx means a part of our immediate body, and "inorganic" means not a part of our immediate body. Given that, what is Marx saying when he states that man makes all of nature his *inorganic* body?
2. Marx next says that an "animal is *its life activity,*" or labor. The same can be said for human beings. But unlike animals, the human species' activity is conscious, not instinctual. Describe a few of the comparisons Marx

makes here between the way the animals and human beings produce things.

3. Based on his comparison of the two, describe your sense of what Marx thinks makes human beings human and not merely animal.

4. Now you can begin to see why labor is so important to Marx–human beings' way of working is who they are as the human species. What does the capitalist mode of production do to tear apart the proper relationship between the worker, his labor, and the products of his labor?

5. How are human beings alienated from each other within the capitalist system?

The Alienation of Ownership In this section, Marx discusses the master-slave-like relationship between the owner of the means of production, the rich capitalist, and the worker. Marx concludes that the idea of private property, treated by some as a fact or absolute truth, is merely the by-product of this unnatural and alienating relationship.

1. Marx writes, "If the product of labor does not belong to me . . . to whom then does it belong?" How does he answer this question?

2. What is the relationship between the worker and the capitalist? How is this yet another form of alienation? Do you get a sense from this discussion of what the relationship of all should be within any production process?

3. How is private property a consequence of "externalized labor," or the way labor is done and by whom it is controlled in a capitalist system?

Conclusions This section is weakened by the fact that the manuscript breaks off in the middle of Marx's conclusions. Another difficulty with this section is that the jargon, which Marx has used throughout, is extensive in these concluding remarks. Still, we can extract from his summations and restatements more clarification of Marx's arguments. In these remarks, Marx mentions Proudhon several times. Pierre-Joseph Proudhon (1809–1865) was a French socialist who came to be known as the father of anarchism. As you will see, Marx contrasts Proudhon's seemingly flawed analysis and proposals with Marx's own.

1. How does Marx argue that "*wages* and *private property* are identical . . ."?

2. Marx takes on two of Proudhon's ideas for helping the workers, an enforced raising of wages and an enforced equality of wages. How does he reject both of these ideas?

3. Marx's ultimate aim is the "emancipation of society from private property," not just the emancipation of the workers. Even though working conditions have drastically improved since Marx's time, could there still be some other value in emancipating society from private property?

4. Marx says in his statement of the second problem toward the end of the essay, "We have already achieved much in resolving the problem by *transforming* the question concerning the *origin of private property* into the question concerning the relationship of *externalized labor* to evolution of humanity." Does this statement help clarify his agenda in writing "Alienated Labor"? Remember, in this essay he has been critical of the idea that private property is some sort of original truth or guiding fact upon which capitalism is based. Rather, he has argued that private property is simply the by-product of the capitalist mode of production.

5. Near the end of the essay, Marx refers to the "non-worker" versus the "worker." Who is the non-worker in the capitalist system? Why do you think Marx chose this terminology to describe this class of people?

GUIDE TO "CRITIQUE OF THE GOTHA PROGRAM"

Part of the difficulty of reading this critique lies in the fact that it *is* a critique—a reaction to someone else's work. From this reaction, the reader must glean what Marx is advocating, not just what he is denouncing. Marx's criticisms can sometimes be petty, other times profound. One of the reader's tasks is to sort out the latter and not be too mired in the former. Marx starts every section off with a paragraph from the Gotha Program. Then, he goes on to critique the ideas embodied in that paragraph. He also sometimes goes beyond this critique to expound on his own teachings.

Part I

First Sentence Marx's critique of the first paragraph of the Gotha Program starts out in a seemingly nit-picking way but ends up making a deeper point.

1. Why does Marx criticize the program's phrase, "Labour is the source of all wealth and all culture" as a "bourgeois phrase"? (Remember what Locke had to say about labor as the source of private property.)

2. Marx offers the following substitute for the first part of the Gotha sentence: "Since labour is the source of all wealth in society also no one can appropriate wealth except as the product of labour. Therefore, if he himself does not work, he lives by the labour of others and also acquires his culture at the expense of the labour of others." How does Marx's sentence improve upon the Gotha sentence?

3. Marx catches a logical problem with the second part of the Gotha sentence, "Useful labour is only possible in society and through society." What is the logical problem?

4. What flaws does Marx see in the Gotha Program's idea that "the proceeds of labour belong equally to all people"?

5. Marx offers two alternative sentences as "incontestable": " 'Labour only becomes the source of wealth and culture as social labour,' or what is the same thing, 'in and through society.' " And, "In proportion as labour develops socially, and becomes thereby a source of wealth and culture, poverty and neglect develop among the workers, and wealth and culture among the non-workers." From these two sentences, are you getting a sense of which themes Marx would have liked the Gotha Program to emphasize.

Second Sentence

1. What is wrong with the idea in the Gotha Program that "the instruments [or means] of labour are the monopoly of the capitalist class"?
2. Marx mentions the rules of the communist International as an alternative source of wording for this sentence. Why is "the monopoly of the means of labour, that is the sources of life" a better wording according to Marx?

Third Sentence

1. How does Marx critique the Gotha phrase "proceeds of labour"?
2. Marx goes on at length to criticize the phrase "equitable distribution of the proceeds of labour." How many different deductions are taken from the "proceeds of labour" before the worker receives his share? Why do you think Marx wants to point out that the laborer will not receive all of the proceeds of his labor?
3. Marx goes on to clarify why he objects to the idea of "proceeds of labour" by discussing what a truly cooperative society with common ownership of the means of production will be like. Why does the phrase "proceeds of labour" lose all meaning in such a society?
4. How will people be "paid" in the initial phase of communist society under discussion?
5. Further along, Marx writes, "In a higher phase of communist society . . . ." Does this paragraph help you to understand better what Marx thought full communism would be like?

Fourth Sentence

1. Why does Marx dislike the phrase "emancipation of labour," and what does he think should replace it?
2. Marx goes on to claim that the bourgeoisie is a revolutionary class, not just the proletariat. In what way is the bourgeoisie a revolutionary class?
3. Why does it seem silly to Marx to lump the peasants, bourgeoisie, and feudal lords into "one *reactionary mass*"?

Fifth Sentence

1. Marx objects to the Lassallian "narrow" view of the worker's movement as a national movement. With what would Marx replace this narrow view?

2. How does Marx link the German worker's party, as it is represented by the Gotha Program, to German leader Otto Von Bismark's "*international policy*" of foreign trade?

Part II   This part discusses one long sentence from the Gotha Program. It takes several swipes at Lassalle and his followers.

1. Ferdinand Lassalle's "iron law of wages" states that the average wage will remain at the level needed for the laborer's subsistence, and no more. Marx would seem to agree with this as a description of wages under capitalism, so why does he discredit Lassalle's idea?

2. "Since Lassalle's death," writes Marx, a new "scientific understanding" of wages has replaced the bourgeois understanding. The bourgeois understanding is that the worker is getting paid for his labor. The new understanding is that he is paid the price of his "labour power." Given what Marx says about the proper understanding in this paragraph, what do you think "the value, or price, of labour power" means, as opposed by simply "labour"?

3. Why does Marx compare the Lassallian understanding of wages to the system of slavery toward the end of this section? Does this analogy help to understand what Marx's disagreement is with Lassalle?

Part III   The main point of this part of the critique has to do with the Lassallians' overreliance, according to Marx, upon the state as the source of change. Does this section shed any light on why Marx was distrustful of state reforms?

Part IV   Here, Marx continues to hammer the Lassallians on their implicit faith in the power of the state to right wrongs.

1. Why does Marx object to the idea of a "free state"?

2. How can Marx say that the "present-day state" is therefore a fiction? How does he modify his criticism of this concept?

3. Marx next asks the question, "What transformation will the state undergo in communist society?" He criticizes the Gotha Program for not really dealing with this question. Then he launches into the program's "political demands." What are these demands?

4. Why does Marx criticize the Gotha Program for making these demands?

5. What is wrong with advocating progressive income taxes as a solution to the people's problems?

6. What is wrong with the Gotha Program's demand for equal education and universal compulsory school attendance? Why is the idea of "[u]niversal and *equal elementary education* through the state . . ." objectionable? Does this discussion help you understand what education would be like in Marx's brand of communism?

7. Why is "freedom of conscience" or religion not a worthy demand, according to Marx?
8. Marx is ambiguous on the issue of female labor, and his comments may be surprising on the issue of child labor. What do you think he is saying about the appropriate place of female labor in the overall workforce, and what do you think is the appropriate place of child welfare in Marx's view?
9. When Marx deals with "Regulation of prison labour," is he saying labor might rehabilitate criminals? If so, is this idea a good one?
10. In general, does reading "Critique of the Gotha Program" give you a clearer idea of Marx's critique of liberalism?

BIBLIOGRAPHY

Sir Isaiah Berlin, *Karl Marx: His Life and Environment,* New York: Oxford University Press, 1996.

Alan Gibert, *Marx's Politics: Communists and Citizens,* New Brunswick, NJ: Rutgers University Press, 1981.

Richard F. Hamilton, *The Bourgeois Epoch: Marx and Engels on Britans, France and Germany,* Chapel Hill: University of North Carolina Press, 1991.

Richard N. Hunt, *The Political Ideals of Marx and Engels,* Pittsburgh: University of Pittsburgh Press, 1974.

Richard N. Hunt, *Classical Marxism, 1850–1895,* Pittsburgh: University of Pittsburgh Press, 1984.

Leszek Kolakowski, *Main Currents of Marxism,* Oxford: Clarendon Press, 1978.

John M. Maguire, *Marx's Theory of Politics,* Cambridge: Cambridge University Press, 1978.

Appendix

THE DISCIPLINE OF POLITICAL THOUGHT: A BRIEF INTRODUCTION

LAURIE M. BAGBY AND MELLISSA KAYE RUNDUS

Political thought is the attempt to understand political phenomena and to solve political problems. The most complex questions for political philosophers are those that are normative. Political thought attempts to answer, for instance, questions about what *should be* the rights and responsibilities of citizens in a democracy, not just what they are at the moment.

The *discipline* of political thought is the academic enterprise of studying various political thinkers, applying their ideas and even formulating new political theories. This section provides a brief guide for how to approach the work of those in the discipline who study political thought, and it supplies some help for writing a paper in this subject.

Interpretation in Political Thought

To interpret is to offer an explanation. The ideas and texts of past cultures and governments are not always easily explained. There are various approaches to interpretation in the discipline of political thought. It will be helpful in your research to know about the existence of various interpretive frameworks. Below we will address four major approaches broadly construed.

Close Textual Analysis   In this approach the primary aim is to understand the thinker as he understood himself. This is done by a thorough reading and close inspection of the text without too much intrusion from other lenses through which the text could be viewed, such as the work's historical or economic context or speculation about the author's psychology. Much time is spent asking whether the author's argument makes sense, whether it is consistent, whether it is logical. In other words, does the argument hang together? But before arriving at any such judgment, scholars who focus on close textual analysis believe greater time must be spent simply figuring out the author's true intent. The author's intent can often be misconstrued, they argue, by the

215

casual reader. Many philosophers wrote their works in such a way that only the discerning reader would fully understand their message, and some even tried to hide their true intent from all but a few for fear of political or religious persecution. Authors and professors who follow this approach will often move through a work line by line or sentence by sentence in an attempt to thoroughly understand the argument of the author. Using this approach, it soon becomes obvious to the student how little of the political thought they read is obvious and how much is a matter of argument. At the end of such an analysis, however, the readers or students are better informed about the philosopher's teaching and more able to make arguments of their own.

The Historical Approach   Scholars who follow this approach believe that to get the most out of a text, they must know the circumstances that surrounded the author. According to these scholars, the meaning of a historical text cannot be understood through a close reading alone.

For political historians to understand the meaning of philosophical works, they must learn and know about the political language and concepts of the time. Such scholars see political texts as forms of political action. Historical reconstruction shows the world the author lived in and the events that influenced his behavior. For example, the historical interpretation of Machiavelli would focus on understanding the impact of Renaissance, Italian politics, the religious beliefs of the time, Machiavelli's personal history, his associations, and his political ambitions. According to this approach, without this type of historical information, we are likely to misconstrue what an author says and therefore miss his or her true intent.

The Relativistic Approach   The relativistic approach disagrees with focusing on the original intentions of the author and thus differs from both approaches above. Relativists believe that there is no fixed truth, because all truths are relative to things such as time, culture, sex, and race. Relativists range from completely giving up on trying to understand an author's intent to attempting to show the numerous factors that influenced the author's intentions to point out how many motives existed for a writing beside those consciously stated by the author. For these scholars, every reader receives and interprets the text differently, and so the reader, in effect, writes the text while reading it.

From the relativist perspective, objective reading is impossible. Everyone has different values and experiences and will gain different insights from the same readings. Relativists believe that what one gains from a text is and should be primarily determined by the reader's current problems and interests.

The Economic Approach   The economic approach is based on the idea that political thought is greatly influenced by the economic institutions and class structures of the time. According to Marxists, political thought is often utilized to justify and legitimize the status quo of the "haves" dominating the "have nots." Marxists interpret all political theories (except their own) as ideological means of hiding and justifying the domination of one class by another.

A scholar following the economic approach might describe the U.S. Constitution as an elitist document framed by the wealthy and guided by their class interests. He might attempt to prove that the founders profited directly from policies initiated under the new constitution. The founders' intentions, seen from this perspective, were to erect a government strong enough to protect the haves from the have-nots. Such a scholar might view the Constitution as actually being a mechanism for protecting property rights, not civil liberties and rights. The liberties and rights enshrined in the Constitution cannot benefit everyone, according to Marxist scholars, only those who have the wealth to invest, trade, and accumulate more wealth.

A Brief History of the Discipline of Political Thought

When doing research in political thought, it may help to understand a particular scholar's argument by understanding a little about the history of the discipline of political thought. The distinction usually made today between political science and political thought is a fairly recent one which came about during the *behavioral revolution*, a movement of a new generation of scholars that emerged after World War II. Members of this movement were intent on studying only what could be counted and tested using empirical methodology. They wanted to completely avoid value judgments. Behaviorists called for the discipline of political science to abandon traditional methods of argumentation, such as those used in political philosophy, in exchange for modern scientific inquiry.

The behaviorist movement led to a temporary and partial rejection of traditional political thought by the discipline of political science. At the same time as there was a great influx of money into academia for more faculty and academic journals, there was a significant decrease in the number of political scientists willing to devote attention and energy to political thought. Many political science departments across the nation even stopped offering classes in political thought, especially at the graduate level. In those departments that still taught political thought, it was treated primarily as political history.

Of course, thinking about and trying to solve important political problems never stopped, and, during the late 1960s and 1970s, the academic discipline of political thought was reborn. There were many social and political issues demanding attention, such as the Vietnam War, the Civil Rights movement, student rebellions, feminism, and unemployment. Academia reacted to these issues by returning again to the attempt to answer the bigger questions that behaviorism could not answer. New journals appeared which specialized in political thought.

Throughout the 1990s, there was continued growth in political thought. Issues such as welfare policies, economic crises, conservation, and sexual and racial equality provided plenty for political theorists to think and write about.

Continued study of the old but timeless ideas of political thinkers on issues such as democracy, justice, and political legitimacy informed their inquiries. The crucial political issues of the future include environmental concerns and the question of our obligation to future generations, and the ethics of government policies on abortion, cloning, and genetic screening.

Selected Journals   The following journals contain articles on political thought that may help you do a research paper for this or another class. It is not meant to be inclusive, but should provide you with a good start in your search for information.

American Journal of Political Science
American Political Science Review
Ancient Philosophy
British Journal for History of Philosophy
European Journal of Philosophy
History and Theory
History of Political Thought
Interpretation
Journal of Politics
Philosophy
Philosophy and Public Affairs
Political Theory
Polity
The Review of Politics
Theory and Society

Valuable Indices   Below are some of the most valuable indices you may find in your library for research in political thought, along with some commentary on what information they provide.

Social Sciences Citation Index   Provides three index guides where one can find articles by citation, source, or subject. This extensive index also provides abstracts and lists additional works by the author and related articles by various authors.

Philosopher's Index   A yearly index that cites journal and newspaper articles by subject and provides the journal titles, volumes, and pages where the articles can be located.

International Political Science Abstracts   A yearly index that cites journal and newspaper articles by author and provides the journal location information and a complete abstract.

Wilson's Humanities Index   A yearly index that cites journal articles and book, film, and journal reviews by author and subject. It includes 400 periodicals.

America: History and Life   This internet index can be located at *http://serials.abc-clio.com*. It contains a humanities menu providing book reviews, journal articles, and dissertations. The search can be limited by specific journal titles, key words, subject, and/or author.

Historical Abstracts This internet index also is located at *http://serials.abc-clio.com*. Its humanities menu provides only journal articles and their complete abstracts. The search can be limited by journal titles, key words, subject, and/or author.

PAIS International This internet index is available at universities that have login access to it. This index provides a social science menu of newspaper and journal articles.

Noesis Philosophical Research Online This internet index is located at *http://noesis.evansville.edu*. This site provides texts, reviews, and reference material categorized by author and subject.

Selected Interpretive Books and Series

Cambridge Studies in Medieval Life and Thought, published by Cambridge University Press.

Cambridge Texts in the History of Political Thought, published by Cambridge University Press.

Copleston, Fredrick Charles. *A History of Philosophy.* Image Books, 1946, 1953, and 1985. New York, New York.

Oxford Readers, published by Oxford University Press.

Philosophy and Political Thought, published by Encyclopedia Britannica.

Political Science Classics, published by the Free Press.

Routledge Studies in Social and Political Thought, published by Routledge Publishing.

Strauss, Leo and Joseph Cropsey. *A History of Political Philosophy.* University of Chicago Press, 1963, 1972, and 1987. Chicago, Illinois.

Studies in Continental Thought, published by Indiana University Press.

SUNY Series in Ancient Greek Philosophy, published by the State University of New York Press.

The Vanderbilt Library of American Philosophy, published by Vanderbilt University Press.

Voeglin, Eric. *Order and History.* Louisiana State University Press, 1956. Baton Rouge, Louisiana.

Bibliography

PLATO AND ARISTOTLE

Allan, D. J., *The Philosophy of Aristotle,* London: Oxford University Press, 1970.

Annas, Julia, *An Introduction to Plato's Republic,* New York: Oxford University Press, 1981.

Barker, Ernest, *The Political Thought of Plato and Aristotle,* New York: Russell & Russell, 1959.

Brickhouse, Thomas C. and Nicholas D. Smith, *Plato's Socrates,* New York: Oxford University Press, 1994.

Burnett, John, *Early Greek Philosophy,* London: A & C Black, 1952.

Edel, Abraham, *Aristotle and His Philosophy,* Chapel Hill, NC: University of North Carolina Press, 1982.

Jaeger, Werner W., *Aristotle: Fundamentals of the History of His Development,* London: Oxford University Press, 1962.

Johnson, Curtis N., *Aristotle's Theory of the State,* St. Martin's Press, 1990.

Kagan, Donald, *The Great Dialogue: A History of Greek Political Thought from Homer to Polybius,* Westport, CT: Greenwood Press, 1986.

Klosko, George, *The Development of Plato's Theory,* New York: Methuen, 1986.

Lord, Carnes, *Education and Culture in the Political Thought of Aristotle,* Ithaca, NY: Cornell University Press, 1982.

Reeve, C. D. C., *Philosopher-kings: The Argument of Plato's Republic,* Princeton NJ: Princeton University Press, 1988.

Vlastos, Gregory, *Socrates, Ironist and Moral Philosopher,* Ithaca, NY: Cornell University Press, 1991.

MACHIAVELLI AND THE RENAISSANCE

Baron, Hans, *The Crisis of the Early Italian Renaissance,* Princeton, NJ: Princeton University Press, 1955.

Burckhardt, Jacob, *The Civilization of the Renaissance in Italy,* New York: Oxford University Press, 1937.

Cantor Norman, and Peter Klein, eds., *Renaissance Thought: Dante and Machiavelli,* Waltham, MA: Baisdell Publishing Company, 1969.

Kristeller, Paul Oskar, *Renaissance Thought: The Classic, Scholastic, and Humanist Strains,* New York: Harper, 1961.

Skinner, Quentin, *The Foundations of Modern Political Thought,* New York: Cambridge University Press, 1978.

Skinner, Quentin, *Machiavelli,* London: Oxford University Press, 1981.

Strauss, Leo, *Thoughts on Machiavelli,* Chicago: University of Chicago Press, 1958.

HOBBES AND ENGLISH HISTORY

Bagby, Laurie M. Johnson, *Thucydides, Hobbes, and the Interpretation of Realism,* DeKalb, Northern Illinois University Press, 1991.

Baumgold, Deborah, *Hobbes's Political Theory,* Cambridge: Cambridge University Press, 1988.

Burgess, Glen, *Absolute Monarchy and the Stuart Constitution,* New Haven, CT: Yale University Press, 1996.

Hampton, Jean, *Hobbes and the Social Contract Tradition,* Cambridge: Cambridge University Press, 1986.

Jessop, Thomas Edmund, *Thomas Hobbes,* London: Published for the British Council by Longmans, Green, 1961.

Johnston, David, *The Rhetoric of Leviathan: Thomas Hobbes and the Politics of Cultural Transformation,* Princeton, NJ: Princeton University Press, 1986.

Martinich, A. P., *The Two Gods of Leviathan: Thomas Hobbes on Religion and Politics,* Cambridge: Cambridge University Press, 1992.

Russell, Conrad, *The Fall of the British Monarchies, 1637–1642,* London: Oxford University Press, 1991.

Skinner, Quentin, *Reason and Rhetoric in the Philosophy of Hobbes,* Cambridge: Cambridge University Press, 1996.

Stone, Lawrence, *The Causes of the English Revolution,* New York: Harper & Row, 1972.

Strauss, Leo, *The Political Philosophy of Hobbes: Its Basis and Genesis,* Chicago: University of Chicago Press, 1952.

Tuck, Richard, *Hobbes,* New York: Oxford University Press, 1989.

LOCKE AND THE ENLIGHTENMENT

Ashcraft, Richard, *Revolutionary Politics and Locke's Two Treatises of Government,* Princeton: Princeton University Press, 1986.

Becker, Carl L., *The Heavenly City of the Eighteenth Century Philosophers,* New Haven, CT: Yale University Press, 1932.

Dunn, John, *The Political Thought of John Locke,* London: Cambridge University Press, 1969.

Gay, Peter, *The Enlightenment,* New York: Knopf, 1969.

Harris, Ian, *The Mind of John Locke: A Study of Political Theory in Its Intellectual Setting,* London: Cambridge University Press, 1994.

Pocock, J. G. A., *Three British Revolutions: 1641, 1688, 1776,* Princeton, NJ: Princeton University Press, 1980.

Shklar, Judith N., *Men and Citizens, A Study of Rousseau's Social Theory,* London: Cambridge University Press, 1969.

ROUSSEAU, KANT, AND HISTORY OF THE FRENCH REVOLUTION

Baker, Keith Michael, *Inventing the French Revolution,* New York: Cambridge University Press, 1990.

Blanning, T. C. W., *The Origins of the French Revolutionary Wars,* New York: Longman, 1986.

Galston, William A., *Kant and the Problem of History,* Chicago: University of Chicago Press, 1975.

Gulyga, Arsenij V., *Immanuel Kant: His Life and Thought,* Boston: Birkhauser, 1987.

Masters, Rodger D., *The Political Philosophy of Rousseau,* Princeton: Princeton University Press, 1968.

Miller, Jim, *Rousseau: Dreamer of Democracy,* New Haven, CT: Yale University Press, 1984.

Palmer, Robert Roswell, *The Twelve Who Ruled,* Princeton: Princeton University Press, 1958.

Palmer, Robert Roswell, *The Age of the Democratic Revolution* (two volumes), Princeton: Princeton University Press, 1964.

Shell, Susan, *The Rights of Reason: A Study of Kant's Philosophy and Politics,* Toronto: University of Toronto Press, 1980.

Shell, Susan, *The Embodiment of Reason: Kant on Spirit, Generation, and Community.* Chicago: University of Chicago Press, 1996.

Shklar, Judith N., *Men and Citizens: A Study of Rousseau's Social Theory,* London: Cambridge University Press, 1969.

Strong, Tracy B., *Jean Jacques Rousseau: The Politics of the Ordinary,* Thousand Oaks, CA: Sage Publications, 1994.

Yovel, Yirmiahu, *Kant and the Philosophy of History,* Princeton, NJ: Princeton University Press, 1980.

MARX AND THE DEVELOPMENT OF COMMUNISM

Berlin, Sir Isaiah, *Karl Marx: His Life and Environment,* New York: Oxford University Press, 1996.

Gilbert, Alan, *Marx's Politics: Communists and Citizens,* New Brunswick, NJ: Rutgers University Press, 1981.

Hamilton, Richard F., *The Bourgeois Epoch: Marx and Engels on Britain, France and Germany,* Chapel Hill, NC: University of North Carolina Press, 1991.

Hunt, Richard N., *The Political Ideas of Marx and Engels,* Pittsburgh: University of Pittsburgh Press, 1974.

Hunt, Richard N., *Classical Marxism, 1850–1895,* Pittsburgh: University of Pittsburgh Press, 1984.

Kolakowski, Leszek, *Main Currents of Marxism,* Oxford: Clarendon Press, 1978.

Maguire, John M., *Marx's Theory of Politics,* Cambridge: Cambridge University Press, 1978.